The Quest for Justice

Educational Policy, Planning, and Theory
Series Editor: Don Adams, *University of Pittsburgh*

The Quest for Justice

The Politics of School Finance Reform

Richard Lehne
The Eagleton Institute of Politics
Rutgers—The State University
of New Jersey

LONGMAN
New York and London

The Quest for Justice
The Politics of School Finance Reform
Longman Inc., New York

Associated companies, branches, and representatives throughout the world.
Copyright © 1978 by Longman Inc.

Developmental Editor: Edward Artinian
Editorial and Design Supervisor: Nicole Benevento
Design: Tim McKeen

Manufacturing and Production Supervisor: Louis Gaber
Composition: American Book–Stratford Press
Printing and Binding: Fairfield Graphics

Library of Congress Cataloging in Publication Data
Lehne, Richard.
    The quest for justice.
    (Educational policy, planning, and theory)
    Includes bibliographical references and index.
    1. Education—New Jersey—Finance. 2. Educational law and legislation—New Jersey. I. Title.
KFN2190.L43   344'.749'076   77–17713
ISBN 0–582–28036–2
ISBN 0–582–28035–4 pbk.

Manufactured in the United States of America

ACKNOWLEDGMENTS

Research projects which examine contemporary events make extraordinary demands on public officials, activists, colleagues, and friends. Almost everyone I approached in the course of this project responded to my requests with a cooperation and courtesy that exceeded my original hopes. From the hundreds of hours of interviews and observation, I have gained a respect for many participants in New Jersey government, which may surprise some readers. I have encountered numerous officials who were capable, concerned, and well-motivated, and very few who appeared to be simply self-serving. Without their cooperation, this analysis of judicial involvement in New Jersey's school finance controversy would have been impossible.

Many people have generously read and commented on all or part of this book: Kenneth Carlson, Anthony Champagne, Susan Kinsey, Julius Mastro, Alan Rosenthal, and Jane Sommer. I have benefited as well from comments by Michael Kirst, Robert Lineberry, and Arthur Wise on an earlier paper presented at the 1976 American Political Science Association meeting. I also appreciate the confidence and encouragement of James Kelly, Gerald Pomper, Roberta Sigel, and Roger Stetson.

This book is based on a project of the Eagleton Institute of Politics at Rutgers University. The project was supported by a grant from the Ford Foundation and was facilitated by other contributions from Rutgers. While preparing this manuscript for publication, I have served as a consultant on specialized activities to the New Jersey State Department of Education and the New Jersey General Assembly. An early version of chapter two appeared in *New Jersey Monthly*, which has granted permission for its publication here.

Many people have helped guide this book through numerous drafts. I am particularly grateful for the patience and understanding of Karen Kecskes and Edith Saks.

CONTENTS

1

Courts and Public Policy

The people of New Jersey celebrated the nation's Bicentennial as the proprietors of the only statewide school system in American history that has ever been totally shut down. The New Jersey Supreme Court had ruled that after June 30, 1976, no public official could spend any funds for the operation of any public school in the state. Until the legislature enacted a constitutional plan for funding elementary and secondary education, the schools would remain closed to the hundred thousand students who expected to enroll in academic summer sessions, to the many handicapped youngsters who participated in special education activities during July and August, and to all the administrators and curriculum planners preparing programs for the 1.4 million children who would normally return to New Jersey's public schools in the fall.

On June 30, numerous public officials were gathered in the state capital trying to cope with the supreme court order. At 11 A.M., eleven federal judges convened in an almost unprecedented session in a courtroom on the third floor of the Trenton post office building to decide if they would stay the state court order. At the same hour, down State Street and across the mall, top leaders of the Democratic majority in the assembly met in the State House to try to devise a legislative package which could satisfy the court. Downstairs in the governor's office, aides discussed the likelihood of urban rioting if the schools were closed for an extended period, and farther down State Street, in the New Jersey State Department of Education, staff members assembled to learn how to apply for unemployment benefits if they were laid off. By the time midnight struck, the federal judges had decided not to overturn the state court order, the assembly leadership had failed to devise a package which would win majority support, and the state supreme court's order closing New Jersey schools went into effect.

The court's stern decision to close the schools was not a petulant reaction to transient events. The justices ordered the schools closed only after years of frustration and controversy had embroiled the state's governing institutions. On April 3, 1973, the New Jersey Supreme Court had declared the existing system for funding elementary and secondary education to be unconstitutional and ordered the state legislature to devise a new school finance plan that would pass constitutional muster. Despite dozens of proposals, scores of sessions, and years of effort, the New Jersey Senate and Assembly were unable to fund a school finance program acceptable to the court. When the legislature failed to adopt an adequate policy to fund education, the state supreme court padlocked the schools until they did.

The involvement of the New Jersey Supreme Court in that state's policy process vividly illustrates the dynamic role that courts have come to occupy in the conduct of public policy in the United States. Hardly a week passes without some state or federal court delivering a notable decision that revamps an important public policy. In the last few years, judicial initiatives in such areas as desegregation, school prayer, welfare, defendant rights, legislative apportionment, and abortion have guided the reformulation of countless public policies. And continuing efforts are underway to use court systems to rewrite public policies governing zoning and land use, the provision of local services, prisoners' rights, the structure of government in metropolitan areas, public access to beaches, and other public amenities.

Law reformers have been attracted to the judicial arena by the stunning victories won there in the name of civil rights and civil liberties. With *Brown* v. *Board of Education* as an implicit model, activist lawyers pursuing egalitarian goals often shun popularly elected legislators and executives and attempt to achieve their objectives through the decisions of judges who are insulated from the majoritarian currents of public opinion. Well-chronicled accounts of successful lawsuits have reinforced the tendency to use litigation as a first step in a strategy of reform rather than reserving the courts as a last resort.[1] Sometimes, however, campaigns to reshape public policies have no choice but to rely on litigation because groups in power may refuse to negotiate with the powerless without the threat of judicial action. Furthermore, reform through legislation is a cumbersome process, which can require financial resources and public support that are beyond the reach of reformers. Under such circumstances, failure to invoke judicial procedure becomes, in effect, a ratification of the status quo. By any standard, reformist litigants have been successful in winning favorable judgments from both state and federal courts in their efforts to alter the content of public policy.

The victories of activist lawyers have inspired not only numerous imitators but also a chorus of critics who denounce court decisions in these policy areas and question the desirability of this type of judicial activism. Since reactions to court decisions often reflect individuals' appraisals of the groups perceived to gain or lose from the judgment, most objections to the role courts play in disputed policy areas are dismissed as complaints from people who do not favor the policy goals being litigated. In recent years, however, a catalog of criticism has been assembled by prestigious commentators whose motives cannot be so easily impugned. Constitutional critics complain that excessive involvement of judges in policy disputes emphasizes the political nature of court decisions and tarnishes the image of neutral competence that is essential for public acceptance of judicial rulings. Without widespread public support for their judgments, it is argued, courts will not only lose the ability to implement innovative policy decisions, but they will also forfeit their capacity to perform the traditional constitutional tasks all agree on assigning to the judiciary. Furthermore, it is urged, reliance on judges to solve public controversies may deaden that sense of individual responsibility for civic well-being essential to a healthy community and enfeeble democratic institutions that are better able than courts to accommodate conflicting political interests.[2]

Pragmatic critics have discarded the constitutional perspective and asserted that courts are sometimes inappropriate vehicles for pursuing policy goals, not because of constitutional inhibitions but because the consequences of court decisions ripple out into the real world in a thoroughly unpredictable fashion. Noble court judgments may both fail to accomplish the goals outlined in the opinions and at the same time produce deleterious consequences which no one favors. For example, a quarter-century after the United States Supreme Court's *Brown* decision, many point out that the patterns of systemwide noncompliance with the ruling leave the country still destructively divided over school integration questions, and they suggest that the courts themselves may have contributed to this situation.[3] One researcher concluded:

> I believe it is unfortunate that the Courts have chosen to follow a precedent leading to imposition of full-scale racial balance in systems that have contained some de jure segregation . . . . In hindsight ten or twenty years hence, these policies designed to desegregate schools may well be seen as highly segregative policies instead, because while their direct and immediate effect is to reduce school segregation, their indirect and longer-term effect is to increase *both* school and residential segregation.[4]

From the radical flank, other judicial critics protest that the legal process in general and the United States Constitution in particular are weighted against the changes which activist lawyers seek. The visionary goals of the original Constitution—a federal system, a national economy, a unified posture in foreign affairs, and a viable military establishment—have all been achieved, and the principles of the Constitution are now more likely to frustrate reformers than assist them.[5] The social service reforms of the New Deal, for example, were opposed, not by an aggressive court overstepping its authority, but rather by a precedent-based court reluctant to modify traditional values.[6] Full realization of the egalitarian goals often espoused by activist lawyers may require a reformulation of constitutional principle more profound than that of the New Deal, and more difficult for a precedent-based court to accept. Despite current victories, constitutional principles may in the future be a barrier to additional reforms rather than a vehicle for achieving them.

Accumulating criticism and the direction of political events may slow the growth of judicial participation in policy controversies in the years ahead, but it is unlikely that they will prevent courts from exercising the vast discretion they already possess in major policy areas. Perhaps the United States has entered a fundamentally new era, in which courts do not simply respond when problems are left untended by other institutions but, instead, display an ongoing activism that continually affects the conduct of public policy.[7] The expansion of government in society and the progressive logic of constitutional positions once taken may have propelled courts beyond the point where they can retreat from a dynamic role in policy debates. And even if these developments have not pushed courts beyond that point of no return, hundreds of advocacy law centers have been established to make it more difficult for courts to avoid the full implications of the constitutional positions they have already taken.

Prospects, for the immediate future at least, are for continuing judicial involvement in important policy questions, yet it remains an involvement the total consequences of which are not well understood. Are many critics simply rationalizing their reluctance to reward groups they do not like or are the eventual results of judicial activism more destructive than reformers acknowledge? Will a review of events reveal evidence on behalf of the activist lawyers or the hesitant critics? The dramatic events of New Jersey's school finance controversy provide an excellent record that can be examined to understand better the implications of judicial participation in the conduct of public policy.

Once, long ago, the building at the corner of Lembeck and Ocean avenues in Jersey City had been an imposing structure in an imposing city. In recent years, it has housed the law firm of Ruvoldt & Ruvoldt, a two-man partnership consisting of Harold Ruvoldt, Sr., now sixty-two years old, a former Hudson County prosecutor, and his son Harold, Jr., a sandy-haired young man with two small daughters and an affinity for sailboats. A few blocks down Ocean

Avenue from the Ruvoldt office is an old-fashioned candy and cigar shop where kids hang out after school. It is the sort of mom-and-pop place that so many exurbanites recall nostalgically, even as they relax on the lawns of their suburban homes. For the kids of Ocean Avenue, though, there has been no escape to the suburbs. Beneath the camaraderie of the neighborhood is the unspoken suspicion that the candy store is going nowhere, the neighborhood is going nowhere, and the kids themselves are going nowhere. The setting of the Ruvoldts' law office, just across the street from a boarded-up meeting hall, vividly depicts the decline of American cities in general and of Jersey City in particular.

Once, Jersey City had been an attractive place with a prosperous history. Alexander Hamilton had foreseen its value as a transit point and helped purchase the land where the city now stands for a transportation company in 1804. As late as the mid-1950s, the value of railroad property had given Jersey City and its 250,000 residents a property tax base per school pupil just below that of the average New Jersey community. By 1970, the declining value of railroad land and the decay of other buildings had lowered the tax base to only two-thirds of the state average. In the mid-1950s, Jersey City schools had spent 40 percent more than the average New Jersey school to educate each child; by 1970 they were spending 10 percent less.[8] Overloaded with aging factories and residential neighborhoods divided by ribbons of highways and railroads, Jersey City seemed helpless to reverse the trend.

Jersey City's predicament typified that of most other American cities. In the early decades of the twentieth century, urban areas had been great centers of personal wealth, valuable real estate, and dynamic economic activity. Throughout the twentieth century, however, suburbs grew up around the nation's central cities and slowly began to drain their vitality. As the migration to the suburbs accelerated after World War II, the financial condition of established urban areas began to deteriorate with alarming speed. By the mid-1960s, the stagnant tax base of many urban areas could no longer pay the escalating costs of municipal services.

The costs of municipal services were rising rapidly in the nation's cities because the patterns of urban development had concentrated large numbers of people who had expensive social service needs within their boundaries. Immigrants, the aged, the poor, and others who placed unusually heavy burdens on municipal services constituted a disproportionate share of central city populations. They required more public assistance of almost every kind than the average middle-class family: health care, employment training, human services, police protection, transportation, sanitation, and fire protection. Furthermore, the costs of providing municipal services are far greater in older, congested communities than in newly built suburbs. The simple fact of age necessitates greater expenditures for the maintenance of roads, buildings, sewers, and the like. This is true for schools as well as other local services. It costs more to maintain a fifty-year-old school than one constructed five years ago; it costs more to build on a site which must be cleared than on vacant land which has never been used before. Unionized public employee groups also appeared first in older urban areas, and the contract negotiation process raised the costs of conducting government in central cities above what it was in surrounding jurisdictions. As a result of all these factors, the residents of older urban centers were often compelled to pay a higher tax bill to provide lower levels of service than were the citizens of other parts of the state.

Local governments in the United States derive almost all of their own revenues from taxes on local real estate. Each municipality decides how much money it needs to fund all its activities, and it then sets a property tax rate to yield the necessary revenues. In the nineteenth century, property taxation served the country rather well as a tax source, because municipal boundaries normally encompassed all the developed neighborhoods in a region, both rich and poor, and because the ownership of real estate was usually an accurate measure of an individual's wealth and income. Property taxation could be used even to relieve the fiscal plight of poor school districts. A century ago, local school bills were usually paid with revenues from local property taxation and tuition charges. Some parents and communities, however, lacked the funds to pay for a full year of schooling. When these communities ran out of money, they would frequently close their schools for the balance of the year.[9] To guarantee an adequate education for students everywhere, many state governments began to pay a share of local school costs by giving all districts a specified number of dollars for each pupil. States later became more concerned about poor districts and adopted "foundation plans" to redistribute school funds from wealthy communities to poor districts, with wealth measured by the value of taxable property per pupil located in each community. Since urban areas then were financially secure, state school aid formulas were designed to shift funds from wealthy urban areas to poorer rural districts.[10]

The magnitude of state programs to aid local school districts increased throughout the twentieth century to such an extent that, by 1970, state governments paid 40 percent of the costs of operating local schools. The turn-of-the-century structure of these programs had remained intact, however, as suburbs had grown up around the nation's central cities and as local property values had become an increasingly inaccurate measure of community wealth. Suburbs with wealthy residents but little business property often qualified for substantial state aid because their property values per pupil were relatively low. Central cities often received little aid for their above-average educational needs and their extraordinary noneducation costs because businesses had chosen to locate there. As a result, in the early 1960s, state programs to aid local districts usually did little to reduce the initial advantage that suburbs had over central cities, and sometimes they even increased that edge. One government study examined a number of state programs to aid local districts and concluded that state governments contributed more money per pupil to suburban schools than to city schools.[11]

All of these factors combined to impair the financial well-being of urban school systems. By the early 1960s, urban schools, which were the traditional avenues of social mobility for immigrant groups and the disadvantaged in the United States, were unable to play their historic role. The burdens of poverty and the discrimination of race were combined handicaps urban schools could no longer overcome. At the same time, suburban areas, generally avoiding staggering bills for police, welfare, and sanitation, and often possessing a growing tax base, could afford rich curricula for their children, even though their needs were not so great as those of inner-city kids. In the words of one best-selling government report from these years, "Despite the overwhelming need, our society

spends less money educating ghetto children than children of suburban families." [12]

Governmental failure to solve the conundrum of urban, racial,
and poverty problems ravaging central city schools, and the occasional action of government which exacerbated those problems,
constituted to many observers a clear denial of equal protection
under the law. In the mid-1960s, important national organizations
began to explore ways of describing the scope of these hardships
and of relieving them through constitutional litigation. Perhaps the
organization most intimately involved was a Washington-based
group called the Lawyers' Committee for Civil Rights Under Law,
an association of established lawyers and law firms formed in
1963.[13] In June of that year, President John F. Kennedy had urged
the two hundred and fifty lawyers present at a large White House
meeting to use their skills to advance the cause of civil rights by
promoting minority job opportunities, supporting the integration
of public facilities, and leading the nation to a more sympathetic
understanding of black demands. The Lawyers' Committee was organized in response. Since a large fraction of the nation's minorities
are educated in urban school systems, the committee assembled a
task force of tax experts and researchers to examine the distribution of educational resources in the country. In subsequent years,
the committee provided many types of assistance to attorneys challenging existing school finance legislation in numerous states. Play-
ing roles that have ranged from co-counsel to clearinghouse, the
committee has attempted to coordinate school finance litigation on
a national basis by drafting model complaints, providing expert
testimony, and hosting conferences on litigation strategies.

Another organization that became involved in the school finance
reform movement was Syracuse University's Maxwell School of
Citizenship and Public Affairs. Recognizing that inequalities in
school resources would be one of the major education issues for
the next decade, research components of the university began to
apply earlier work on education and metropolitan finance to the
issues of school finance reform. Personnel who are or once were at
the Maxwell School continue to prepare much of the fiscal data
relied on in school finance litigation. The National Urban Coalition
initiated projects to guarantee that urban interests were adequately

represented in the reformulation of school finance programs, and the League of Women Voters was enlisted to disseminate "educational" material in states where school finance reformers were active. Furthermore, the Education Commission of the States and the National Conference of State Legislatures undertook their own programs to provide technical expertise for states engaged in preparing new school funding systems. Personnel in these organizations and researchers from university departments were woven into a loose network through the judicious distribution of foundation grants. Thus constituted, the nationwide school finance reform movement evolved into a notable force in the politics of education in the 1960s and 1970s.

This pattern of national backing for school finance suits confirms the well-documented belief that most major constitutional litigation movements receive organizational sponsorship.[14] Attempts to persuade judges to amend policies governing abortion, race relations, capital punishment, minimum wage laws, and public support for Catholic schools have all been aided by organized resources. School finance reformers probably differ from other constitutional litigants only in their willingness to acknowledge the organizational backing that frequently assists their efforts.

The national school finance reformers argued that state programs for funding elementary and secondary schools were unconstitutional because they violated the clause of the Fourteenth Amendment to the federal Constitution that guarantees each citizen equal protection before the law. Government action often entails classification of citizens, taxing various income groups at different rates, providing health care and housing to some and not to others, and admitting some persons to state universities and rejecting the applications of others. Equal protection cases generally require a court to decide whether specific classifications can be justified by their relationship to a legislative purpose. The cases ask whether there is a rational relationship between the classificatory means that have been established and the legislative ends the program is designed to achieve. Courts have found "suspect" legislative classifications resting on characteristics such as race and religion and have required states to demonstrate a "compelling" reason for using such classifications. Courts have also held that the equal protection clause protects certain "fundamental rights" more rigorously than other interests.[15] When cases involve restrictions on voting rights, for example, courts weigh not just the rationality of a program but also its effect on society. When cases involve debate on "fundamental interests," courts pass judgment on both the classifications and the purposes of legislation.

Early school finance reformers pleaded that state programs for funding education violated the equal protection clause of the Fourteenth Amendment, because reliance on local property taxation constituted a classification of students according to a suspect characteristic, the wealth of their communities, and this could not be justified by any compelling state purpose. They also argued that students have a fundamental right to education and that this right must not be any less available in one community than another. Unequal financing was a denial of equal protection. Reformers extended their arguments further.

Americans live under a dual system of laws, one set written by the national government and another set drafted by each state. A New Jersey citizen must adhere to state law when getting married and federal law when transporting goods among states. Some activities are normally governed by state law and others by federal law, but an increasing number of activities are subject to the requirements and protections of both. When a hotel rents a room or a restaurant serves a meal, the owner must respect the provisions of state law and the public accommodation sections of federal civil rights law. Provisions of both state and federal law frequently govern a citizen's conduct in a particular situation and often protect a citizen's rights. Many state constitutions have clauses which are the functional equivalent of the equal protection clause of the federal Constitution, and, in these states, reformers argued that the existing school finance systems violated the requirements of both the federal and state constitutions.

The basic thrust of the legal arguments of the proponents of school finance reform has been apparent from the start, but they have had difficulty clarifying the details of their position in specific cases. The first school finance case to be decided at the appellate level, *McInnis* v. *Ogilvie*, was launched by poverty lawyers in Chicago in 1968.[16] Plaintiffs argued that students were denied equal protection by the existing system of funding public schools, because the educational benefits received by students in different communities were unrelated to their educational needs. The suit claimed that varying levels of per pupil expenditures in different communities constituted an arbitrary and unreasonable classification of students. The district judges replied, and the United States Supreme Court affirmed, that "educational need" was not a sufficiently precise standard for courts to use in making sweeping judgments about the constitutionality of state school finance systems and indicated that a more intelligible standard was required.

This decision touched off a search for a legal standard that the reformers could present to sympathetic judges, and so far this quest has yielded two possible answers. The first has been called the "fiscal neutrality" principle.[17] Its proponents claim that the quality of education in individual communities is enhanced when local people support and run their own schools. What must be assured, however, is that their decisions about school operations and school funding are not restrained by the wealth of their locality; in other words, the quality of education must not be a function of the wealth of the local community. "Fiscal neutrality" can be achieved by a school funding device called "district power equalizing." Under this scheme, all property values in a state are considered part of one pool. Taxes set at a given rate will produce the same number of education dollars for each community in a state, regardless of the property values actually located within its boundaries. The local community is free to decide what property tax rate it will select to support its own schools, but the number of dollars that rate will yield depends on statewide property values. This mechanism permits localities to determine the level of effort they will make to support local schools and, at the same time, frees their decision from the constraints or advantages of the wealth of the community. The simplicity of this proposal has won considerable judicial support, but it has received less than enthusiastic endorsement from many reformers. They protest that the technique ignores the extraordinary nonschool needs of cities, which deny them a genuine opportunity to make the same effort to support education as communities without such costs can put forth, and they contend that the quality of a child's education is too important to be left to the whims of local citizens. Opponents assert that local communities do not have the right to provide an inadequate education for their students, regardless of their own wishes.

The second approach to formulating judicially manageable standards for education implicitly concedes that the right to a general education is too broad to define but assumes that certain elements can be specified.[18] According to this position, standards of educational quality can be anticipated by asserting that students have the right to a "minimum education." People presumably can agree more easily on the content of a minimum education than on that of a full education. Once this principle has been established, states could be compelled to pay for that minimum program for students everywhere in the state, and the quality of that minimum program would quickly escalate toward the provision of a general right to education.

The school finance reformers achieved their first notable legal victory on August 30, 1971, in a case captioned *Serrano* v. *Priest*. On that day, the California Supreme Court ruled that the state's school finance program violated the equal protection clauses of both the United States and California constitutions. The system's substantial dependence on local property taxation caused wide disparities in local school revenues and meant that the quality of a child's education was a product of the wealth of the child's parents and neighbors. The California court endorsed the fiscal neutrality principle by declaring that the quality of public education could not be "a function of the wealth of . . . [a pupil's] parents and neighbors." The reformers were ecstatic. The highest court in the nation's largest state had adopted their position. In a flurry of activity, actions challenging the constitutionality of state school finance programs were soon filed in more than thirty states.[19]

Events in New Jersey had not waited for the court decision in *Serrano*, however, because the plight of the state's urban schools was even more acute than that found elsewhere. New Jersey generally permits its local governments greater discretion than other states in providing public services, but it also forces them to pay more of the bill. Public education is no exception. In 1970, New Jersey communities paid about 67 percent of school costs, the state government contributed only 28 percent of the funds, and the federal share averaged only 5 percent. Cities in New Jersey also have a more fragile property tax base than most urban centers. In most parts of the country, the urban property tax base is strengthened by a concentration of high-value commercial and office property, but in New Jersey such facilities are broadly scattered throughout the state. Unlike most central cities where business properties help support high cost school needs, New Jersey cities have relatively little property value to finance the education of each student. New Jersey cities, therefore, have fewer resources to shoulder a burden heavier than most American cities bear.

The decade of the 1960s had been a tumultuous one for most of the nation's cities, but it had been especially difficult for the citizens of Jersey City. The inspiring view of the Statue of Liberty and the New York City skyline faded before the grim reality of urban rioting and the machinations of a mayor who would soon be sent to a federal penitentiary. Unfinished urban renewal programs and vigorous suburban development had drained the life from many local neighborhoods, and nothing, it seemed, could revive them. The conditions in the city's schools had deteriorated so badly that some urged the Ford Foundation to take over the operations of the entire system to demonstrate how urban schools could be improved, but even the Ford Foundation replied that it did not want to become involved in Jersey City.[20] For many people, Jersey City had become a place to escape from.

Not for Harold Ruvoldt, Jr., however. Ruvoldt could relate to the problems of places like Jersey City on a personal level, because the city had nurtured his family and his friends when he was growing up: Ruvoldt lived only two blocks from one of the oldest schools in Jersey City and in the state. He said he has never been able to forget the sight of "those broken windows, that terrible lighting, those kids huddled there." He remembered as well the students who attended P.S. 16, the Cornelia F. Bradford School. To get to P.S. 16, students went south from Journal Square along Kennedy Boulevard, past the Jersey City Armory and downhill past some housing projects. Standing in the shadow of the elevated roadway of the New Jersey Turnpike, P.S. 16 enrolls a student body of approximately five hundred students a year which is predominantly black and Puerto Rican. Ruvoldt believed that the students in these schools were not getting an adequate education because Jersey City lacked the tax base to pay the bill. Years before the *Serrano* decision, young Ruvoldt had read a newspaper story about an early school finance suit in Detroit. The Detroit suit sought to require the state of Michigan to equalize school opportunities for all the state's students, regardless of where they lived. It occurred to Ruvoldt that the same argument could be applied to New Jersey. Jersey City and Detroit had much in common: their housing and public buildings were not up to modern standards, businesses and well-to-do citizens were reluctant to locate within their boundaries, and the community tax bases could no longer meet the needs of an increasingly dependent citizenry. Both cities suffered from advanced cases of the decaying-city syndrome. As Ruvoldt read the newspaper article, he vowed to himself that sometime he would file a suit challenging the constitutionality of New Jersey's school finance program.

When American government textbooks discuss court systems, they often compare courts and judges to umpires and referees. When people need a judgment about facts or rules in a sports match, the umpire makes the decision. When a dispute arises about the meaning of a statute or constitutional provision, a court determines what it means and how it will be applied to a particular situation. Most attempts to appraise the role of courts in the policy process agree with the textbook that concludes, "Clearly, judges are decision makers." [21] Courts render a decision, and it is then the obligation of the parties to the case and the community at large to obey that decision with greater or lesser speed. As befits the formal rules of a community, the written decisions of courts are assembled and indexed and their contents are then carefully analyzed to trace doctrinal heritage and to evaluate future significance.

This view of courts as decision makers has prompted many scholars to attempt to explain why individual judges vote as they do on specific cases, balancing the impact of legal precedent against the importance of such extralegal factors as social background, judicial ideology, and personal interaction among judges.[22] This same view of courts also leads to examination of patterns of public compliance with court rulings and to analyses of the determinants of that compliance; numerous studies have tried to explain why some court decisions are promptly obeyed while others are bitterly denounced and generally evaded. These studies highlight the features of the court decision itself, the mechanisms to enforce the ruling, the resources of the groups affected by the judgment, and the sensitivity of the public values being litigated.[23]

However important these questions are for the conduct of public policy, this view of courts as decision-making institutions can overlook as much as it brings into focus. It assumes that the meaning of a decision is apparent to any informed reader, while, in practice, the actual meaning of a court ruling is often determined, not by the text, but by the manner in which the final judgment is implemented.[24] It does not account for the fact that a judicial statement may affect policy officials in ways that have little to do with its specific content, altering their attitudes, changing the relationships among the institutions they administer, and involving them with previously disregarded groups. Institutions themselves may also be transformed in response to court action, causing them to change their priorities, redeploy their resources, and restructure their organizational patterns. Judicial participation in a policy dispute can raise previously unrecognized issues, enhance some institutions at the expense of others, and even reform the contours of the total policy area. Numerous questions beyond the extent of compliance with a court decision need to be asked to determine the full significance of judicial involvement in policy controversies.

An alternative perspective on the role of courts in public policy has emerged in past decades from changes in the nature of the court rulings themselves. Archibald Cox has noted that landmark decisions have generally shifted from "mandates directing the government to refrain from a particular form of regulation" to judgments that require states "to make some changes in the *status quo* —some alteration of a widespread and long accepted practice, some improvement from the standpoint of human rights."[25] While judicial decisions have traditionally been negative statements proscribing specified actions, in recent decades, courts more frequently demand positive actions from government to achieve specified goals. The judiciary is now more likely to require the executive, the legislature, and the public to deal with an issue but also to leave them an uncertain latitude to determine exactly how to deal with it.

Jonathan Casper captures the essence of this process in his analysis of *Lawyers Before the Warren Court:*

> The typical image of litigation as a conflict-resolving process, a mechanism for settling overt disputes . . . may be by now simply a straw man. . . . litigation served not only to win cases but also to raise issues. In a sense it was as much a conflict-generating as a conflict-resolving process. This is not to say that the conflict that emerged after judicial decisions did not exist before. . . . What the Court can and did do was to insure that these basic political issues were placed upon the agendas of other political institutions. . . . Courts cannot determine political outcomes in issue areas. . . . but they can . . . take steps that make it essential for other institutions—legislatures and executives—to participate in the process of collective decision. . . . The Court functions as a kind of access point and agenda-setter, not a final decision-maker.[26]

Thus, courts can be viewed as agenda-setting institutions in policy disputes rather than decision-making agencies, institutions that specify which issues will be considered rather than agencies that impose concrete policies and principles.

This view of the judiciary as an agenda-setting mechanism is a particularly appropriate perspective from which to examine school finance litigation, both nationally and in New Jersey. Some school finance litigants themselves viewed the judicial system in just this way, expecting that genuine victories would be won, not in the courts, but from the reactions of other political institutions to judicial initiative. Courts were used to prod legislatures and executives to reform the state programs that financed elementary and secondary schools, but the judges were not asked to grant additional aid to individual school districts and income groups on their own authority.

Many courts as well accepted this agenda-setting role in the school finance litigation.[27] They delivered declaratory judgments in school finance cases, which ruled statutes unconstitutional, but, because of the newness of the law in this area and the forbidding position of legislatures in the taxation and appropriations process, they were hesitant to define clear remedies. The New Jersey Supreme Court has consistently asserted that the legislature must exercise its judgment about the issues of school finance and school governance, but it has imposed few restrictions on the policies that could emerge. The court initiated a momentous dispute that would entangle the state's policy-making institutions for more than three years, but the ruling did not command any particular solution to the problem. That was left to the legislature and the executive. Furthermore, the court's ruling launched these far-reaching events without establishing a constitutional standard that would inevitably limit its discretion in future cases. The decision that would convulse the state in the years ahead was politically aggressive, but its strict constitutional assertions were quite modest. The actions of judges and litigants, as well as those of legislators and executives, demonstrate that in school finance cases, courts can be more accurately viewed today as setting public policy agendas rather than determining the content of public policies.

Most discussions of agenda setting try to determine why some items are seriously considered by public officials while other topics fail to win governmental attention, why government considers the issue of television blackouts of football games but ignores problems of hunger, discrimination, and exploitation.[28] Since the number of potential topics far exceeds individual or institutional ability to make policy decisions, choices about topics to be considered have to be made. Success in placing issues on the public agenda is sometimes related to the characteristics of the groups that might benefit from consideration of the issues; some think that such attributes as high social status, economic mobility, institutional position, stable residence in a community, and large membership are particularly helpful in getting a topic considered.[29] Others argue that issues typically arise in small groups and receive governmental consideration only if they can attract widespread public attention. Topics which can be expected to arouse public interest are usually those that affect many aspects of society, can be stated in simple language, appear to have long-term consequences, arise suddenly, and resist solution by traditional means. Issues may also win agenda status by a variety of routes other than public attention. Resourceful groups and individuals, the media, governmental agencies, experts, private institutions, and even day-to-day events can all nominate issues for serious policy attention.[30] Courts also have long been used by minority interests to increase official awareness of their plight.

The view of the court system as an agenda-setting technique leads beyond the questions of how and why issues are raised for policy consideration to the evaluation of the impact of specific agenda-setting techniques on subsequent policy debates. What are the consequences of the fact that an issue arose through the court system rather than from more traditional agenda-setting sources such as public opinion? Are there specific characteristics of court actions as agenda-setting procedures, as opposed to the features of other agenda-setting techniques, which affect the attitudes, objectives, and activities of participants in policy debates? In sum, how does a court's involvement as an agenda-setting institution in a policy controversy reshape the politics of that controversy? Looking at New Jersey's situation, did the fact that the issues of education funding and governance came before the New Jersey legislature because of a court decision affect the way in which those issues were considered? Were the responses of the general public and the department of education to the problem determined more by the nature of the issues or the involvement of the court? How importantly did the participation of the court in the controversy influence the approach of the governor and the education groups to the events of 1973 to 1976?

The Chronology, "New Jersey School Finance Events," records the highlights of the controversy that preoccupied New Jersey's governing circles for more than three years. As the chapters which follow indicate, these events involved all the state's political institutions in a protracted minuet of pronouncements, proposals, and rejections. This study examines the complicated history of the period to help us understand the implications of judicial participation in public disputes. Chapter two explores the dynamics of the original court action. The motivations of litigants, the problems of governments as defendants in public policy cases, and the significance of organized litigation are all discussed from the perspective of the New Jersey case. Some traditions and procedures of the trial court and the state supreme court are explained as background for an analysis of the decisions. The attitudes of the public, state

CHRONOLOGY

NEW JERSEY SCHOOL FINANCE EVENTS

1970	February 13	Ruvoldt files original *Robinson* v. *Cahill* complaint
1971	August 30	California Supreme Court decides *Serrano* v. *Priest*
	November 1–9	Trial court hearings on *Robinson*
1972	January 19	Judge Botter's decision in *Robinson*
1973	January 9	*Robinson* argued before New Jersey Supreme Court
	March 21	United States Supreme Court decides *San Antonio* v. *Rodriguez*
	April 3	New Jersey Supreme Court decides *Robinson*
	April 4	State Board of Education establishes task force to plan response to *Robinson*
	June 5	Governor Cahill defeated in primary election
	June 19	In *Robinson* II, New Jersey Supreme Court establishes timetable for compliance, which requires legislative action by December 31, 1974
	December 18	Richard Hughes sworn in as Chief Justice of New Jersey Supreme Court
1974	January 15	Brendan Byrne takes office as Governor
	January	Byrne Administration task force on education, finance, and taxation established
	April 9	Joint Education Committee created
	June 13	Report of Joint Education Committee to the New Jersey legislature
	July 24	Byrne Administration program withdrawn in senate
	December 31	Supreme court deadline passes

1975	January 23	In *Robinson* III, New Jersey Supreme Court establishes October 1 date for legislative action
	May 13	In *Robinson* IV, New Jersey Supreme Court rules that it will redistribute aid if the legislature does not act by October 1
	May 27	Senate passes Wiley-Burstein education bill
	September 29	Assembly passes Wiley-Burstein education bill
1976	January 30	In *Robinson* V, New Jersey Supreme Court upholds constitutionality of Wiley-Burstein bill
	February 19	In *Robinson* VI, New Jersey Supreme Court schedules new hearings
	March 15–16	Assembly passes tax package
	May 13	In *Robinson* VII, New Jersey Supreme Court orders officials to stop expending funds for elementary and secondary education on July 1 if the legislature has not acted
	June 30	Federal district court meets to review *Robinson*
	July 1	New Jersey schools close
	July 9	Legislature passes tax package

legislators, members of the New Jersey State Department of Education, and the personnel of interest groups all helped shape the way New Jersey responded to the court. In chapter three, the opinions of these groups about courts, education, and taxes are described, and then the extent to which the decision itself reshaped their original viewpoints is analyzed. Chapter four outlines the procedures used by the governor's office, the legislature, and the state department of education to develop a policy response to the court ruling and evaluates the proposals. Chapter five reviews the seething events that preceded the eventual adoption of an educational finance program and examines the role played by the state supreme court in New Jersey's legislative process. The impact of the events on school funding, education interest groups, the state department of education, and New Jersey's policy process is appraised in chapter six. The final chapter briefly discusses the role of courts in the conduct of public policy, litigation strategies for programmatic reform, and the importance of the agenda-setting process in the analysis of public affairs.

The story of the events in New Jersey is not a story of simple justice. Justice is simple only when it focuses on a single principle and disregards adjacent principles and only when it examines the assertion of a position and ignores its implementation. The history of events does not record the inevitable victory of good guys over bad guys, because such victories are usually inevitable only in hindsight. This study is an account of numerous persons, diligent and well-meaning, acting out their beliefs and struggling with their limitations. But more than anything, this is the story of the quest for justice. It is an account of citizens and officials working to devise equitable programs to accommodate the divergent standards and conflicting purposes of a self-governing community.

NOTES

1. Anthony Lewis, *Gideon's Trumpet* (New York: Alfred A. Knopf, 1964); Richard Kluger, *Simple Justice: The History of Brown v. Board of Education and Black America's Struggle for Equality* (New York: Alfred A. Knopf, 1976); Michael Meltsner, *Cruel and Unusual: The Supreme Court and Capital Punishment* (New York: Random House, 1973); Dan T. Carter, *Scottsboro: A Tragedy of the American South* (Baton Rouge: Louisiana State University Press, 1969); David R. Manwaring, *Render Unto Caesar: The Flag Salute Controversy* (Chicago: The University of Chicago Press, 1962).

2. Archibald Cox, *The Role of the Supreme Court in American Government* (New York: Oxford University Press, 1976), pp. 75, 88, and 103.

3. Harry P. Stumpf, *Community Politics and Legal Services: The Other Side of the Law* (Beverly Hills, Cal.: Sage Publications, 1975), pp. 276–77; Stuart A. Scheingold, *The Politics of Rights: Lawyers, Public Policy and Political Change* (New Haven: Yale University Press, 1974), pp. 95–96; Charles V. Hamilton, *The Bench and the Ballot: Southern Federal Judges and Black Voters* (New York: Oxford University Press, 1973).

4. "Testimony of James S. Coleman before the Senate Judiciary Committee, October 28, 1975," pp. 4 and 22. See also James S. Coleman, "Recent Trends in School Integration," *Educational Researcher* 4 (July–August 1975): 3–12.

5. Scheingold, *Politics of Rights*, p. 99.

6. Ibid., p. 94.

7. Nathan Glazer, "Towards an Imperial Judiciary?," *The Public Interest* 4 (Fall 1975): 104–23.

8. In 1955, Jersey City's equalized property valuation per pupil was $24,-672, or 90 percent of the state average of $27,486. The current expenditures per pupil for the same year in Jersey City were $460, 140 percent of the state average figure of $328. In 1970, Jersey City's equalized valuation of $26,675 constituted only 70 percent of the state average valuation of $38,172. The current expenditures per pupil for that year in Jersey City were $688, which was only 86 percent of the state average expenditures of $800 (New Jersey Commissioner of Education *Annual Report, Financial Statistics of School Districts*, vol. 4 and 19).

9. William Aloysius Shine, "Ellis Apgar: Educational Leadership in New Jersey in an Era of School Change" (Dissertation in the Graduate School of Education, Rutgers University, 1964).

10. Joel S. Berke, *Answers to Inequity: An Analysis of the New School Finance* (Berkeley, Cal.: McCutchan, 1974).

11. U.S. Commission on Civil Rights, *Racial Isolation in the Public Schools* (Washington: Government Printing Office, 1963), p. 26.

12. National Advisory Commission on Civil Disorders, *Report* (New York: Bantam Books, 1968), p. 434.

13. This paragraph is based, verbatim in parts, on Lawyers' Committee for Civil Rights Under Law, *10 Year Report* (Washington: The Committee, 1973), pp. 8, 9, 65, and 66.

14. Clement E. Vose, *Constitutional Change: Amendment Politics and Supreme Court Litigation Since 1900* (Lexington, Mass.: D. C. Heath, 1972). For a sharply contrasting view, see Nathan Hakman, "The Supreme Court's

Political Environment," in *Frontiers of Judicial Research*, ed. Joel Grossman and Joseph Tanenhaus (New York: John Wiley & Sons, 1969), p. 246.

15. See "Developments in the Law—Equal Protection," *Harvard Law Review* 82 (March 1969): 1065.

16. *McInnis* v. *Shapiro*, F. Supp. 327 (N.D. Ill. 1968), *aff'd mem. sub nom. McInnis* v. *Ogilvie*, 394 U.S. 322 (1969).

17. John E. Coons, William H. Clune, and Stephen D. Sugarman, *Private Wealth and Public Education* (Cambridge, Mass.: Harvard University Press, 1970).

18. Frank Michelman, "Foreword: Protecting the Poor Through the Fourteenth Amendment," *Harvard Law Review* 83 (November 1969): 7–59.

19. *John Serrano, Jr. et al.*, v. *Ivy Baker Priest*, 5 Cal. 3d 584. For subsequent filings, see Betsy Levin, "Foreword," *Law and Contemporary Problems* 38 (Winter–Spring 1974): 295.

20. National Advisory Commission on Civil Disorders, *Report*, pp. 70–71.

21. Stephen V. Monsma, *American Politics: A Systems Approach* (Hindsdale, Ill.: The Dryden Press, 1973), p. 354.

22. See works cited in chapters 2 and 3 of Charles H. Sheldon, *The American Judicial Process: Models and Approaches* (New York: Dodd, Mead, 1974).

23. Stephen L. Wasby, *The Impact of the United States Supreme Court: Some Perspectives* (Homewood, Ill.: Dorsey Press, 1970).

24. Jack W. Peltason, "After the Lawsuit is Over," in *Federal Courts in the Political Process*, ed. Jack W. Peltason (New York: Random House, 1955).

25. Archibald Cox, "Forward: Constitutional Adjudication and the Promotion of Human Rights," *Harvard Law Review* 80 (November 1966): 91–92.

26. Jonathan D. Caspar, *Lawyers Before the Warren Court: Civil Liberties and Civil Rights* (Urbana: University of Illinois Press, 1972), pp. 20 and 160. See also other works which discuss courts and setting agenda, for example, Neal A. Milner, *The Court and Local Law Enforcement: The Impact of Miranda* (Beverly Hills, Cal.: Sage Publications, 1971), p. 18; and Kenneth M. Dolbeare and Phillip E. Hammond, *The School Prayer Decisions: From Court Policy to Local Practice* (Chicago: University of Chicago Press, 1971), pp. x–xi.

27. See *Van Dusartz* v. *Hatfield*, 334 F. Supp. 872 (SD Minn. 1971).

28. See Roger W. Cobb and Charles D. Elder, *Participation in American Politics: The Dynamics of Agenda Building* (Boston: Allyn-Bacon, 1971); and Peter Bachrach and Morton S. Baratz, "Two Faces of Power," *American Political Science Review* 56 (December 1962): 947–52.

29. See Robert Crain et al., *The Politics of Community Conflict: The Fluoridation Dispute* (Indianapolis: Bobbs-Merrill, 1969); Joseph Gusfield, *Symbolic Crusade* (Urbana: University of Illinois Press, 1966); Norman Nie et al., "Social Structure and Political Participation," *American Political Science Review* 63 (June 1969): 361–78; and Sidney Verba et al., "The Modes of Democratic Participation: A Cross-Cultural Comparison," *Sage Professional Papers in Comparative Politics* (1971).

30. Cobb and Elder, *Participation in American Politics*; Roger Cobb, Jennie

Keith-Ross, and Marc Howard Ross, "Agenda-Building as a Comparative Political Process," *American Political Science Review* 70 (March 1976): 128; Jack L. Walker, "Setting The Agenda in the U.S. Senate: A Theory of Problem Selection," Paper prepared for delivery at the 1976 Annual Meeting of the American Political Science Association, September 2–5, 1976; Barbara Deckard Sinclair, "Party Realignment and the Transformation of the Political Agenda—The House of Representatives, 1925–1938," unpublished paper; and John H. Kessel, "The Parameters of Presidential Politics," *Social Science Quarterly* 55 (June 1974): 8–24.

2

No Thicket Too Political

Jimmy Ryan was Corporation Counsel of Jersey City. For some time, he had known Harold Ruvoldt as a locally prominent lawyer, with close ties to Hudson County's political establishment, who was active in bar association activities. He also knew his son, Harold Ruvoldt, Jr., and an article the son had drafted for the *New Jersey State Bar Journal* entitled "The Right to Learn." In that article, young Ruvoldt argued that the federal and state constitutions implied the right to an education and, therefore, the state's system for financing public schools had to secure that right.[1] Most lawyers who bothered to read the article agreed with the attorney who told Ruvoldt at the time, "If that were the law, obviously someone else would have recognized it sometime in the last 130 years."

But Jimmy Ryan did not agree. For years he had believed that the state had treated Hudson County and Jersey City unfairly by taking away tax dollars and then refusing to help pay the costs for the poor. Certainly, Jersey City's high property tax rates were a consideration, but Ryan believed that other towns were spending twice as much educating each student as Jersey City was spending, and that was unfair to Jersey City kids. Ryan was thus one of the few lawyers in the state of New Jersey in 1969 who thought Ruvoldt's article had some merit. As it happened, however, that was sufficient, for Ryan had the ear of Jersey City's mayor, Thomas J. Whelan.

Through Ryan's urging, Ruvoldt was invited to the mayor's office in November 1969 to meet with Ryan, Mayor Whelan, City Council President Thomas Flaherty, the mayor's secretary, Warren Murphy, and three lawyers in private practice. Young Ruvoldt distributed his materials, and, for an hour, the eight men sat around a large conference table while Ruvoldt outlined his arguments. Jersey City should sue the state, he said, on the ground that the school finance system is unconstitutional, because it denies Jersey City children the right to equal educational opportunity. The others peppered Ruvoldt with questions, but, except for Ryan, none thought the idea was worth pursuing. One lawyer said that such a suit would be an indefensible waste of money. "The case would be thrown out of court in six weeks," he predicted. The matter was unceremoniously dropped, and Ruvoldt's idea was set aside.

In November 1969, however, Mayor Whelan faced a dilemma. He was already being criticized in some quarters for the extraordinarily high property tax rate in the city, and, at the same time, he was being warned by others that the city's school teachers were about to go on strike for a large pay increase. Furthermore, other high priority public services including police, fire, health, and sanitation were also demanding substantial budgetary increases, and the mayor did not know where to turn to get the needed funds. Something was needed to dramatize Jersey City's plight. As Warren Murphy, the mayor's secretary and public relations adviser, mulled over this problem, a thought occurred to him: even if the suit proposed by Ruvoldt couldn't be justified on legal grounds, perhaps it was worth trying for its public relations value.

So it happened that one evening, early in January 1970, Harold Ruvoldt, Jr., read in the *Jersey Journal* that Mayor Whelan would refuse to provide funds to operate Jersey City's schools for the coming year.[2] Instead, the local board of school estimate would insist that the state was obliged to provide funds to operate public schools in Jersey City and elsewhere throughout the state. The city would press its point in a law suit challenging the constitutionality of the state school aid program.

No one had mentioned a word to Ruvoldt about the suit. He had heard nothing from City Hall since his meeting there two months earlier. "Looks like the mayor got someone else to do it," Ruvoldt remembers thinking to himself. The following night, Mayor Whelan called Ruvoldt. As it turned out, Whelan had made no plans to file a suit; he had apparently used the litigation as a pretext for his refusal to appropriate the education funds. Now the *New York Times*, the *Daily News*, and the *Jersey Journal* were besieging him with questions about the suit. He needed Ruvoldt to provide the answers. Over the objections of Jersey City's two independent councilmen, who argued that the legal fees were a waste of money, Ruvoldt was hired and the suit moved ahead.

Most legal actions usually do not begin in quite this way. Classically, someone has a specific problem with another person or organization and seeks out a lawyer to help solve it. The judicial system is designed to handle such controversies between two parties who are both striving to make the best possible argument to win their position. Court decisions are generally binding only on the parties to the specific case. Today, however, much litigation is not initiated simply to solve a problem of a single party, but aims instead to alter the public policies that affect all citizens.

The challenge to New Jersey's school finance scheme was a genuine controversy with real interests, but it was "managed" litigation inspired by clear policy goals. Ruvoldt's objectives and much of his litigation strategy were formulated before he was retained by Jersey City and before other plaintiffs were recruited to lend their positions to the case. Even though the suit sought to change public policy, the law required Ruvoldt to present it as a dispute between individual parties. The young attorney decided that Jersey City's plaintiff would be a student who would claim that, because he lived in Jersey City, he was deprived of an education comparable to that received by students residing in more affluent areas of the state. He set out to find one.

Ideally, Ruvoldt figured, the plaintiff should be young, so he would still be in school even if the litigation took years. He should come from a middle-class family that owned property in Jersey City and was thus subject to local property taxes. The income-producing parent of the student should have a job that required residence in the city, such as that of a city employee. In the end, Ruvoldt settled on eleven-year-old Kenneth Robinson, a sixth-grader at P.S. 16, the Bradford School. Robinson filled the particulars: his mother, Ernestine Robinson, worked for a federal school program in Jersey City, owned her own house, and was willing to cooperate. Joining Robinson as plaintiffs were the mayors of Jersey City, Plainfield, Paterson, and East Orange, the boards of education of all four cities, and Jersey City's board of school estimate.

The defendants, too, would be individuals, even though the real targets of the litigation were the suburbs around the state that enjoyed lower tax rates than Jersey City yet had better schools for their children. In legal form, Ruvoldt's suit was filed against Governor William Cahill. Cahill had himself already embraced the type of property tax reform sought by Jersey City officials, but he was chosen as a defendant on the theory that as governor he was partially responsible for the state's school finance structure. Other state officials were also named as defendants in the suit. Thus, when Ruvoldt filed the complaint of February 13, 1970—a Friday, incidentally—the case was captioned *Robinson* v. *Cahill.*

Ruvoldt's legal arguments resembled those of school finance reformers in other states.[3] Students in some school districts received an education that cost substantially less than that received by children in other school districts in the state. Ruvoldt contended that education was a fundamental interest and that delegation of responsibility for education by the state to localities whose property wealth varied widely constituted a classification of students on the basis of wealth, a constitutionally suspect distinction among citizens. The court, he argued, must strictly scrutinize the state's education finance system to determine if it denied some students equal protection of the laws as guaranteed by the Fourteenth Amendment of the United States Constitution and by the New Jersey Constitution. The quality of a child's education may not be a function of the wealth of the community in which he lives, the complaint alleged. Ruvoldt reinforced this position by contending that the youngsters harmed by the state's education finance scheme were predominantly minority group members. New Jersey created and maintained a school finance system, it was charged, that provided disproportionately fewer educational opportunities to black children such as Kenneth Robinson than to white children. The New Jersey Constitution assigned the responsibility for public education to the state government, and any failure to meet that obligation must be remedied by the state itself.

When courts try public policies rather than private disputes, government, too, can play an unaccustomed role in the litigation. Traditionally, governments defend challenges against the constitutionality of policies enacted by legislatures. However, in suits between nongovernmental parties that contest the validity of established policies, government can sometimes choose sides. At the national level, the United States Solicitor General frequently intervenes in cases before the Supreme Court or files an amicus curiae brief supporting the interests represented by one of the original parties.[4] Since the solicitor general now participates in most cases that are argued on their merits before the Supreme Court, this official's opportunity to influence the direction of the court is substantial. Reapportionment and civil disobedience cases saw the government favor constitutional arguments that furthered the policy goals of one group at the expense of the policy preferences of others. In civil rights litigation the solicitor general often placed the government on the side of civil rights advocates, even though Congress was unwilling to take such positions.[5]

In rare cases in New Jersey, government agencies have apparently used the court system to secure policy objectives that could not be achieved in traditional ways. One agency may seek authority from the courts to make decisions which another branch of government opposes. In the mid-1960s, the New Jersey Supreme Court had accepted cases in which the powers of the commissioner of education were debated. In its decisions, the court chastised the commissioner for taking a narrow view of his administrative powers.[6] A few years later the commissioner asserted in a related case that he would like to use his authority to make a decision which was socially and educationally desirable but that he lacked requisite powers. An official close to the situation explained the strategy:

The Commissioner encouraged the . . . case knowing all along that he had the power, because he wanted the court to back him up. The court had already said that he had the power in previous cases. Many governmental officials find the legislative process so slow and painful that they come to rely on the courts. Sometimes you need an ally and you look around and all you see is the court. You make a political judgment that you need the court to reinforce your options. Government officials are constantly sued to do things they really want to do anyway.*

In deciding this case, the supreme court again condemned administrative narrowing of grants of authority and again ordered the commissioner to act.

Defense of government policies is not always an easy task, even in cases totally independent of official instigation. Conflicting views among agencies can complicate the chore of formulating the legal positions of public defendants. Even a single government agency may have so many different interests that it is fearful of making an argument in one situation that may spill over into another arena. School officials in Detroit, for example, became committed to racial integration of the city's public schools, but public support for integration was so fragile that they were restrained in court testimony from candidly discussing problems in the schools.[7] Officials may not vigorously oppose an interest group's claim in one law suit, because they need that group's assistance in other contests which do not involve the legal system.[8] Finally, officeholders may be reluctant to defend established policies simply because they do not support them. Kansas officials were reportedly slow to defend the state's statute that permitted segregated schools in *Brown* v. *Topeka*, and West Virginia authorities apparently did not care to defend the practice of saluting the flag in that state's public schools.[9] Public policies are often litigated when relevant traditions and attitudes are in flux, and public officials themselves often share these changing attitudes. All these considerations complicate the assignment of attorneys to defend the constitutionality of public statutes.

* Unattributed quotations come from personal interviews by the author. See Appendix A.

Defendants in *Robinson* included the governor, the legislature, and the commissioner of education. The governor's counsel, legislative officials, and lawyers from the attorney general's office concluded that all the defendants in *Robinson* would be represented by the personnel in the attorney general's office who normally represented the department of education.

Education department officials undoubtedly welcomed the *Robinson* litigation because they agreed that schools in places like Jersey City deserved more state support. The administration also favored increased state support for schools in older urban areas, and the legislature would soon enact a program which would provide just such assistance. However, while most state officials endorsed the policy objectives of the litigation, their legal position opposed judicial involvement. School finance decisions were historically a legislative prerogative, the defense asserted, and the court should respect established precedent. Defense attorneys had to defend a state finance system they really did not believe in. An official close to the defense explained their thinking:

> There was really no way to fight the facts of the case. There *were* hundred year old schools in Jersey City where kids were taught in rooms without windows. Those were the facts. I suppose the defense could have found people from a district with the same expenditures as Jersey City where the schools were doing a good job, but Jersey City's situation was clear. It was a claim that had a lot of sympathy to it. The defense tried to blunt the impact of the facts by emphasizing the separation of powers argument. The defense pointed to recent legislative action and said, see, the legislature recognizes the problem, and they are doing something constructive about it. Leave the problem alone. These are legislative questions.

The defense presented a sound legal argument to the trial court, but it was presented with a sense of inevitability. While Jersey City officials thought their litigation was a long shot, the defense was less certain. The tone of a conference of attorneys defending state school finance programs from the equal protection attack was captured by a New Jersey lawyer who attended the sessions:

> The attorneys all thought that they had the law on their side, but they felt they were fighting a rear guard action. The suits

represented an idea whose time had come. The New Jersey
court might agree. The legislature would not act to reform
the tax structure and something had to be done. There was
nothing standing in the way of reform except political realities. . . . The law was clear, but if the judge wanted to make
a decision he would and nothing would deflect him.

The consensus of participants in the original examination of
Robinson in New Jersey is that the attorney general's office offered
a legally sound defense of the state's school finance system, but the
participants generally agree that the defense was not strenuously
developed or forcefully presented. Did this perceived lack of diligence affect the trial's outcome? One observer asserted that there
was no vigorous adversary process and lamented, "I often thought
that the ends we were trying to achieve were being degraded by
shabby means." Another mused that if aggressive effort had replaced defeatist assumptions, the defense might have been more
successful. Although it is impossible to be sure, few participants
believe that the final outcome would have been very different. A
display of passion and commitment might 'have influenced the
judge, but the relevant arguments were clearly presented in the
record and in easily accessible legal and scholarly writings.[10] The
policy positions of the official defendants and evolving trends in national events could not be altered by the attorney general's defense,
regardless of its vigor, and these background circumstances formed
an important aspect of the case.

Background events have nothing to do with the merits of a case.
They do, however, encourage resourceful interest groups to take
part in court proceedings they might otherwise ignore. In recent
decades, numerous groups have sponsored campaigns to change
public policies through litigation.[11] As groups recruit individuals to
file test cases, however, the interests of the individual can become
confused or occasionally subordinated to the policy goal of the
group. A lawyer may focus on the policy objectives of a case at the
expense of the immediate interests of the party involved.[12] In court
challenges to the death penalty, for example, it is a close question
whether the futures of particular clients were aided or jeopardized
by linking their fates to a general campaign to abolish capital punishment.[13]

The well-being of individuals is compromised less when groups turn from managing specific cases to filing "amicus curiae" briefs. Originally, an amicus curiae ("friend of the court") was a neutral party without a direct interest in a case who provided argument or information to the court that it would not otherwise receive.[14] The role of the amicus was to assist the court in reaching a sound decision. These days the role of amicus has shifted from a neutral observer to a forceful advocate of a specific viewpoint. The typical amicus brief today champions a line of argument that a resourceful group wants to bring to the court's attention, not to enrich the court's decision, but to further its own purposes. Amicus curiae briefs are often solicited by lawyers to demonstrate the breadth of support for a controversial position, as was done in the United States Supreme Court cases that expanded the right to counsel and examined the validity of restrictive convenants on the sale of real estate.[15] The use of amicus briefs to register the support or opposition of groups for specific positions is so common that it can enable a court to gauge the likely political response to a decision. Some argue that the presence of amici in policy litigation reflects the fact that courts now perform a legislative as well as a judicial role in many constitutional cases.[16]

A major amicus curiae brief in *Robinson* was filed on behalf of the Education Committee of the Newark Chapter of the National Association for the Advancement of Colored People (NAACP) and the American Civil Liberties Union (ACLU) of New Jersey. The 126-page document did argue that New Jersey's system for funding elementary and secondary education violated the equal protection guarantees of the state and federal constitutions, but the brief focused its attention on the education clause of the New Jersey constitution. Amici were concerned about the inability of the state's inner cities to raise sufficient funds on their own to finance an adequate education. They believed that New Jersey's existing statutes did not satisfy the state's obligation to all children in local school districts, as specified in the state constitution. That obligation extended beyond the simple doctrine of fiscal neutrality, the brief argued. It required the state to guarantee to each youngster in the state an education of some indeterminant quality, regardless of the preferences of local voters, taxpayers, and officials. Adequate funding and necessary supervision of the implementation of education programs both were needed to meet the state's constitutional obligation.

The catalyst behind the NAACP-ACLU brief was a professor at the Rutgers law school in Newark, Paul Tractenberg. Some time earlier, and completely independently of Ruvoldt, Tractenberg, too, had concluded that New Jersey's school finance scheme was unfair, and he had his students explore the issue as a semester project. Throughout most of 1970, Tractenberg hesitated to become directly involved in the litigation, as Ruvoldt and the attorney general's office gathered depositions and made cross motions. But in 1971, when the *Serrano* case in California resulted in a ruling that largely supported Ruvoldt's theory, Tractenberg decided to cast his lot with Jersey City's case. Later, Tractenberg would become director of an advocacy law center concentrating on education topics. This shift from university professor to interest representative personifies the transformation of amicus curiae from a neutral observer to a champion of a specific policy viewpoint.

The traditional legal roles of plaintiffs, the government, and amicus curiae were formed at a time when courts focused on adversary disputes between private parties. Judicial scrutiny of public policy requires departures from those standard roles, not only by the parties but also by the courts.

Harold Ruvoldt filed the *Robinson* complaint in the Law Division of the New Jersey Superior Court in February 1970. The complaint went first to Judge Peter Artaserse, who was then in charge of assigning cases to specific superior court judges in Hudson County. Like most state constitutions, the New Jersey Constitution vests the state's judicial power in a supreme court, a superior court, and other lesser courts. The superior court is divided into an appellate division, which is the state's intermediate court, a chancery division, which hears matrimonial and equity cases, and a law division, which handles general suits involving state law. Even though Ruvoldt's suit alleged violations of both the state and federal constitutions, the state court system was the appropriate arena to hear it, because state court systems in the United States are allowed to interpret both state and federal law. As it turned out, Artaserse was an old friend of Ruvoldt's father. He normally assigned cases to other judges on a rotating basis, but he also took many of them himself. Since he was going to retire later that year, however, Artaserse decided not to keep the *Robinson* case. Instead, it went to a stranger to Ruvoldt, Judge Theodore I. Botter. Ruvoldt had never argued a case in Judge Botter's courtroom before, and there were indications that his first suit would not be taken very seriously. When Artaserse gave the case to Botter, he reassured him, "This will be an easy one."

Botter had been a judge of the New Jersey Superior Court for almost six years when he was handed the *Robinson* case. He was regarded by some as a typical Hudson County politician who owed his legal career solely to the local Democratic organization, but, in *Robinson*, Botter would demonstrate that he was far from the usual machine product. A man of animated vitality, Botter was educated in the Weehawken public schools, attended several colleges while in the Army Air Force during World War II, and finally emerged with a law degree from Columbia in 1949. He practiced law privately in New York and Union City and appears to have made a respectable living at it. In 1958, Botter became a New Jersey deputy attorney general, and in short order was promoted to assistant attorney general and then first assistant attorney general. In these posts he handled some cases that touched on education matters and others that involved taxation disputes—all of which gave him some background for evaluating the issues raised by the *Robinson* suit. In May 1964, Theodore Botter became a judge of the New Jersey Superior Court, where he was sitting when Ruvoldt filed *Robinson* v. *Cahill.*

During the course of numerous conferences before the actual trial, Botter offered Ruvoldt few of those hopeful signs that attorneys seek. The first major problem the court faced was narrowing the issues to be litigated in *Robinson*. Ruvoldt's complaint implied consideration of the racial, educational, and economic conditions in each of the state's six hundred school districts, a task which would necessitate many months of testimony. The volume of testimony had to be made manageable. First, the charges of racial segregation and discrimination were set aside, with the plaintiffs agreeing to a dismissal of the issues if they won their case on other grounds and with the court accepting the possibility that the charges could be reintroduced for later appeal if the decision went against the plaintiffs.

The original complaint in *Robinson* was filed on behalf of each named plaintiff as well as all others who were similarly situated as deprived students, overburdened taxpayers, or local officials unable to discharge constitutional obligations.[17] Ruvoldt adopted this class-action technique because he wanted to forestall a quarrel over the mootness of the case, if the original plaintiffs lost their standing to sue in the years ahead.[18] Regardless of the reasons, Botter would not accept the class-action approach. Botter asked Ruvoldt about his plans for listing and notifying each of the students who were deprived by the existing school finance system and all those that the complaint implied were unfairly advantaged by it, an enormous task; Ruvoldt took the hint and abandoned the class-action technique. Ruvoldt then requested a jury trial for the case, so the court could assess damages for the students who had been harmed by the state's school finance system, but Botter flatly denied the request.

Botter's most stinging denial came after Ruvoldt asked that Governor Cahill be required to give a deposition in the case. Shortly after *Robinson* was filed, Governor Cahill made a special address to the legislature, calling for a restructuring of the entire educational finance system.[19] In that speech, Cahill made many of the same points that Ruvoldt had raised in his suit, and Ruvoldt wanted him to repeat them for the court record. Botter was asked to order the reluctant governor to give a deposition when the governor's counsel refused to provide one voluntarily. Botter not only refused to issue such an order, but his refusal seemed to indicate that he doubted the merits of the entire *Robinson* suit. The case was, Judge Botter said, "highly speculative at best," and he would not force the governor to testify. Ruvoldt left the courtroom that day thoroughly dejected and convinced that *Robinson* was a lost cause, at least in Judge Botter's court.

It did not take long for word to get around on the ninth floor of the Hudson County Administration Building that Judge Botter had finally put the brash young lawyer in his place. "See," another judge across the hall told Ruvoldt later that day, when the attorney appeared to argue a different case, "you got what you deserved."

Nevertheless, ever so gradually, friends and supporters of Ruvoldt's cause began to appear, and events in Botter's courtroom became more favorable. To expedite the proceedings and monitor the quality of the defense, Judge Botter allowed most information to be filed through depositions and cross motions. The court would then concentrate its attention on the issues in dispute. Since the case was triggered by easily documented conditions in schools and among taxpayers, few points of factual dispute remained. The attorney general acknowledged the differences in per pupil expenditures caused by variations in district wealth and conceded the presence of inadequate schools. Ruvoldt agreed that financial discrepancies among districts would be reduced by the full funding of a new state program and conceded that conditions in some deprived school districts would be improved.

Robinson's major factual dispute concerned the relationship between expenditures and educational quality. The plaintiffs charged that some students received an inadequate education, because local school districts lacked necessary funds, and they asserted that actions to improve the quality of education in these districts required additional moneys. The attorney general responded that unequal expenditures do not prove that the quality of the education offered to pupils is unequal. During the first two weeks of November 1971, the court heard twelve expert witnesses and held six days of hearings to help it decide the issue.[20]

The plaintiffs assembled ten witnesses to testify that the quality of education was related to the amount spent. Taking care to represent a wide spectrum of educational opinion, Ruvoldt flew in expert witnesses from major universities and recalled another from a cross-county tour in a converted mail truck. The defense called on one present and one former official in the state department of education, both of whom were noted for their expertise in the school finance area.

The transcript of the proceedings reads like a discussion between the judge and the witnesses, with only an occasional interruption to remind the court that there were lawyers present. Botter appeared to be grappling with the perplexing issues involved in the case. During the course of the trial, experts testified from their experience and from their research about the correlation between educational expenditures and pupils' achievement. Ruvoldt did not direct his few questions to the general relationship, however. Instead, he asked if improvements in the quality of inadequate educational programs required additional funds. Even the defense witnesses agreed that they did. Authorities from the department of education could hardly do otherwise, because the official budgetary actions of the commissioner of education and the public positions of the department assumed that increased expenditures improved the quality of the educational program.[21] Ruvoldt had won his most important point. When the decision was rendered, the expert testimony was recounted at length, but that testimony probably did not affect Botter's decision very greatly.

The presumption that a statute is constitutional is a well-established judicial tenet, but a trial court judge can sometimes be more adventuresome. Even though constitutional precedent should be overturned with great reluctance, a trial court judge knows that someone else will have an opportunity to review any decision made in his or her court. An appellate court judge must compromise opinions with the other members of the bench or the harmony needed to perform the court's work will be lost, and a supreme court justice must compromise first with other justices and then with the legislature and the public. Some trial court judges, however, believe that they can occasionally give viewpoints their rein. When a trial court judge decides a constitutional case, he or she has no need to compromise sentiments and has every assurance that a higher court will review the decision before it is imposed on society.[22]

When the attorneys assembled in Botter's chambers on January 19, 1972, to receive the *Robinson* decision, they found a state trooper waiting in the room. Botter explained that he had agreed to send a copy of the ruling to Trenton. Once the trooper had received a copy of the judgment and was on his way, the judge turned to the anxious attorneys.

The decision had been a time-consuming one for Botter to write. He had first studied the mountains of material submitted as evidence. The judge devoted most of a Christmas recess to *Robinson* and then delayed his January cases five or six days while he completed the writing. The written opinion first noted that *Robinson* was similar to cases in other states which alleged violations of the equal protection clause.[23] Botter then summarized the factual evidence presented at the trial and examined the financial characteristics of 144 school districts in New Jersey to demonstrate that the problems he was discussing were not just those of Newark and Jersey City. He quoted with confidence the testimony of a former acting commissioner of education in New Jersey and the analyses of an officer of the Educational Testing Service to support his conclusion that the relation between educational expenditures and pupil achievement was positive but not strong.[24] Botter then held that New Jersey's education finance scheme violated the equal protection guarantees of both the state and federal constitutions and adopted the fiscal neutrality position of the school finance reformers:

> Education is a fundamental interest, vital to the future of every citizen. . . . Lines drawn on the basis of wealth or property, like those of race, are traditionally disfavored. . . . Thus where fundamental rights are asserted under the Equal Protection Clause, classifications will be closely scrutinized . . . . Public education cannot be financed by a method that makes a pupil's education depend upon the wealth of his family and neighbors as distinguished from the wealth of all taxpayers of the same class throughout the state. . . . No compelling state interest justifies New Jersey's present financing system. It is doubtful that this system even meets the less stringent "rational basis" test normally applied to the regulation of state fiscal or economic matters. . . . The New Jersey system of financing public education denies equal protection rights guaranteed by the New Jersey and Federal Constitutions.[25]

Botter humbly acknowledged the complexities of education finance reform.[26] Educational standards, he admitted, were difficult to identify and education programs time consuming to prepare. Furthermore, he feared that his decision might simply increase the cost of the existing educational system without improving its quality or its equity.

Yet Botter's decision did not focus on education alone. In a surprising departure, the opinion also stressed the equal protection rights of *taxpayers*. While Botter was not sure of the exact relationship between equal expenditures and equal protection for schoolchildren, he was more confident of the relation between equal burdens and equal protection for taxpayers. He pointed out that education was a state responsibility and that the taxation clause of the state constitution required taxes to be imposed uniformly on all members of the same class. The decision asserted: "There is no compelling justification for making a taxpayer in one district pay a tax at a higher rate than a taxpayer in another district, so long as the revenue serves the common state educational purpose." [27] Botter concluded that New Jersey's heavy reliance on local property taxation to finance education violated the equal protection rights of overburdened taxpayers and the state constitution's clause requiring uniform standards for taxation. Discharging the state's obligation to provide each student an adequate education was a subtle and indeterminant objective that would demand lengthy effort, but equalization of the tax burden was a specific goal which could be accomplished in a short period. [28] Botter ordered the state to devise a tax program that would pass constitutional muster by the end of the year and granted a longer period for enacting an education program.

The attorney general protested that the timetables Botter had outlined were unrealistic and the substance of his decision was in error. The parties and the court cooperated to move the case quickly to the New Jersey Supreme Court.

The New Jersey Supreme Court normally hears oral arguments on cases every other Monday and Tuesday in its courtroom on the top floor of a state office building in Trenton. Located along the Delaware River, west of the State House in New Jersey's capital complex, the supreme court shares the building with judges of the superior court and personnel of the attorney general's office. On January 9, 1973, the lawyers from the attorney general's office left their offices on the second floor to go up to the fourth floor and join the other lawyers who had assembled there for the oral arguments in the *Robinson* case.

Despite the red velvet drapes on the windows, the chandeliers adorned with brass eagles, the arched and latticed ceiling, and the portraits of earlier justices on the walls, the courtroom appears simply—almost starkly—furnished. Above all else, it conveys the sense of authority traditionally associated with New Jersey's highest court. In a state whose governmental institutions generally receive low marks, the New Jersey Supreme Court has been one of the most respected in the nation.

The New Jersey Supreme Court operates within the context of a dual political and judicial heritage that combines legal professionalism and a long history of innovative policy decisions. The tone of New Jersey's modern court system was established in 1947, when the state adopted a new constitution. The drafting of its judiciary section was dominated by Arthur T. Vanderbilt, a nationally prominent figure in court reform, who believed that a supreme court should provide both administrative and policy leadership to help the state respond to pressing public problems.[29] Vanderbilt was given an opportunity to impress his views on the newly reformed supreme court during almost a decade as the new system's first chief justice. His success has been evident. A recent study measured the legal professionalism of state court systems by examining the patterns of judicial recruitment, court organization, and judicial administration and rated New Jersey second out of the fifty states.[30] The legal stature of New Jersey's court is demonstrated by the facts that Vanderbilt was a serious candidate for Chief Justice of the United States Supreme Court in the early 1950s and that the last state supreme court justice promoted to the United States Supreme Court, William Brennan, came from the New Jersey court.

Also, the New Jersey Supreme Court has rarely been bashful about assuming an active policy role. Almost twenty-five years before John Marshall's Supreme Court established the authority of federal courts to invalidate an act of Congress in 1803, a New Jersey court had already become the first in the nation to strike down a legislative act.[31] New Jersey's justices still hold the view that they should do more than simply dispose of cases. Each year the seven justices on New Jersey's highest court generally write full decisions in less than seventy-five cases, about half the number written by the justices of the United States Supreme Court. By writing fewer decisions, they are better able to consider the policy implications of each case.[32] In a recent poll, the justices of the supreme courts of New Jersey, Massachusetts, Pennsylvania, and Louisiana were asked whether they believed that courts should be restricted to a formal role of interpreting and applying existing law or whether they believed that the judges should feel free to make policy judgments. In Massachusetts, Pennsylvania, and Louisiana, more than two-thirds of the justices asserted that the task of a supreme court was to interpret law.[33] In New Jersey, only one of the seven justices replied that they should simply interpret the law; the other six contended that fashioning public policy was an essential part of their job. Not long ago, a former New Jersey justice elaborated on the court's policy role:

> In *Asbury Park* v. *Woolley* [an early reapportionment case], people raised the political thicket argument contending that we should stay out because the questions were too political, but they should have known better. They should have known that no thicket was too political for us. . . . The questions of law are settled [in the Appellate Division] before cases come to us. . . . Decisions should not change law every year because there should be some stability; perhaps every five years. But decisions must change law sometime, because law is largely policy anyway.

A third political tradition in New Jersey is not unique to the supreme court, but it frequently envelops some members of the court and other personnel in the governor's office. In New Jersey, these are often the same persons, because lawyers who serve in the governor's office are commonly appointed to the supreme court and law students who become clerks for judges frequently find prominent roles in subsequent administrations. This third tradition can best be called the antilegislative tradition. Many court cases, it is said, result from the fact that the legislature lacks the will or the capacity to write good legislation, and its work must be corrected by the judiciary. Legislators sometimes ask the court to specify problem areas where laws need to be amended, but when the justices make recommendations in decisions or in person, the recommendations are ignored and nothing is done. The legislature frequently scuttles the governor's programs, because legislators lack the staff to understand policy questions and lack concern for anything except their own political interests. "New Jersey has a good court system," one proponent of this view concluded, "a good, but certainly not the best, executive branch, but a punk legislature." While there is some truth to this biting characterization of the legislature, the antilegislative tradition in New Jersey politics probably emerges from the inevitable tension between the legal and the democratic modes of conducting public business and the frustrations that result from defeats at the hands of the legislature. These three court traditions of legal professionalism, an active policy role, and a low regard for the legislature might not have been equally shared by each of the seven members of the court on that Tuesday morning in January 1973, but they would have been acknowledged by most of them.

The justices of New Jersey's highest court, led by the court's most junior member, file into the courtroom through a door in the front of the room. The chief justice sits at the center of the bench, flanked by the senior associate justice on his immediate right, and the second-ranking associate justice on his immediate left.

In January 1973, the court was still headed by Joseph Weintraub who was coming to the end of his fifteen-year tenure as chief justice. Under Weintraub, the New Jersey Supreme Court became famous as a critic of the precepts and decisions of the United States Supreme Court in the field of criminal justice. Although they did not join the efforts to assault the court by constitutionally altering its jurisdiction, New Jersey justices freely ridiculed the national court's decisions on criminal procedures as unrealistic and unconcerned with questions of guilt or innocence.[34] This was not simply a policy dispute. The disagreement reflected a profound conflict between the federal and state supreme courts about the desirability of basing judicial decisions on the provisions of the constitution or on the tenets of common law.

Common law is not a fixed body of written rules codified in a legal handbook, but a series of unwritten principles based on custom and tradition that attempts to express a sense of equity in the context of a changing society. Common law is not enacted by legislators but is articulated from the bench by judges, and it stands below both constitutional provision and legislative statute on the hierarchy of legal authority. Common law possesses a practical quality that enables it to be changed and adapted to the developments in society. In *The Common Law,* Oliver Wendell Holmes justifies this quality:

> The life of the law has not been logic; it has been experience. The felt necessities of the time, the prevalent moral and political theories, intuitions of public policy, avowed or unconscious, even the prejudices which judges share with their fellow-man, have had a good deal more to do than syllogism in determining the rules by which men should be governed. . . . The very considerations which judges most rarely mention, and always with an apology, are the secret root from which the law draws all the juices of life.[35]

By the 1960s, a majority of the Warren Court had moved away from the traditional common law premises of criminal procedure to seek constitutional rules on which to base their decisions.[36] Questions of guilt and innocence in particular situations were sacrificed to the need to define rules preserving constitutionally based individual rights. The New Jersey court objected, first on the grounds that the United States Supreme Court was too far removed from local circumstances to develop a clear set of rules to govern the police activities that disturbed it, thus making confusion and judicial involvement inevitable; and, second, the New Jersey justices contended that decisions based on constitutional provision possessed a timelessness that made them difficult to reverse if future conditions warranted. Decisions which rested on the common law, in contrast, reflected a sense of humility that acknowledged that justices might not be able to anticipate all future problems. Such rulings could easily be adjusted by the court or superseded by the legislature if they generated hardship in the present or became unworkable in the future. This common law orientation permitted the New Jersey Supreme Court to champion its view of equity in sensitive policy disputes and, at the same time, to accommodate the exigencies of legislative and executive behavior.[37]

The Weintraub Court, as it had come to be called, touched every aspect of New Jersey law during Joseph Weintraub's long tenure,

but its time was passing. While the full membership of the Weintraub Court had remained unchanged for more than a decade, by
1973 its ranks had begun to thin. Only three of the members who
had served throughout the 1960s would participate in the *Robinson*
decision, and none of them would be a fully active member of the
court by the fall of 1974. *Robinson* v. *Cahill* was to be the last major decision of the Weintraub Court and certainly one of its most
prominent.

When New Jersey's justices arrive in the morning for oral argument, they enter a robing chamber between the courtroom and the
conference room. More than anything, the court's conference room
in Trenton resembles a movie set for a banquet hall in a modest
castle. The long narrow conference table sits in the center of
the dark-paneled, high-ceilinged room. The narrow windows, embedded with stained-glass replicas of the New Jersey seal, look out
on the State House and across the Delaware River to Pennsylvania.
When the justices meet, the chief justice sits at the head of the
table, facing the huge fireplace at the far end of the room. A small
table for the court's clerk has been placed on the chief justice's
left. Bookcases containing volumes of statutes and bundles of current court papers line one wall.

When *Robinson* was first argued before the New Jersey Supreme
Court, Harold Ruvoldt, Jr., represented Jersey City and the other
plaintiffs, the attorney general's office represented the governor and
other defendants, and the NAACP and the ACLU were represented
as amici curiae. Chief Justice Weintraub presided. We do not know
what specifically transpired when the justices conferred on the *Robinson* case, but retired Justice John Francis has described the typical conference procedure of the Weintraub Court:

> After the argument and before the conference, it was the duty
> of each justice to consider each case and reach a tentative
> conclusion. . . . When the justices assembled for the Tuesday
> conference, not one of them knew until the Chief Justice
> called on him to discuss a particular case that he would write
> the opinion if the views he expressed received the support of
> the majority. . . . After the justice called upon reviewed the
> appeal and announced his feelings about the desirable result,

Chief Justice Weintraub continued the discussion, suggesting his own views. Each of his colleagues then set forth his opinion, normally in order of seniority, until a majority decision was reached.[38]

The scene sounds like a classroom in which Weintraub the teacher quizzed his students to see how well they had done their homework. Thus supreme court decisions under Weintraub were not simply a matter of each justice announcing his vote. Instead, the decisions emerged in a consensus after discussion, in which Weintraub often vigorously pushed his own views.[39] Even though the chambers of the seven justices were scattered in different parts of the state, the justices would normally write or telephone comments about the draft of an opinion back and forth before the next conference. Dissenting opinions were usually circulated before the majority draft, to permit the majority the opportunity to accommodate conflicting views. Characteristically, decisions of the Weintraub Court stressed areas of agreement within the court and avoided unnecessary topics of dispute. As a result, the Weintraub Court produced a deceptively large number of unanimous decisions.[40]

After the oral arguments in January 1973, Chief Justice Weintraub took upon himself the task of writing the court's judgment in *Robinson* v. *Cahill*.[41] The justices sometimes held a conference on a case in which the issues were clearly defined; one justice went off to draft a decision, and then all the other justices quickly assented to the draft. Apparently, writing the court's decision in *Robinson* was not so easy. The United States Supreme Court was then participating actively in the school finance controversy, the questions of law involved in the case were inchoate, and the diversity of judicial opinion was substantial. The court's decision in *Robinson* clearly articulated certain principles, but the logic offered in support of some of its conclusions was more murky.

The trial court had relied heavily on the equal protection guarantees of both the state and federal constitutions to invalidate New Jersey's school finance program. Two weeks before the New Jersey Supreme Court delivered its decision in *Robinson*, the United States Supreme Court handed the school finance reformers a stunning defeat in *San Antonio Independent School District* v. *Rodriguez*. In a five-to-four decision, the nation's highest court rejected the argument that existing state school finance programs violated the equal protection safeguards of the federal constitution. The narrow United States majority ruled that the Texas school finance system did not discriminate among children on the basis of wealth and that the federal Constitution did not guarantee a fundamental right to education. Because of these findings, Texas was required to show only that its program for financing elementary and secondary education was rational, not to demonstrate that it was the necessary result of some "compelling state interest."

With this assistance, Weintraub easily found that the New Jersey statute was rational and thus did not violate the federal equal protection guarantees.[42] But he did not stop there. Having disposed of the specific claim in *Robinson*, Weintraub went on to attack the United States Supreme Court's approach to equal protection litigation in the same terms he used elsewhere to denounce the high court's rulings in the criminal justice area.[43] He complained that the concepts of "fundamental rights" and "compelling state interest" were too vague to be applied successfully, and, even if the concepts could be adequately defined, such mechanical standards for judicial action diverted attention from the merits of the issues being considered.

The New Jersey Supreme Court was also unwilling to accept the contention that the state's school finance scheme violated the state equal protection guarantees. Education, they pointed out "is handled no differently than sundry other essential services" such as police, fire protection, and public assistance. All are basic and essential to the people who receive them. State uniformity in one would imply state uniformity in the others, and that would require a fundamental change in the state's political structure. The court rejected plaintiffs' argument that, if the state decided to provide a service, that service automatically became a fundamental right.

Having rebuffed the state and federal equal protection arguments, Weintraub then considered the trial court contention that the school finance system violated the taxation clause of the state constitution that asserted that all property should be taxed uniformly.[44] Plaintiffs argued that this provision was violated because property of equal value in different communities was taxed at different rates to support schools. Education is a state obligation, yet support for education comes primarily from a tax on local property, which is imposed at widely divergent rates throughout the state. The court simply said no. The tax clause did not prevent the state from delegating functions to municipalities and having those functions funded by local taxation. The clause meant that, if the state provided a service at the state level which was supported by a property tax, the tax must be imposed on all property in the state rather than on property in only one or two regions of the state; and, if the state assigned a responsibility to local governments, the localities must tax all property within their boundaries at the same ratio to support the task. The school finance system, the court ruled, did not violate the taxation provision of the state constitution.

That left only one of Ruvoldt's arguments still standing: the state's program for funding elementary and secondary schools violated the education clause of the New Jersey Constitution: "The legislature shall provide for the maintenance and support of a thorough and efficient system of free public schools for the instruction of all the children in this state between the ages of five and eighteen years." [45] To determine exactly what this provision meant, Weintraub reviewed the history of public education in New Jersey. Based on nineteenth-century practice, the opinion concluded that the education clause did not prevent the use of local taxation to meet the state's constitutional obligation.[46] What was that constitutional obligation? The decision goes on:

> The Constitution's guarantee must be understood to embrace that educational opportunity which is needed in the contemporary setting to equip a child for his role as a citizen and as a competitor in the labor market . . . we do not doubt that an equal educational opportunity for children was precisely in mind. The mandate . . . can have no other import.[47]

Having failed to find an equality requirement in the explicit provisions of the state or federal constitution, the court discovered a similar mandate in the education clause. If the quality of instruction in any school district in the state falls short of the constitutional command, it is the state's obligation to restore it to a "thorough and efficient" level. This construction enabled the court to avoid the pitfalls of a comprehensive equal opportunity standard and yet permitted it to inquire whether New Jersey's school finance system reached a comparable standard. The decision stated:

> The trial court found the constitutional demand had not been met and did so on the basis of discrepancies in dollar input per pupil. We agree . . . [it is] clear that there is a significant connection between the sums expended and the quality of the educational opportunity. . . . we accept the proposition that the quality of educational opportunity does depend in substantial measure upon the number of dollars invested. . . .[48]

Ignoring the disputes among social scientists, the court adopted this clear position on the contentious cost-quality debate. The cost-quality relationship then enabled the court to discover limitations within the education clause on the state's ability to delegate its educational responsibilities to local government. The court held that the education clause could impose restrictions on per pupil expenditure variations, even though general variations in educational expenditures were sanctioned by other clauses in the constitution.

What were the circumstances that enabled the court to find in the education clause restrictions not found elsewhere in the constitution? First, the state had never explicitly defined its obligation under the education clause, and it had not enacted a program to guarantee that the obligation would be met. The state's existing education finance program was unconstitutional, because it was a "patchy product reflecting provincial contests rather than a plan sensitive only to the constitutional mandate." [49] The standards implicit in the education clause required that the state's school funding system be more than simply rational. The court scrutinized the program closely to determine if it overcame discrepancies in funds available to support education in local communities. It did not.

Then, there were the variations in expenditures themselves. The discrepancies in education funds, the court held, reflected a general inequality caused by the state's heavy reliance on local property taxation to fund public services. The court commented at length:

> It is undeniable that local expenditures per pupil do vary, and generally because other essential services must also be met out of the same tax base and the total demands exceed

what the local taxpayers are willing or able to endure. But for that same reason similar discrepancies, both as to benefits and burdens, can be found with respect to the other vital services which the State provides through its local subdivisions. . . . The case now before us was not tried or argued in terms that local government as a political institution denies equal protection in New Jersey because unequal demands upon unequal tax bases result in statewide inequality as to benefits or as to tax burden. In these circumstances we will not pursue the equal protection issue in the limited context of public education. Nor do we consider a question of parties have not projected, whether, apart from the equal protection guarantee, there is an implicit premise in the concept of local government that the State may not distribute its fiscal responsibility through that vehicle if substantial inequality will result. It may well be that at one time there was a rough correlation between the needs of an area and the local resources to meet them so that there was no conspicuous unfairness in assigning State obligations to the local units of government. Surely that is not true today in our State. Problems are now mobile. They have settled intensively in limited areas. Statewide there is no correlation between the local tax base and the number of pupils to be educated, or the number of the poor to be housed and clothed and fed, or the incidence of crime and juvenile delinquency, or the cost of police or fire protection, or the demands of the judicial process. Problems which are in no sense local in origin have become the special burden of those who cannot find a haven elsewhere.[50]

The stunning implication was that perhaps the whole structure of local government itself was unconstitutional.

In its decision, the court did not indicate which of these two factors was more important: the state's failure to define the content of its educational obligation or its heavy reliance on local property taxation. There is an admirable reluctance among justices to be too assertive in new areas of the law where standards and doctrines are only beginning to take shape, and education finance was just such an area. Perhaps more to the point, the contortions Weintraub went through to reach his conclusion in *Robinson* hinted at tensions between the "fiscal" and "educational" perspectives that existed among the justices themselves. For some, *Robinson* was essentially an educational statement, requiring the state to be sure that school programs in local districts measured up to a constitutional standard. This viewpoint was later reflected by one of the justices who voted in favor of the original ruling, when he complained that the public discussion of *Robinson* had "extravagantly overemphasized the fiscal aspects" of the decision.[51]

From the other perspective, analyses of *Robinson* could not overemphasize the fiscal aspects of the judgment, because those were the essence of the ruling. *Robinson* became an educational decision, not because of the substance of the issues, but because of the development of the law. Decades of cases dealing with flag salutes, prayer in schools, civil rights, student conduct, and the rights of the handicapped had deeply involved courts in school district operations. Although courts had volumes of precedent for adjudicating educational issues, legal doctrines dating from the New Deal had all but barred justices from evaluating standards of taxation. Those economic decisions had been surrendered to the legislative branch. Thus, even though *Robinson* was primarily directed at the destructive consequences of the state's heavy reliance on local property taxation, especially for older cities, prudence and precedent compelled the court to rest its opinion on the education clause of the state constitution. A justice who endorsed the original *Robinson* decision conveys the tax-oriented perspective:

> The court did not say that you had to have an income tax, but anyone with an ounce of sense would know that the only possible solution to the problem was the adoption of an income tax or something much worse [such as increased sales or statewide property taxes. A later decision] . . . was even more direct. There, some communities argued that they would be hurt by the burdens of development, but the decision pointed out that relief from the consequences of the existing tax system in the state was to be sought from other branches of government. A clear endorsement of an income tax.

The Weintraub Court, true to its form, worked hard to prepare a written opinion that all the justices could support. On occasion, this meant avoiding divisive issues. Some justices argued that the logic of the decision would prevent local school districts from spending local funds to give their own children a better-than-equal opportunity to get a good education. Limitations on local school expenditures must be imposed, they contended. Others replied sternly that they would have to dissent from legal principles that had such implications. As a consequence, the court's formal decision did not directly address the issue of local expenditure leeway.

One justice summarized the court's general strategy for preparing opinions in cases like *Robinson:*

> The quality of judicial writing is one of encouraging the legislature, setting activities in motion which will have secondary consequences to lead the senators and assemblymen to act. This is the essence of democracy. We can encourage the legislature to pass laws or taxes without directing them to do that. This is the wonder of our system, and besides it works to accomplish judicial objectives.

Robinson was used to ignite a controversy that consumed much of the energy of the legislature and the executive for the next three years, but it did not command the state to enact a specific program. The shape of the state's response to the judgment was a matter for legislative and executive determination. Even though they were troubled by the consequences of the state's existing policies, the justices believed that courts should be very timid about imposing their own programs on society. True to the admonition, "If you look at the constitution and see only your own image, you know you're in trouble," the court's judgment in *Robinson* did not erect rigid constitutional tests that would have had unfortunate implications for the future. The court integrated a forceful political strategy with a restrained legal philosophy. Weintraub placed the issue of tax reform on the governmental agenda without establishing constitutional doctrines that would hinder future courts—once the issues of *Robinson* were resolved.

The genius of the *Robinson* decision was that it could say different things to different people. To federal judges, it would say that the ruling rests on provisions of the state constitution, and there is no need for their involvement. To the legislature and the public, the court would say that heavy reliance on local property taxation to fund education and for other purposes should be reduced. To the New Jersey Education Association and the New Jersey School Boards Association, it indicated that additional state support for local schools was in the offing. Once the controversy ignited by

Robinson had passed, the judgment would remain a mandate for judicial action that future state justices could invoke or ignore at their pleasure.

Robinson climaxed the career of Justice Weintraub, advanced the career of Judge Botter, and launched the career of Harold Ruvoldt, Jr. On June 30, 1976, dozens of state officials were crowded into a federal courtroom trying to unravel the consequences of Ruvoldt's argument, which they would have ridiculed seven years earlier. No longer an unknown Jersey City lawyer, Ruvoldt would be invited by groups to speak about the *Robinson* case on an average of twice a week. He has recently been appointed Hudson County attorney and named to the editorial board of the *New Jersey State Bar Journal,* the magazine which had printed his first article in 1969. He is busier now, but still shares the two-man office with his father in that dingy neighborhood along Ocean Avenue in Jersey City. Having won his case before the New Jersey Supreme Court in April 1973, Ruvoldt could look back over the events of the previous years with some satisfaction, in the hope that the opportunities for the kids who congregated at the candy store down the block would be enhanced. He would not have been so sanguine, however, if he could have anticipated the three years of contention and stalemate that lay ahead.

The fate of school finance decisions, even more than most judicial rulings, depends on activities outside the courtroom. *Robinson* did not liberate discussions of education and tax policy from the premises of previously established state programs. On the contrary, the debates initiated by the court reflected the contours of existing state policies and echoed the sentiments of contemporary public attitudes. Those debates might have been different if developments in law had permitted the justices to make an explicit tax decision, but they had not. The controversies might have been precluded if the state's policy institutions could have addressed the issues quickly, but they could not. The New Jersey Supreme Court's decision in *Robinson* v. *Cahill* reflected an uncertain blend of concern about education policy, school finance, and property tax rates, and somehow the governing institutions of the state would have to respond to it.

NOTES

1. Harold J. Ruvoldt, Jr., "The Right to Learn," *New Jersey State Bar Journal* 51 (January 1970): 16.

2. New Jersey Commissioner of Education, decision in *Board of Education of Jersey City et al.* v. *Board of School Estimate of the City of Jersey City, Hudson County,* 24 March 1970.

3. Harold J. Ruvoldt, Jr., Plaintiff's Complaint as filed on 13 February 1970.

4. See Note, "Government Litigation in the Supreme Court: The Roles of the Solicitor General," *Yale Law Journal* 83 (July 1969): 1442.

5. Randall W. Bland, *Private Pressure on Public Law: The Legal Career of Justice Thurgood Marshall* (Port Washington, N.Y.: Kennikat Press, 1973); Richard Kluger, *Simple Justice: The History of Brown v. Board of Education and Black America's Struggle for Equality* (New York: Alfred A. Knopf, 1976).

6. See *Booker* v. *Board of Education, Plainfield,* 45 N.J. 161 (1965); also, *Board of Education, East Brunswick Township* v. *East Brunswick Township,* 48 N.J. 94 (1966).

7. Eleanor P. Wolf, "Social Science and the Courts: The Detroit Schools Case," *The Public Interest* 42 (Winter 1976): 102–20.

8. Joel L. Fleishman and Carol S. Greenwald, "Public Interest Litigation and Political Finance Reform," *The Annals of the American Academy of Political and Social Science* 425 (May 1976): 114–23.

9. Kluger, *Simple Justice,* p. 547; David R. Manwaring, *Render unto Caesar: The Flag Salute Controversy* (Chicago: University of Chicago Press, 1962), p. 234.

10. John E. Patton, *While New Jersey Slept: The Botter Decision Revisited* (Belleville, N.J.: privately printed, 1976).

11. Perhaps the best single account remains Clement Vose, *Caucasians Only: The Supreme Court, the NAACP, and the Restrictive Covenant Cases* (Berkeley: University of California Press, 1959); for an early discussion, see also, Note, "Private Attorneys-General: Group Action in the Fight for Civil Liberties," *Yale Law Journal* 58 (March 1949): 574.

12. Jonathan D. Casper, *Lawyers Before the Warren Court: Civil Liberties and Civil Rights, 1957–1966* (Urbana: University of Illinois Press, 1972), pp. 198 ff.

13. Michael Meltsner, *Cruel and Unusual: The Supreme Court and Capital Punishment* (New York: Random House, 1973), p. 107.

14. Samuel Krislov, "The *Amicus Curiae* Brief: From Friendship to Advocacy," *Yale Law Journal* 72 (March 1963): 694.

15. Anthony Lewis, *Gideon's Trumpet* (New York: Random House, 1964); Bland, *Private Pressure on Public Law,* p. 52.

16. See Phillip Kurland, *Politics, the Constitution and the Warren Court* (Chicago: University of Chicago Press, 1970), esp. chap. 5, "Problems of a Political Court"; also, Lucius Barker, "Third Parties in Litigation," *Journal of Politics* 29 (February 1967): 41–71.

17. Note, "Expanding the Impact of State Court Class Action Adjudications to Provide an Effective Forum for Consumers," *UCLA Law Review* 18 (May 1971): 1002; L. Ashe, "Class Action: Solution for the Seventies," *New England Law Review* 7 (Fall 1971): 1.

18. Harold J. Ruvoldt, Jr., "Educational Financing in New Jersey: *Robinson v. Cahill* and Beyond," *Seton Hall Law Review* 5 (Fall 1973), n. 27.

19. Special Message to the Legislature by Governor William T. Cahill, "Toward Excellence in Education in the Seventies," 9 April 1970.

20. Patton, "While New Jersey Slept," p. 4.

21. The expert witnesses called by the plaintiffs were: Dr. Henry M. Levin, Associate Professor of Economics and Education at Stanford University, who had received a Ph.D. in Economics from Rutgers University; Dr. Mark Hurwitz, Executive Director of the New Jersey School Boards Association; Dr. Harold Seamon, Director of Special Services for the New Jersey School Boards Association; Dr. James Guthrie, Assistant Professor of Education at the University of California; Dr. Richard Rossmiller, Professor of Education at the University of Wisconsin; Henry S. Dyer, Consultant to the New Jersey State Department of Education; Steven Michelson, Lecturer at Harvard Graduate School of Education; Robert P. Martinez, Staff Counsel to the New Jersey School Boards Association; Aaron Schulman, Manpower Planner for the City of Jersey City; and Neil Gold, Director of the Suburban Action Institute. The defense presented Dr. Edward Kilpatrick, New Jersey Assistant Commissioner of Education, and Dr. Joseph Clayton, former Acting Commissioner of Education. See material cited in Wolf, "Social Science and the Courts"; and Patricia E. Stivers, "Social Science Data and the Courts," *Educational Researcher* 5 (May 1976): 11–13.

22. See Henry J. Abraham, *Justices and Presidents: A Political History of Appointments to the Supreme Court* (New York: Oxford University Press, 1974).

23. 118 N.J. 223, at 227.

24. Ibid., at 253.

25. Ibid., at 275, 274.

26. Ibid., at 248.

27. Ibid., at 278.

28. Ibid., at 281.

29. Arthur T. Vanderbilt II, *Changing Law: A Biography of Arthur T. Vanderbilt* (New Brunswick: Rutgers University Press, 1976); Richard J. Connors, *The Process of Constitutional Revision in New Jersey: 1940–1947* (New York: National Municipal League, 1970); and N. Baisder, *Charter for New Jersey: The New Jersey Constitutional Convention of 1947* (Trenton: State Library, New Jersey Department of Education, 1952), pp. 40–41.

30. Henry Robert Glick and Kenneth N. Vines, *State Court Systems* (Englewood Cliffs, N.J.: Prentice-Hall, 1973), p. 11. This rating is based upon their "index of legal professionalism." This is a composite score including five major factors of state court systems: (1) method of selection for judges in all courts—states were scored for approximation to American Bar Association model plan of selection; (2) state courts organization and the approximation to the A.B.A. model court structure; (3) judicial administration in the states—states were scored for presence of professional administration and size and nature of staff; (4) tenure of office for judges of major trial and appellate courts and approximation to A.B.A. recommendations; (5) level of basic salary for judges of major trial and appellate courts exclusive of fees and local payments. Each factor involved scoring the states

on a five-point scale according to how closely judicial features in the state approached the A.B.A. model.

31. "State Supreme Court: A New Team," *New York Times,* 12 April 1976, New Jersey Section 16, pp. 28–29.

32. In 1973–1974, the justices of the United States Supreme Court wrote decisions in 147 cases, while the justices of the New Jersey Supreme Court wrote decisions in only 63 cases.

33. Glick and Vines, *State Court Systems,* p. 61.

34. *Newark Evening News,* 24 April 1968.

35. Oliver Wendell Holmes, *The Common Law* (Boston: Little, Brown, 1881), pp. 1–2; see also, Roscoe Pound, *The Spirit of the Common Law* (Boston: Little, Brown, 1921).

36. Dominick A. Mazzagetti, "Chief Justice Joseph Weintraub: The New Jersey Supreme Court, 1957–1973," *Cornell Law Review* 59 (January 1974), esp. pp. 203–8; "Judicial Federalism: Rights of the Accused in New Jersey," *Rutgers Law Review* 23 (1969): 530 ff. Stanley H. Friedelbaum, "Constitutional Law and Judicial Policy Making," in Alan Rosenthal and John Blydenburgh, eds., *Politics in New Jersey* (New Brunswick: Eagleton Institute of Politics, Rutgers University, 1975), esp. pp. 232–34.

37. *In the Matter of Karen Quinlan: An Alleged Incompetent,* New Jersey Supreme Court, A-116, September Term, 1975, decided 31 March 1976; Thomas Julius Anton, "The Politics of State Taxation: A Case Study of Decision-Making in New Jersey Legislature" (Ph.D. dissertation, Princeton University, 1961).

38. John J. Francis, "Joseph Weintraub—A Judge for All Seasons," *Cornell Law Review* 59 (January 1974): 188–89.

39. Francis, "Joseph Weintraub," p. 188; Henry J. Abraham, *The Judicial Process* (New York: Oxford University Press, 1962), pp. 205–6.

40. Robert J. Sickles, "The Illusion of Judicial Consensus," *American Political Science Review* 59 (March 1965): 100.

41. 411 U.S. 1 (1973).

42. 62 N.J. at 488–489.

43. *State* v. *Funicella,* 60 N.J. at 68–84.

44. See 1044 N.J. State Constitution, as amended in 1075, Article IV, Section 7, clause 12; also, 1947 Constitution, Article VIII, Section 1, clause 1.

45. 1875 Amendment to Article IV, Section 7, clause 6 of 1844 N.J. State Constitution.

46. 62 N.J. at 510.

47. 62 N.J. at 515, 513.

48. 62 N.J. at 515, 516, 481.

49. 62 N.J. at 519, 520.

50. 62 N.J. at 499–501.

51. Oral argument of 24 November 1975.

3

Robinson in the News

In New Jersey, supreme court justices do not read their decisions aloud to the assembled litigants and the press.[1] Instead, written copies of their rulings are normally distributed at 10 A.M. in the office of the court's clerk. The Trenton press corps, headquartered on the first floor of the State House, is usually warned twenty-four hours in advance of the announcement of a major decision. On minor cases, wire service newswriters pick up copies of the decision and pass them out to other State House reporters; on major decisions, reporters will jam the clerk's office to get copies of the ruling and then hurry off to file stories as their individual deadlines dictate.

On the morning of April 3, 1973, more than a dozen reporters were crammed into the narrow waiting space in front of the counter in the clerk's office. On the previous day, they had received a confidential memorandum from the court notifying them that a decision in *Robinson* v. *Cahill* was forthcoming. Breaking with custom, some reporters had ignored the "confidential" stamp on the court's release and written stories alerting their readers that the long-awaited decision on school funding was due. On that Tuesday morning, several newspeople anxiously glanced up at the wall clock; the decision was to be released at 10 A.M. Reporters on afternoon papers would have no more than thirty minutes to grab a copy of the decision, scan the pages of intricate legal argument, write a three-hundred-word story, and then phone it in to their editors.

The first news accounts of a court decision usually break the story with a hard-news lead: "The New Jersey Supreme Court ruled today. . . ." After filing their announcements of a decision, reporters often prepare more comprehensive stories by securing evaluations of the opinion from the parties and public officials involved. The original press stories then give way to second-day articles recording how the various luminaries viewed the ruling: "Generally cautious reaction greeted yesterday's supreme court decision . . . ." Even with years of hindsight, those initial, rushed accounts of *Robinson* have proven to be remarkably accurate, and the second-day stories correctly highlighted those aspects of the ruling which would become the most controversial in the years ahead. When reporters questioned the governor, the commissioner of education, legislators, and interest group representatives about *Robinson*, they all pointed out that the ruling placed the complex issues of tax reform, equal opportunity, and the quality of education squarely before the state's policy institutions.

Without the pressure of deadlines, more systematic appraisals of New Jersey's initial reactions to *Robinson* are possible. Understanding of the state's response to the ruling first requires knowledge of New Jersey politics and government and then demands careful analysis of the attitudes of the people involved in the controversy. For this study, structured interviews were conducted with samples of the state's residents, legislators, educators, and interest group leaders. During these discussions, people's assessments of the *Robinson* decision were recorded, and their opinions about the issues involved in the ruling were explored. These opinions about New Jersey's courts, the state's system of public education, its taxation policies, and fiscal equity guided New Jersey's reaction to *Robinson*, and these opinions, in turn, were then reshaped by the events that followed the decision. Information gathered during these interviews forms the basis of this chapter, but professional readers may want to examine the actual data, which are summarized in Appendix B.

TRENTON, April 3—The New Jersey Supreme Court struck down the state's system of financing public school education today on the grounds that it failed to fulfill an 1875 mandate in the state's constitution for equal educational opportunity.
—New York Times, 4 April 1973

A fundamental principle of democratic government is that public policies which affect large numbers of people should be influenced by public opinion. A major dilemma in using public opinion to direct public policy, however, is that the general public usually has well-developed opinions on very few issues. Furthermore, the opinions that the public does hold are frequently so vague and undefined that they cannot serve as a meaningful guide to specific policy choices in concrete situations. This is particularly true of public policy choices facing state governments. States exist as intermediate units of government in a limbo between city and nation, too big and too remote to permit much direct citizen participation and yet too small and unimportant to capture the attention of the national news media.[2] Trapped between the immediacy of local government and the televised glamour of Washington, states generally lose out in the struggle for public notice. As a result, citizens are usually less knowledgeable about the policies and personalities of state government than about similar aspects of either local or national politics.[3]

Public affairs in New Jersey stand out as being peculiarly invisible, even within this nationwide pattern of low salience for state politics. New Jerseyans do not possess any strong sentiments or special like-mindedness on which a sense of statehood can rest. They are a diverse group who look first to their local communities for solutions to day-to-day problems. The state's residents are no less interested in public affairs than citizens of other states, but their access to political information is more limited. Sandwiched between New York City and Philadelphia, New Jersey has lacked its own statewide newspapers and its own commercial television stations to focus public attention on state politics. Consequently, fully developed views on public events, contemporary political figures, and important institutions are even rarer in New Jersey than they are in other states.[4]

Reporters called the *Robinson* decision a "landmark" opinion, and their editors ran the stories under banner headlines on the front page. Thoughtful second-day articles were published, analyzing the implications of the ruling for the state's education, taxation, and school finance programs. The average New Jersey resident is a well-educated, well-paid suburbanite, but despite this newspaper treatment, *Robinson* never captured the public mind. Public opinion polls showed that few state residents followed the case during its stormy three-year history, and even fewer could explain what it meant.[5] Aside from the dearth of political information in New Jersey, the *Robinson* case itself had a limited impact on the public consciousness, because the activities of state supreme courts are generally quite remote from people's lives.[6] Most citizens are only dimly aware of the existence of a state supreme court, and few can supply the name of its chief justice. For them, a court decision in a specific case is understandably even more obscure. Like its counterparts in other states, the New Jersey Supreme Court is more the object of elite attention than generalized public interest, and its rulings usually escape the scrutiny of all but the most concerned citizens.

Even after the years of extraordinary publicity which surrounded the *Robinson* case, the typical citizen's view of the New Jersey Supreme Court still rested more on vague impressions than on careful appraisals of court actions.[7] Popular evaluations of the supreme court were not based on ideological or policy grounds. Indeed, they appeared to be almost random. Republicans held basically the same opinion of the court as Democrats, liberals differed little from conservatives, and no major variations appeared among age, education, or income groups. Instead, perceptions of the court appeared to be related to broad evaluations of governmental institutions in general. People who believed that the state supreme court was doing a good job were also likely to believe that the United States Supreme Court, New Jersey's governor, and the state legislature were also performing well. Those who had negative views of the court were usually the same ones who condemned other governmental institutions. The prominent events of the *Robinson* years made the New Jersey Supreme Court somewhat more visible to the public than it had been in the past, but the popular images of the court remained impressionistic and poorly developed.

The lack of solid information about public events did not halt the decline in public confidence in governmental institutions that had characterized public opinion in both New Jersey and the United States since the mid-1960s.[8] The traumas of Vietnam and Watergate had undermined public confidence in the national government, and accounts of congressional impropriety had frustrated attempts to rebuild it. The impact of these national scandals was compounded in New Jersey by the spectacle of a series of state and municipal officials being indicted for criminal wrongdoing, convicted, and sent off to prison. In 1975, less than one-quarter of the state's residents had a favorable view of their governor, the state legislature, or even the United States Congress. Popular ratings of the New Jersey Supreme Court were somewhat more favorable than those of other governmental institutions, but the over-all view was still negative. Citizens complained that courts were too involved in political controversies and too lenient with criminals. Three residents criticized the performance of New Jersey's highest court for every two who praised it.[9] The years of the mid-seventies were ones of great distrust of governmental institutions in New Jersey, but the state's supreme court remained more highly esteemed than any other institution. During the *Robinson* years, in fact, popular approval of the New Jersey Supreme Court actually edged slightly higher.

The *Robinson* decision itself got mixed reviews from New Jersey's citizens.[10] When pollsters explained the ruling to a cross section of the state's voters, a narrow but consistent majority expressed their opposition. Despite the fact that the case was triggered by the financial plight of urban centers, most residents of the state's growing suburbs praised the decision, while two-thirds of those living in established urban areas condemned it. Citizens' evaluations of *Robinson* were only loosely related to their policy preferences on other issues. Liberals did approve of the decision more frequently than conservatives, but people who were most concerned about the conditions of the poor and disadvantaged backed it no more strongly than those who did not acknowledge such concern. New Jerseyans who applauded *Robinson* were no more willing to shoulder the burden of increased taxes to assist less fortunate communities than Garden State residents who had opposed the ruling all along.

Sometimes citizens who follow public events more closely than their neighbors develop distinctive attitudes about those events.[11] Often the viewpoints of attentive citizens are more carefully thought out and more closely integrated into their general policy preferences than those of ordinary citizens. This was not so with *Robinson*. Approval of *Robinson* by attentive citizens did not coincide with great concern for the poor, great willingness to pay new taxes to finance social programs, or great respect for the New Jersey Supreme Court as an institution. The opinions of these better-informed citizens did differ from those of the general public in one crucial respect. The attentive citizenry was initially more critical of the court's ruling than the typical New Jerseyan, but then a shift took place. As one season gave way to the next, the citizens who followed *Robinson* most closely became more favorably disposed toward it. The attentive public warmed to *Robinson* and accommodated itself to its implications, while the general public became increasingly antagonistic; by the spring of 1976, a clear but small majority of elite citizens supported the court's ruling.

Even this degree of limited support for *Robinson* probably would not have survived if individuals' interests had been thought to be genuinely endangered. Reformers believe that they can build support for a cause by enlisting the aid of the judiciary. Respect for the courts, reformers assume, will enhance the legitimacy of their position and win new converts to their standard. On an abstract plane this may be true. Polls show that a large majority of New Jerseyans would support a hypothetical supreme court ruling awarding compensatory state aid to poor and disadvantaged communities, even though they disagree with the principle implied by such a ruling.[12] If the aid is to come out of their own communities, the tune changes. If they are to pay the tab, most citizens reply that they would then abandon their respect for the court and their compassion for the poor and urge their local officials to oppose the justices. Public attitudes toward the New Jersey Supreme Court are not sufficiently well developed nor sufficiently well embedded in people's philosophies to persuade them to sacrifice their own interests in concrete situations. In most instances, court decisions alone are too distant and too intangible to lead people to relinquish values or interests that are important to them. Would this be the case with *Robinson*?

State House reporters knew that New Jersey's ultimate response to *Robinson* would be influenced less by public attitudes toward the court than by how people felt about the issues of taxation and education. Prior to the 1970s, New Jersey had gained a national reputation for levying low taxes and providing meager financial support for its public services, and, by and large, this reputation had been deserved.[13] By the beginning of the 1970s, however, Trenton lawmakers had begun to expand the state's catalog of public services, and New Jersey had been compelled to follow the lead of most other states and adopt its first permanent, broad-based tax —a sales tax—to pay the cost. Even before *Robinson* had been decided, though, taxpayers were beginning to wonder aloud whether the new public money was being well spent. By the mid-1970s, state residents told pollsters that they were already paying enough taxes and that it was time for the state to hold the line on governmental spending. New Jerseyans believed, inaccurately, that they were paying more taxes than citizens of other states, and they felt that they were getting back less in services for their money.[14]

A notable exception to the pattern of low support for public services was the generous financing New Jersey had long lavished on its elementary and secondary schools. By relying on one of the nation's highest local property taxes, New Jersey's schools had long ranked among the half-dozen best funded in the United States. Now that the court had ruled that such heavy reliance on local property taxation was unconstitutional, other taxes would have to be raised to replace local taxes. Under the best of circumstances, raising taxes in New Jersey has never been an easy matter. Three different governors had tried to impose a state income tax and use part of the revenue to reduce property taxes, but, since New Jerseyans are strong opponents of tax increases and only lukewarm backers of tax reform, all three efforts failed. State residents indicated that they would accept the adoption of a personal income tax if the revenues were used to reduce property taxes, but few believed that lasting property tax relief would result. Furthermore, in the early 1970s, the circumstances for raising taxes in New

Jersey were far from the best. The stagnation of the national economy struck New Jersey with special vehemence, and the record inflation that accompanied one of the nation's highest unemployment rates made the state's citizens particularly reluctant to assume new financial obligations.

In New Jersey, support for public education had once been a sacrosanct item on the public agenda, potent enough to overcome even adverse economic conditions. These days had passed, however, by the time the supreme court had delivered its *Robinson* decision. Declining student scores on standardized examinations had shaken public confidence in educators. Citizens were reading and reacting to newspaper stories quoting academic researchers as saying that the features of modern school programs did not contribute to levels of student performance. "Basic skills" became a rallying cry for many New Jerseyans who believed that permissive schools were getting too far from standards, discipline, and the "three R's." After years of widespread support for public schools and ever-increasing educational expenditures, a 1975 poll showed New Jersey residents divided evenly in their evaluation of the performance of the public schools—half believed that the schools were doing a good or excellent job and half termed school performance inadequate.[15] Public schools were not thought to be teaching students essential skills as well as they once did, and, most ominously for educators, it was the better-educated, better-informed, more attentive citizens who were now the most critical. While scholars continued to debate the relationship between educational expenditures and student performance, the question seemed settled in the minds of New Jersey residents. Most told pollsters that the schools did not need any more money and that further increases in state aid would not mean better student performance. The decisive rejection of most local school budgets at public referenda in the mid-1970s further documented public opposition to additional school spending.

Unusual public hostility toward the institutions of government, education programs, and tax increases made the mid-1970s a difficult time for Trenton officials to set about formulating a new school finance program. When most issues are placed on governmental agendas, legislators and executive officials can delay their consideration until the climate of the times becomes favorable. Sometimes a blue-ribbon commission can be established, a resolution passed, or cosmetic reforms enacted to deal with the politics of an issue without addressing the substance of the original controversy. Court-initiated agenda issues are different. A question placed on the agenda by a court has staying power and frequently a deadline demanding action. Policy-making institutions are generally not permitted to wait until conditions favor action. Trenton officials had to face the *Robinson* issues and face them within a relatively short time, and, when they did, it would be the state legislators who shouldered the bulk of initial public criticism for unpopular proposals.

> *A state income tax proposal may be revived as the best way to finance public education, according to the chairman of a legislative schools commission.*—Jersey Journal, 7 April 1973

> *State Senate President Alfred Beadleston said . . . the case "is not a green light" for an income tax, which Beadleston termed "stone cold dead."*—Trenton Times, 24 October 1973

The size of the State House news force in Trenton has doubled in recent years, as newspapers throughout New Jersey are devoting more resources to the coverage of state politics. Seasoned reporters who once appeared in Trenton only when the legislature was meeting are now assigned there full time, and young people have been hired to expand the bureaus even further. Increasingly, the State House itself has become the news focus of the state, and department heads and politicos from throughout New Jersey often troop in when they want to make an announcement for statewide consumption. Each day, the administration usually distributes about two dozen releases to the unpretentious press offices that line State House corridors, and two dozen more releases are mailed into the bureaus from resourceful groups and organizations all over the state.

On legislative days, the pace in Trenton quickens considerably, and the State House comes alive. Stories that weary reporters are lethargically developing are set aside as the newspeople concentrate on the events breaking around them. There are committee meetings to attend, caucuses to monitor, and the legislative sessions themselves to cover. In addition, members of the legislature can be buttonholed in the hallways for a quick comment on whatever subject is of immediate interest. Most New Jersey lawmakers are starved for media coverage, and they are usually willing to take time from the most hectic day to speak with newspeople.

The vigorous growth of the State House press corps reflects the profound transformations that have been occurring in New Jersey politics in the past decade. Traditionally, New Jersey has relied on local communities rather than the state to control, finance, and maintain essential public services. The state's politics, too, were county based rather than defined around statewide issues and statewide personalities. More than anything, New Jersey's unsavory political reputation throughout the nation has been shaped by the actions of local party organizations in the counties. Typified by Boss Frank Hague's machine in Jersey City, local party activities in New Jersey have frequently been colorful, occasionally dictatorial, and all too often corrupt. A comprehensive study of political cultures in the United States described New Jersey as the only major state whose political traditions were predominantly localistic.[16] As a consequence of this localism, the policy institutions of the state government long remained underdeveloped. The governor's office, the legislature, and the executive departments all lacked the resources, the professionalism, and the expertise that characterized similar institutions in comparable states. New Jersey's policy institutions often served as little more than an arena where local figures worked out agreements to protect local interests.

Historically, the New Jersey legislature has been dominated by party caucuses.[17] Before each day's session, party members would gather in secluded State House meeting rooms to decide which measures would pass and which would pass away. The only significant groupings within the party caucuses were composed of the county party delegations. In fact, even the seating on the floor of the senate and assembly was assigned by county unit. Traditionally, legislative committees met infrequently and rarely considered bills on their merits. Leadership positions in both chambers usually rotated each year, so no continuing legislative expertise was acquired. This system did allow the majority party to balance the interests of its important members, but it left the legislature with little capacity to formulate its own policy proposals on critical issues. Major legislative programs were traditionally initiated by the executive and ratified by the legislature only if the governor had built the necessary support among local party officials. In most cases, the primary allegiance of members of the senate and assembly was to a local party organization or perhaps to the governor but not to the legislature.

The last decade has been a period of active change in both New Jersey politics and legislative operations. Increased mobility of population, changing demographic patterns, legislative districting reforms, and aggressive legal prosecutions have combined to reduce the power of local party organizations. At the same time, the prominence of the state's governing institutions has increased with the assignment of new public service responsibilities and the development of new revenue sources. In recent years, the number of special interest associations in the state has multiplied dramatically, and the associations' growing politicization has made the governing milieu profoundly more complex. During the past decade as well, numerous national organizations have devoted themselves to improving the operations of state legislatures throughout the country.[18] In many states, their impact has been apparent. New Jersey's legislature now meets more often than it did in the past, and its committees have begun to play a meaningful role in policy deliberations.[19] Numerous staff members have been hired to serve the legislature as committee aides, fiscal analysts, leadership staff, and assistants to individual legislators. Proceedings are now better publicized and opportunities for public participation greatly expanded. In the last decade, the New Jersey legislature has slowly built up its capacity to shape the state's public policies, but, when the supreme court delivered the *Robinson* decision in 1973, the legislature had yet to prove whether it could translate the new legislative capacity into performance.

Lawmakers' initial reaction to the *Robinson* decision reflected cautious support for the court's judgment and stressed the problems that lay ahead in responding to it. Yet, even this cautious support was something of a judicial victory, for the ruling embodied a classic, constitutional confrontation between the legislature and the judiciary. Rarely have the fundamental tensions between separate but equal branches of government been more graphically displayed than in this decision. In the extended analysis of taxes, schools, and the obligations of the state to all its citizens, legislative prerogatives to establish policy and appropriate funds were pitted squarely against the power of the state supreme court to realize its interpretation of the constitution.

Most legislators approached their incipient confrontation with the judiciary with a generalized sense of respect and esteem. Whether they were lawyers or not, most legislators praised the legal skills and normal conduct of the New Jersey Supreme Court.[20] Within this broad pattern of favor, however, lawmakers expressed two specific reservations about the court. First, despite the fact that New Jersey's highest court has been nationally respected for more than two decades, many legislators believe that it is too quick to become involved in policy controversies. They argue that the court sometimes attempts to resolve problems it is not equipped to handle and tries to assume responsibilities that properly belong to the legislature.

A second, perhaps more important, reservation about the court is the legislators' perception that the judiciary today lacks public support.[21] Legislators are almost unanimous in feeling that their constituents are unhappy with court actions, even though poll data are not quite so conclusive. Courts have been cast as advocates for liberal social policies, the lawmakers explain, at a time when such good intentions have been given a bad name. The United States Supreme Court has been subjected to sharp criticism in the past decade, public confidence in governmental institutions in general has waned, and the New Jersey court has become another victim of these same dissatisfactions. While some legislators are quick to disassociate themselves from their constituents' viewpoints, many paint a stark picture of public disenchantment with the court in saying, "There is simply no respect left for courts."

Would these perceptions affect how lawmakers responded to *Robinson*? Once, a court ruling could protect officials from public criticism and enable them to adopt principled but unpopular positions on controversial issues, but New Jersey legislators say that this day has passed.[22] Since the reservoir of judicial respect has dried up, a court judgment today is no longer an effective shield against public criticism. In addition, court rulings have lost some of their power to compel lawmakers to accept court objectives. The lack of public esteem for the court means that lawmakers can pick and choose which decisions they will rush to obey. Public disenchantment with the court system grants legislators something of a license to ignore the judiciary with impunity.

The supreme court's decision in *Robinson* came as little surprise to the members of the senate and assembly who had followed the case since Judge Botter's time back in Hudson County. Once they had examined the written opinion, lawmakers said that they favored the decision by a margin of almost two to one.[23] Legislative respect for the supreme court as an institution contributed to the degree of support the decision initially received in Trenton. Whether legislators praised *Robinson* or condemned it, however, their evaluations were usually based on policy preferences rather than legal judgments. Some spoke of the judicial intrusion into the legislative domain, and others discussed technical deficiencies of the decision, but such constitutional commentary usually masked more fundamental policy desires. In most instances, lawmakers applauded *Robinson* if it boosted their policy objectives and criticized the ruling if it jeopardized them. What type of policy statement was the ruling?

First and foremost, for New Jersey legislators, *Robinson* was a fiscal decision, and it was evaluated in those terms.[24] Members who favored a personal income tax gave the court high marks for *Robinson,* and those against the tax were uniformly critical of the ruling. Legislative attitudes toward the decision were based more on assessments of its impact on tax policy and the financial condition of urban areas than on analyses of its implications for the quality of education. Only secondarily was *Robinson* an educational statement, and educational considerations had little to do with lawmakers' overall appraisals of it. Legislators who believed that New Jersey's schools were performing poorly were no more likely to praise the reform-oriented ruling than legislators who felt the schools were doing a fine job.

Traditionally, many state legislators have interpreted their roles in educational policy making as passive rather than active.[25] The historic tenet that there should be "no politics in education" stigmatized the actions of elected officials in the educational arena as partisan and served to restrict their influence. Furthermore, legislators were usually not eager to plunge into education policy debates because they viewed the issues as extremely sensitive ones, where the pitfalls and potentialities for headaches outweighed the possibilities of reward. In the 1950s, the only education issues that usually involved governors and state legislators were fiscal ones. In the past decade, numerous factors have combined to propel legislatures into a more active—and occasionally assertive—role in the conduct of education. The selection of schools as the primary subject for the constitutional struggles over both desegregation and public religion introduced elected officials to education policy. The organized militancy of school teachers emerged at a time when student performance on standardized exams showed the first signs of decline. Furthermore, changes in students' life style and conduct led many citizens to begin to wonder what schools were actually spending their time teaching. Because of constituents' unhappiness with the educational system, some state legislatures began to use their expanding institutional resources to scrutinize educational issues more closely than they had in the past.

The New Jersey legislature was no different from most others.[26] Its educational activities were concentrated on finance issues rather than on educational policy questions. The education committees of the senate and assembly shared only one staff aide, and committee members usually backed whatever program the incumbent administration proposed. In Trenton as well as the other state capitals, however, education politics were changing.

At the time of the *Robinson* decision, New Jersey lawmakers were more critical of the operations of the state's schools than ordinary citizens.[27] A majority believed that the schools were not doing a good job educating New Jersey's children, and almost all agreed that the schools had forgotten how to teach rudimentary skills. Many fumed when they recounted how ineffectively local school districts expended funds. Without prompting by interviewers, they related horror stories about expensive band uniforms, unnecessary supervisors, lavish football fields, and extraneous public relations personnel, topped only by one incredulous legislator who told of local school officials complaining that their new planetarium was not so well equipped as they had desired because of unreasonable fiscal constraints. One important lawmaker summarized the change in legislative attitudes toward education with these words: "When I first came to the legislature, funds for education were sacrosanct, and I thought that I was doing good by supporting them unquestioningly. No more." Legislators had once trusted schoolteachers and appreciated their underpaid dedication to the state's service, but that attitude has passed, too. In another contrast with years gone by, teachers are no longer viewed by New Jersey lawmakers as a hard-working group, selflessly committed to the children's best interests. Asked to select which group received the best treatment from government from a list that included business corporations, the wealthy, suburbanites, and labor unions, legislators picked schoolteachers.

Money alone is not the answer to school problems, legislators agree. With hardly an exception, lawmakers reject the notion that increased educational expenditures will in themselves improve the quality of education in the state's schools. The problem is how the money is spent, they say, not how much money is available. In the words of one assemblyman:

> New York City's schools are better funded than the schools in New Jersey's richest suburbs, but you certainly cannot tell me that the schools in the Bronx work better than schools in the suburbs. Clearly factors other than the level of funding are involved and until someone can explain to me what they are and what benefits will come from increased educational expenditures, why should I support them?

Such views are not simple rationalizations for opposition to increased school funding; these views are voiced equally by those lawmakers who favor new educational expenditures and those who vote against them.

Many legislators also expressed unanticipated views about home rule. Local governments have traditionally provided the bulk of public services in New Jersey, and local party organizations have long set the tone for the state's politics. Thus, protection of home rule has been an article of faith for generations of New Jersey officials. Despite this tradition of localism, most legislators privately expressed skeptical or downright hostile opinions about home rule in education.[28] Local control, they complain, frequently becomes a defense for inadequate performance. Proposed increases in state control over local schools pose no problem for the legislators who argue that increased state control would stimulate innovation in local school districts that are now all too set in their ways. Even legislators defending home rule avoid discussion of its positive qualities and attack instead what they see as the heavy-handed administrative procedures of the state department of education. As long as there is no frontal assault on the symbols of local participation in schools, many lawmakers appear willing to support any state action which promises to improve the quality of education in New Jersey. This does not necessarily mean that legislators will seek out opportunities to vote against schoolteachers and home rule when they gather in the senate and assembly chambers in Trenton, but it does mean that doubts, suspicions, skepticism, and distrust have gnawed away at the almost universal support education once enjoyed.

Many State House reporters in New Jersey and elsewhere are frustrated lawmakers themselves.[29] Their conversations are filled with unflattering remarks about the members of the senate and assembly and with accounts of how they themselves would deal more capably with political and governmental problems. But reporters and legislators both knew that *Robinson* was unlike most issues that come before the senate and assembly. It was not raised by the governor, an interested legislator, or some specialized group, but by the state's highest court. The issue, one legislative aide recalls, "had an air of law about it, a feeling that it was somehow special."

The court demanded legislative action on *Robinson* during the troublesome period from 1973 to 1976. New Jersey's lawmakers were required to concentrate on education issues when there was more public antagonism toward the schools than there had been in years, and they were required to raise additional school revenues when the state's economy was in its most sluggish condition since the Great Depression of the 1930s. These factors apparently had little effect on the attitudes of those legislators who had formed their views of education before the court had acted—they remained traditionally supportive and approving. But the difficult conditions weighed heavily on the minds of legislators who had never considered education policy before the *Robinson* years. Such legislators grew to accept the critical views of school performance which prevailed in the mid-1970s. Lawmakers appear to adopt the opinions about schools which characterize the period in which they first scrutinize education policy. Members of the senate and assembly who first examined education policy when schools were seen as a solution to social problems still praise New Jersey's schools, but, in sharp contrast, those whose opinions date from the *Robinson* years are profoundly critical of school operations. The Trenton legislators who acquired their hard-line views of education during the mid-1970s will probably persist in those attitudes in the years ahead, even if popular sentiments toward education again turn more favorable. If they do, these questioning opinions must be considered one consequence of the court's mandate in *Robinson.*

Party lines are very important in the New Jersey legislature, but judicial involvement in *Robinson* apparently diluted their significance for the educational aspects of that issue.[30] Even though formal votes generally followed party lines, legislative discussions of school operations and even school aid betrayed fewer traces of the calculation of partisan advantage than is normal. In addition, the court's decision made some lawmakers slightly more conscious of the considerations of fiscal equity than they had been in the past and somewhat less narrowly concerned about the financial well-being of their own constituencies.[31] In fact, so long as their districts were not financially hurt by specific provisions of a program to respond to *Robinson,* legislators' evaluations of the ruling were not closely related to its impact on their constituencies at all. *Robinson*'s timing taught new attitudes to lawmakers without previously established opinions, and its judicial mantle altered the ways other legislators perceived the issues the decision had raised, but it was clear that no quick consensus would emerge among legislators on what to do about the ruling.

Many disagreements among the people's representatives would block quick action on a response to the *Robinson* decision. The senators and assemblypersons who dominated the legislature's education committees had traditionally supportive views of education, while most rank-and-file legislators questioned the accomplishments of educators. The state's lawmakers divided rather evenly on the desirability of enacting a personal income tax, with half in favor and half opposed. Regardless of their personal views, however, all legislators knew that the enactment of an income tax would be a difficult chore, because it would be unpopular in their districts. Their mail, they said, usually ran six or eight to one against the tax, and the audiences they addressed were usually hostile to the idea. All lawmakers agreed that government has a special obligation to aid poor and disadvantaged communities, but many backed off when discussion shifted from general principles to proposals for specific legislative action. The supreme court had ruled that New Jersey's educational system and school finance policy had to be revised, but the shape of the new programs that could win legislative support remained elusive and undefined.

> *Education Commissioner Carl L. Marburger said yesterday the decision reflects "the state's basic responsibility for providing equal educational opportunity." The state will now have to develop "the mechanism for providing support and defining equal educational opportunity."*—Newark Star Ledger, 4 April 1973

Today most state constitutions make local education a state responsibility.[32] In fact, support for local education today is the greatest single financial obligation of most state governments, but this was not always the case. In the early decades of the nation's history, public schools were few, scattered, and small, and the only support that state governments usually provided was moral. Provisions were added to state constitutions, in the first quarter of the nineteenth century, assigning states a greater role in assuring that all students could attend public schools, but state governments still lacked the administrative structure to accomplish this. It was not until the middle of the nineteenth century that most states appointed state boards of educations, established departments of education, and selected chief state school officers. Once this administrative mechanism was in place, states slowly began to set minimum standards regulating local school operations, teacher qualifications, and the nature of school programs, while at the same time encouraging local districts to surpass those minimum standards. At the end of the nineteenth century, states began to aid local school districts financially, again by setting minimum financial standards and inviting localities to exceed them. From this perspective, the *Robinson* decision was part of a long-term trend that was increasing the role of state governments in elementary and secondary education.

The New Jersey State Board of Education met in its fifth floor conference room in the state education building in Trenton on the day after the *Robinson* opinion was released. The board welcomed the ruling and created a task force to analyze its implications and help the department prepare for its newly revitalized constitutional obligation.[33] The New Jersey State Board of Education is appointed by the governor, unlike many state boards of education whose members are popularly elected, but the New Jersey board shares with its counterparts elsewhere the weaknesses of most part-time lay boards. Even though state boards of education nominally possess comprehensive powers and great discretion, their activities are usually dominated by the full-time professionals of the state departments of education. Chief state school officers and departmental civil servants normally prepare the analyses and make the recommendations which guide most important actions of state boards.[34]

The most frequent criticism of state departments of education is that they reflect the interests of professional educators rather than the needs of schoolchildren. In the words of James B. Conant, a prestigious commentator on the American educational scene:

> The major weakness of all state departments of education I have encountered, with perhaps one or two exceptions, is that they are too much a part of the educational establishment. That is, I found many of these agencies . . . to be no more than "willing tools" of the interests and clientele, particularly the education association (that is, the state NEA affiliate). A grave shortcoming of our educational leadership at the state level, in my opinion, is often its unwillingness or incapacity to respond to forces outside the establishment.[35]

The consequences of this inbreeding are seen in educators' evaluations of the performance of the New Jersey school system. Despite the fact that the skeptical 1970s persuaded many citizens and legislators to scrutinize school operations more closely, officials in the New Jersey State Department of Education still retained confidence in the state's schools.[36] Almost without exception, personnel in the state education department praised New Jersey's schools, and most asserted that instruction in essential skills was as good today as it ever was, if not better.

An earlier governor had viewed the New Jersey State Department of Education as stodgy, entrenched, and capable of doing little more than listlessly defending an inadequate status quo.[37] To revitalize the department, Dr. Carl Marburger had been selected as commissioner of education in 1967. Carl Marburger had fulfilled that intention—but all too well. Recruited from a federal post in Washington over a popular hometown candidate and selected without real consultation with the state's educational establishment, Marburger's tumultuous tenure could well be symbolized by the urban riots that began throughout the country after he assumed office.[38] During his reign, controversial issues involving busing, community control of schools, students' rights, racial balance, and teacher accountability arose, and Marburger did little to reassure conventional educators that he would defend their positions in grappling for solutions. Declaring that New Jersey's schools were in a rut, Marburger assumed the role of agent of change, and many of the groups that were to be changed did not applaud his performance.

Marburger drafted a four-part blueprint for educational improvements in New Jersey; each component might have enriched the quality of education in the state, but each was also guaranteed to offend at least one established educational group in the process. A cornerstone of Marburger's design was meaningful public involvement in the setting of goals, priorities, and programs for the state's schools. The emphasis on nonprofessional participation in school activities alienated many teachers and administrators without demonstrating to citizens that their involvement in school projects was productive.[39] The second component of Marburger's plan was an assessment program designed to reveal the areas where schools were making inadequate progress toward their stated goals. Regardless of intentions, assessment was quickly denounced by the state's major teachers group as a mechanism for blaming societal problems on teachers under the guise of promoting accountability. Once goals were defined and deficiencies documented, Marburger created a Division of Research, Planning and Evaluation in the department to develop ways of remedying school shortcomings. The division was to formulate and field test innovative programs to combat local failures. This proposal was not enthusiastically received in the department's established Curriculum and Instruction Division, which viewed itself as perfectly capable of formulating and testing its own innovative teaching techniques.

These three components of Marburger's design—goal setting, assessment, and remediation—operated at the state level, while the fourth component was to be locally based. In 1970, the Cahill Administration had proposed and the legislature had enacted a new education program which established five ascending categories of school districts based on the quality of their offerings; it then offered local communities financial incentives to upgrade their programs. Districts were encouraged to use a goal-setting process with broad citizen participation, develop curricula to meet the desired goals, and then assess their progress—thereby implanting in each district a homegrown version of Marburger's statewide blueprint. The prospect of the implementation of this program in local communities aroused the same anxieties and excited the same groups that fought Marburger's plan at the state level. The commissioner's repeated assertions that conventional education programs were inadequate, his careless treatment of important education groups and legislators, and his public identification with busing and integration all contributed to the defeat of his nomination for a second term as education commissioner when it was presented to the state senate in 1972.

Carl Marburger left the department of education the day before the New Jersey Supreme Court rendered its decision in *Robinson*. He was succeeded by a caretaker commissioner, from within the ranks of the department, who served on a temporary basis for a full fifteen months. The creative tension, which typified the department at its best under Marburger, became a great deal less creative during this period, as agencies and divisions downgraded departmental concerns and concentrated on their own activities. A veteran of those days remembers:

There was an outbreak of empire-building. . . . People were trying to consolidate power to pressure the new commissioner. Partly it was a difference over how things should be run and partly a question of who was in and who was out, which divisions take precedence. . . . The Research, Planning and Evaluation people were people outside the system, and Curriculum and Instruction tended to be people inside the system.

The tensions brought on by educational reform in the 1960s were relieved, in part, by a great influx of federal and state funds into schools. In the 1970s, cutbacks in new funds and increasing criticism of education combined to inflame hostilities within the leaderless New Jersey education department. In many ways, *Robinson* was a ruling of the 1960s being worked out in the 1970s. It reflected the anxieties of the 1960s about the plight of urban areas and the disadvantaged, and it assumed that improvements in educational quality would follow increased educational expenditures. By the 1970s, concerns for the problems of urban areas and the disadvantaged were not so prominent in New Jersey education circles—or anywhere else—as they had been. The flow of new federal and state funds for education slowed to a trickle, and challenges were mounted to the assumption that more money meant better schools. The chances that *Robinson* would yield a comprehensive reform of educational policy in New Jersey would have been greater in the mid-1960s than in the early and mid-1970s. Like most citizens, New Jersey educators accepted the *Robinson* decision, without analyzing its logic or debating its wisdom.[40] They thought it would produce more funds for education, and they wanted to get it implemented, but they did not know precisely how to do so.

> *The court supports what educators have been saying for the past four decades in campaigns to improve state school aid. The New Jersey Constitution makes the State Legislature responsible for guaranteeing a good education for all children. Today's decision will not block local school districts from raising their own taxes to underwrite innovations or support unique programs. It will, however, assure full state support for the basic quality education that all children should receive, wherever they live.—Statement of the New Jersey Education Association*, New York Times, *4 April 1973*

The New Jersey Education Association, befitting its stature as one of the state's most celebrated interest groups, is housed in its own imposing building at 180 West State Street, halfway between the State House and the department of education building. With one hundred thousand members, the NJEA is the major teachers' organization in the state, and its eminent role in New Jersey education activities leads some observers to describe it caustically as "the Department of Education at 180 West State." The NJEA collected $6 million in dues in 1975 and boasted an effective leadership and a talented staff. Its 65 professional employees are assigned to a Field Services Division, which concentrates on labor-management relations, or to other divisions that focus on research, instruction, communications, and government relations. The association's operations are characterized by widespread membership participation and free internal communications, which give the NJEA a reputation as a good place to work. The NJEA is noted for an adept blending of classroom education and political action. It endorsed its first gubernatorial candidate in 1973, and it established political committees in local legislative districts to back other NJEA-endorsed candidates. With thousands of members in each legislative district, many lawmakers openly curry NJEA favor by respecting its position on school-oriented legislation and by attending NJEA-sponsored legislative dinners.

Located farther down West State Street, somewhat removed from the center of governmental activity, is the New Jersey School Boards Association. Every local board of education in the state is required by law to join the association and pay dues, which provide the association a steady income of more than $1 million a year. While the NJEA is composed of educators who have undergone similar training and may have worked as teachers for fifteen or twenty years, the membership of the school boards association is extremely diverse. Serving on a school board is normally a part-time responsibility, which usually must be fitted into some other full-time job. The average term of a school board member is three years, and the turnover of association membership is so great that one staffer confided, "We say we are always talking to a moving parade." Its heterogeneous membership often makes it difficult for the association to adopt forceful positions on controversial issues.

The association has recently established local committees to review proposed legislation with individual lawmakers, but the governmental composition of the school boards association precludes its direct involvement in electoral politics. While the New Jersey School Boards Association has a prominent place in the state's educational politics, it is usually unable to speak with compelling authority.

The state's third major educational association, the Council of School Administrators, is a coalition formed by the New Jersey Association of School Administrators, the New Jersey Association of Elementary School Principals, the New Jersey Association of Secondary School Principals, and the New Jersey Association of Business Administrators. In the last half-decade, the four groups have augmented their individual resources and combined their operations to achieve some economies of scale, but, even together, the four groups do not approach the size or political status of the NJEA or the New Jersey School Boards Association. Even though the council has little professional research capability and no involvement in electoral politics, some knowledgeable officials look to it for practical and usually even-handed advice on complicated proposals.

The New Jersey Education Association is the state affiliate of the National Education Association, the New Jersey School Boards Association is a chapter of the National School Boards Association, and the New Jersey administrators' groups are also affiliated with national organizations of school administrators. In New Jersey, as in other states, education associations have often formed ad hoc coalitions to press for increases in state aid to education and to endorse tax proposals needed to raise the revenues to fund the aid increases.[41] In some states, these temporary coalitions have become almost permanent, and leagues of professional educators have emerged to set the tone for the politics of education in the state. Differences among teachers, school boards, and administrators about both financial and educational questions were resolved by the associations themselves, and a unified professional position was then presented to the rest of the state. This pattern of relationships among interest groups permitted educators to appear to be objective, nonpolitical, selfless, and concerned only about the best interests of the state's children. In other states, the structure of relationships among the educational groups took on a different form, however, as the groups were unable to agree on common policy positions. Here, the groups presented their disagreements to the governor and legislature for resolution and thus undermined their image as professionals who were above politics. Once immersed in political conflict, education associations appeared no different from all the other groups who beseeched the legislature to improve the lot of their members.

Relationships among New Jersey's educational interest groups remain in a state of flux and transition. In the late 1950s and early 1960s, New Jersey was cited as an example of a state where the politics of education were harmonious and where professional schoolpersons dominated the field.[42] The leadership of the major groups met quarterly with the commissioner of education, as the "Princeton Group," to discuss important issues confronting the education community and to formulate common positions for dealing with them. Relations between the NJEA and the department of education were so intimate that some thought that the NJEA "knew what the commissioner was thinking before the commissioner thought it."[43] This educational consensus was ruptured in the late 1960s by the unsettling tenure of Carl Marburger, by the volume of contentious issues that arose, and by a collective bargaining system that pitted teachers against school boards. As the labor-management negotiation process became institutionalized in local school districts, each side came to regard the other as an enemy, whose demands were unreasonable and whose intentions were suspect. By the time of *Robinson*, educational harmony in New Jersey had given way to corrosive infighting among the statewide groups. The Council of School Administrators and the New Jersey School Boards Association were seen as allies, which were separated from the NJEA by programmatic distance and leadership animosity.

New Jersey's response to *Robinson* engaged other organizations that were not composed of professional educators: the New Jersey Congress of Parents and Teachers, the New Jersey League of Women Voters, and the Advocates for Education; and additional groups which spoke for minority communities: the New Jersey

National Association for the Advancement of Colored People, the Puerto Rican Congress, and the New Jersey Education Reform Project. With the exception of NJERP, these groups rely on volunteers, because they do not have professional staffs to devote themselves exclusively to education issues. Two business-oriented groups, the New Jersey Taxpayers Association and the New Jersey Manufacturers Association, took an active part in the debates prompted by *Robinson*, because they were concerned about the quality of future employees' educations and because schooling was the state's most expensive public service. These organizations all welcomed *Robinson*, because they believed that New Jersey's education and school finance policies needed thorough review, even though some feared that the ruling might simply increase the costs of education without reforming the tax structure or improving the quality of school programs. The one issue which divided the civic and business groups from the educational associations was the evaluation of the current effectiveness of the state's schools. While the education associations all agreed with departmental officials that New Jersey schools were doing a good job in teaching essential skills and providing a solid general curriculum, noneducators refused to accept either position.[44] Fundamental criticisms of the quality of education expressed by groups of noneducators and the enmity among leaders of the state education associations were hurdles that officials charged with designing a policy response to *Robinson* would have to overcome.

> *Governor Cahill said this evening that the State Supreme Court's ruling against reliance on local property taxes for financing New Jersey's public schools "translated into reality the need for state tax reform. . . ." One reason given for the Governor's reluctance at this time to use the decision as a springboard for a state income tax is the Legislature's dislike for such an innovation. An income tax would be a major way to transfer school costs from local property taxes.*—New York Times, 4 *April 1973*

The news bureau offices in New Jersey's State House are wired with buzzers. When the governor wants to meet with the press, the buzzers summon the reporters to the governor's ceremonial outer office, where press conferences are normally held. American governors are clearly the centers of political attention in most states. They are usually the leaders of their political parties, the heads of the executive branch of government, the representatives of their states in dealings with the national government and neighboring states, and the primary influence on the activities of the legislature. In many ways, governors can have a greater impact on their states than the President can have on the national government, because the competing political institutions in states are less fully developed than are their national counterparts. Furthermore, since Congress has authorized massive programs for sharing national revenues with states and for expanding the discretion of states in the provision of other domestic services, the importance of governors in the policy process may well grow in the years ahead.

The governor's office in New Jersey has long been the focus of policy development and legislative enactment. Well-positioned to tap the technical expertise of the executive branch and to collect legislative majorities in both the senate and assembly, the actions of the governors have determined the tone and direction of public policy during each gubernatorial administration. Without the leadership of the governor, little moved in New Jersey. William Cahill, governor when the supreme court delivered its opinion in *Robinson*, had assumed office two years earlier. He promptly demonstrated his concern for education by fashioning a major new school funding program and then winning legislative approval for it. Interest group leaders soon started calling Cahill "the best governor education ever had," and many thought that his constructive education policies would be the hallmark of his administration. *Robinson* would provide Cahill his greatest educational challenge, most believed. With citizens and legislators abandoning their traditional support for education and the educational community split over a range of institutional, programmatic, and personality issues, a catalyst such as Cahill would surely become necessary for responding to *Robinson*. Reports from other states indicated that a skilled chief executive was the most important ingredient for successful school finance reform, and with Cahill New Jersey had a proven and attractive leader.[45]

Policy-making institutions in the United States usually focus on subjects when the climate of the times favors those functions.

Housing, transportation, and environmental programs, for example, are usually formulated when the patterns of public preference and the dispositions of relevant institutions are supportive. Courts, on the other hand, are not always mindful of the currents of opinion when they place an issue before a state's traditional policy institutions. The New Jersey Supreme Court delivered *Robinson* into a time when public and official attitudes toward education, taxation, and the court system were unfavorable, and when the state's policy institutions were in worse shape to manage divisive issues than they had been in the past or would be in the future. To compound the difficulties, events then conspired to remove Governor Cahill from office.

Much of the support for Cahill's moderate policies came from rank-and-file members of the opposition party, and early in 1973 the governor was looking past his own party's June primary toward the upcoming general election in November. A series of political reversals then struck, and Cahill suddenly found himself challenged by a member of his own party's extreme wing. In June 1973, New Jerseyans awoke to find that their governor had been denied his party's nomination for a second term. The person who was expected to overcome the intramural controversies of educators and to orchestrate the necessary support from suspicious legislators had been defeated in a primary by a man who would go on to lose the general election by the largest margin in New Jersey gubernatorial history. Instead of forceful leadership from the governor's office toward the *Robinson* challenge, policy developments were shelved and initiatives delayed by the lame-duck executive. June, July, August, September, and October elapsed before the electorate even selected Cahill's successor, and then November and December would pass before the new governor assumed office. The one office that could coordinate the discordant participants in New Jersey's educational affairs became, for policy purposes, vacant for months shortly after *Robinson* was decided.

The New Jersey Supreme Court decided *Robinson* at a time when all the state's governing institutions, not just the governor's office, were experiencing a change of leadership. The long and distinguished career of Joseph Weintraub as chief justice was coming to a close, and a new court would assume office before the implications of *Robinson* would become clear. State legislators were all up for election in 1973, and dozens of defeats would guarantee that new faces in both the senate and the assembly would draft the legislative response to the decision. A new legislature would have to be totally reorganized before it could turn its attention to substantive policy issues. The department of education—charged with carrying out *Robinson*'s mandate—was immersed in its own succession controversy. The department was being run by an acting commissioner, whose predecessor had been dropped by the legislature at the behest of some elements of the educational community and over the objections of others. *Robinson* could hardly have come at a worse time. New leaders would have to take control of the state's policy institutions and learn the intricate tasks of governing, before New Jersey could respond to the challenging mandate of the court.

NOTES

1. Some of the information on the State House press corps in this chapter was assembled with the assistance of and in a seminar paper prepared by James Simon, "Press Coverage of the New Jersey Supreme Court" (Department of Political Science, Rutgers University, May 1976). See also, Bertha Clark, "A Study of Efforts from 1947 to 1962 to Obtain a Broad-Based Tax for New Jersey" (Master's thesis, Montclair State College, 1964); W. A. Hatchen, "Journalism and the School Prayer Decision," *Columbia Journalism Review* 1 (Fall 1962): 108–22; Howard A. James, "The Crisis in Our Courts," *Nieman Reports* 30 (Spring 1972): 19–22; David R. Manwaring, *Render unto Caesar: The Flag Salute Controversy* (Chicago: The University of Chicago Press, 1962), chaps. 7 and 11.

2. Robert A. Dahl, "The City in the Future of Democracy," *American Political Science Review* 61 (December 1967): 968.

3. M. Kent Jennings and Harmon Zeigler, "The Salience of American State Politics," *American Political Science Review* 64 (June 1970): 523–35.

4. Stephen Salmore, "Public Opinion," in Alan Rosenthal and John Blydenburgh, eds., *Politics in New Jersey* (New Brunswick: Eagleton Institute of Politics, Rutgers University, 1975), pp. 59–77.

5. Appendix B, "Public Attitudes," questions 18 and 19.

6. William K. Muir, *Prayer in the Public Schools: Law and Attitude Change* (Chicago: University of Chicago Press, 1967); Kenneth M. Dolbeare and Phillip E. Hammond, *The School Prayer Decisions: From Court Policy to Local Practice* (Chicago: University of Chicago Press, 1971); Walter F. Murphy and Joseph Tanenhaus, "Public Opinion and the United States Supreme Court: A Preliminary Mapping of Some Prerequisites for Court Legitimation of Regime Changes," *Law and Society Review* 2 (May 1968): 357–84; Gregory Casey, "The Theory of Presidential Association: A Replication," *American Journal of Political Science* 19 (Feburary 1975): 19–25; John H. Kessel, "Public Perception of the Supreme Court," in T. L. Becker and M. M. Feeley, eds., *The Impact of Supreme Court Decisions* (New York: Oxford University Press, 1973), pp. 89–201; Walter F. Murphy and Joseph Tanenhaus, "Public Opinion and Supreme Court: The Goldwater Campaign," *Public Opinion Quarterly* 325 (Spring 1970): 31–50; Gregory Casey, "Popular Perceptions of Supreme Court Rulings," *American Politics Quarterly* 4 (January 1976): 3–45; Kenneth M. Dolbeare and Phillip E. Hammond, "The Political Party Basis of Attitudes Toward the Supreme Court," *Public Opinion Quarterly* 32 (Spring 1968): 16–30.

7. Appendix B, "Public Attitudes," questions 1, 3, and 4.

8. Roberta S. Sigel and Marilyn Brookes Hoskin, "Affect for Government and Its Relation to Policy Output among Adolescents," *American Journal of Political Science* 21 (February 1977): 111–34; and material cited therein.

9. Appendix B, "Public Attitudes," question 2.

10. Appendix B, "Public Attitudes," questions 18–26.

11. V. O. Key, Jr., *Public Opinion and American Democracy* (New York: Alfred A. Knopf, 1961).

12. Appendix B, "Public Attitudes," questions 5–7. See also, Harrell R. Rodgers, *Community Conflict, Public Opinion, and the Law: The Amish Dispute in Iowa* (Columbus, Ohio: Charles E. Merrill Publishing Co., 1969); Harrell Rodgers and Edward B. Lewis, "Political Support and Compliance

Attitudes: A Study of Adolescents," *American Politics Quarterly* 2 (January 1974): 61–77; Harrell Rodgers, Jr., and Roger Hanson, "The Rule of Law and Legal Efficacy: Private Values Versus General Standards," *Western Political Quarterly* 27 (September 1974): 387–94.

13. Richard Lehne, "Revenue and Expenditure Policies," in *Politics in New Jersey,* pp. 243–71.

14. Appendix B, "Public Attitudes," questions 11–17.

15. Appendix B, "Public Attitudes," questions 8–10. See also reports prepared by George Gallup on national attitudes toward education in *Phi Delta Kappan* 51 (1969): 157, 163; 52 (1970): 99–112; 53 (1971): 33–48; 54 (1972): 33–46; 55 (1973): 38–51; 56 (1974): 20–32; and 57 (1975): 227–40. Robert E. Agger and Marshall N. Goldstein, *Who Will Rule the Schools: A Cultural Class Crisis* (Belmont, Cal.: Wadsworth Publishing Company, 1971).

16. Daniel J. Elazar, *American Federalism: A View from the States* (New York: Thomas Y. Crowell, 1972), pp. 193–205.

17. Dayton McKean, *Pressures on the Legislature of New Jersey* (New York: Columbia University Press, 1938).

18. Examine the activities of the Ford Foundation, the National Municipal League, Legis-50, the National Conference of State Legislatures, the American Assembly, and the Eagleton Institute of Politics at Rutgers University.

19. Alan Rosenthal, "The New Jersey Legislature: The Contemporary Shape of an Historical Institution: Not Yet Good But Better Than It Used to Be," in William C. Wright, ed., *The Development of the New Jersey Legislature* (Trenton: New Jersey Historical Commission, 1976), pp. 72–119; Richard Lehne, "The New Jersey Legislature in the Past Decade: Developments and Deficiencies," *Seton Hall Legislative Journal* 2 (Spring 1977).

20. Appendix B, "Legislative Attitudes," questions 1, 3, 4, and 5. See also, Michael W. Giles, "Lawyers and the Supreme Court: A Comparative Look at Some Attitudinal Linkages," *Journal of Politics* 35 (May 1973): 480–86; and Justin J. Green et al., "Lawyers in Congress: A New Look at Some Old Assumptions," *Western Political Quarterly* 26 (September 1973): 440–52.

21. Appendix B, "Legislative Attitudes," question 2.

22. Appendix B, "Legislative Attitudes," question 6.

23. Appendix B, "Legislative Attitudes," questions 19 and 24.

24. Appendix B, "Legislative Attitudes," questions 25, 27, and 28.

25. Thomas H. Eliot, "Toward an Understanding of Public School Politics," *American Political Science Review* 53 (December 1959): 1032–51; Stephen K. Bailey et al., *Schoolmen and Politics: A Study of State Aid to Education in the Northeast* (Syracuse, N.Y.: Syracuse University Press, 1962); Nicholas A. Masters, Robert H. Salisbury, and Thomas H. Eliot, *State Politics and the Public Schools* (New York: Alfred A. Knopf, 1964); Mike M. Milstein and Robert E. Jennings, *Educational Policy-Making and the State Legislature: The New York Experience* (New York: Praeger Publishers, 1973); Roald F. Campbell and Tim L. Mazzoni, eds., *State Policy Making for the Public Schools: A Comparative Analysis* (Columbus: Educational Governance Project of the Ohio State University, 1974).

26. Donald Ernest Langolis, "The Politics of Education in New Jersey: A Study of Legislator Behavior and Four Major Interest Groups" (Doctoral dissertation, Teachers College, Columbia University, 1972).

27. Appendix B, "Legislative Attitudes," questions 7–11.

28. Appendix B, "Legislative Attitudes," question 13.

29. Delmer D. Dunn, *Public Officials and the Press* (Reading, Mass.: Addison-Wesley, 1969).

30. Appendix B, "Legislative Attitudes," question 33.

31. Appendix B, "Legislative Attitudes," questions 19–23.

32. This paragraph relies heavily on Frederick M. Wirt and Michael W. Kirst, *Political and Social Foundations of Education* (Berkeley, Cal.: Mc-Cutchan, 1972), pp. 111–12.

33. Minutes of the meeting of the New Jersey State Board of Education, 4 April 1973.

34. James Koerner, *Who Controls American Education?* (Boston: Beacon Press, 1969); and Dean Bowles, "The Power Structure in State Education Politics," *Phi Delta Kappan* 49 (1968): 337–40.

35. James B. Conant, *Shaping Educational Policy* (New York: McGraw-Hill, 1964), pp. 37–38, as quoted in Wirt and Kirst, *Political and Social Foundations*, p. 119.

36. Appendix B, "Departmental and Interest Group Attitudes," questions 1 and 3.

37. Richard C. Leone, "The Politics of Gubernatorial Leadership: Tax and Education Reform in New Jersey" (Ph.D. dissertation, Princeton University, 1969); for an alternative view, see "Higher Education in New Jersey, 1945–1967, An Accounting by the State Board of Education of its Stewardship of Higher Education" (July 1967).

38. Kenneth David Pack, "The New Jersey Department of Education: The Marburger Years" (Ph.D. dissertation, Rutgers University, 1974).

39. Alexander Plante and Michael Usdan, "Evaluation of the 'Our Schools' Project," (17 October 1971). This was a report prepared for the New Jersey State Department of Education (mimeo).

40. For an exception, see Dr. Gordon Ascher, "'Thorough and Efficient' and Equal Educational Opportunity: The New Jersey Mandate," Report to the New Jersey Department of Education, Divisions of Research, Planning, Evaluation and Field Services (September 1973).

41. Laurence Iannaccone, *Politics in Education* (New York: Center for Applied Research in Education, 1967).

42. Bailey et al., *Schoolmen and Politics*.

43. Pack, "The New Jersey Department of Education," see pp. 139 and 157.

44. Appendix B, "Departmental and Interest Group Attitudes," questions 1 and 3.

45. Joel S. Berke, *Answers to Inequity: An Analysis of the New School Finance* (Berkeley, Cal.: McCutchan, 1974); Joel S. Berke, John J. Callahan, and James A. Kelly, *Financial Aspects of Equality of Educational Opportunity and Inequities in School Finance,* Committee Print, Senate Select Committee on Equal Educational Opportunity (Washington, D.C.: U.S. Government Printing Office, 1972); Donna E. Shalala, Mary F. Williams, and Andrew Fishel, "The Property Tax and the Voter: An Analysis of State Constitutional Referenda to Revise School Finance Systems in California, Colorado, Michigan, and Oregon in 1972 and 1973" (Syracuse, N.Y.: Syracuse University Research Corporation, 1973).

4

Policy Formation in the Court's Shadow

Tourists usually enter New Jersey's State House from West State Street. The porch at the front of the limestone building is supported by six pillars of polished granite and backed by a double set of heavy glass doors. Through the doors, visitors first pass the offices of the state treasurer on the right and the secretary of state on the left, and then enter the rotunda, which connects the newer part of the capitol with the sections built in earlier years. Heavy-framed portraits of long-forgotten state leaders surround the rotunda and look down on a recently installed bust of Woodrow Wilson, the most recent United States President to come from New Jersey. Passing through the rotunda, the offices of the governor, watched over by state troopers, are on the immediate right and those of the governor's aides are on the left. Farther down the dim corridor, the lights of a newspaper and candy stand mark the entrance to the west wing of the State House, where the senate chambers are located, and the hallway to the east wing, which houses the general assembly and its support personnel.

One day Harold Ruvoldt, Jr., the Jersey City lawyer, journeyed to Trenton to discuss the *Robinson* litigation with some state legislators. The supreme court had not yet established any timetable for compliance with its ruling. Ruvoldt explained what he hoped would happen:

> The best thing in the world that can happen for us is for the court to do nothing more than to declare the system unconstitutional. . . . In fact, we filed for judgment before the trial started in which we offered to accept a judgment which declared the statute unconstitutional and let the legislature have a year—I think it was—to come back with a method of financing which would not discriminate on the basis of wealth.

One senator cautioned, "Maybe that's not generous enough with a year—I think it will take several years frankly." A member of the assembly agreed, "I hope you're right. If the judges know how the legislature works, I'm sure they would give us more than a year." [1]

In June 1973, the justices of the supreme court delivered a second decision in the *Robinson* case that established the timetable for legislative action. They granted the legislators more than the year they wanted to design a new school finance program—but not much more. The supreme court had ruled that the legislature had to enact a constitutional method of funding the state's elementary and secondary schools by December 31, 1974, eighteen months away, for implementation during the 1975–1976 school year. [2] Much of this time, however, was destined to be lost because of electoral instability. The primary election had already displaced the incumbent governor, and most commentators accurately predicted that the November 1973 general election would end the Republican control of the legislature. For a bill to become a law in New Jersey, it must be adopted by both houses of the state legislature and signed by the governor. Yet, as electoral uncertainty gave way to legislative confusion in Trenton, during the second half of 1973, little constructive legislative action took place on education issues or on anything else.

Two talented legislators, elected in November 1973, came to spearhead legislative efforts to reply to the *Robinson* decision, but on election day neither of the two would have predicted that involvement. Stephen Wiley was a Democrat returned to the senate on the governor's coattails from a woodsy suburban district in Morris County that traditionally elects Republicans. Wiley was a graduate of Columbia Law School, who had been the governor's counsel in a previous administration and then became the former governor's law partner when the term ended. Even though his father had been a local school superintendent, Wiley himself had little familiarity with school programs except what he had picked up as a school district lawyer. He thought that his legal background qualified him to chair the Law and Public Safety Committee, but he eventually agreed to chair the Senate Education Committee.

Likewise, Albert Burstein had not intended to devote himself to the Assembly Education Committee in the months and years ahead. Burstein was first elected to the assembly from suburban Bergen County in 1971 and reelected in November 1973. He had been born and brought up in Hudson County, trained as a lawyer at Columbia University, and had practiced law in Jersey City ever since. Burstein wanted a leadership post in the assembly in 1974 and became chairman of the education committee as a consolation prize after he was defeated for the post he really wanted. Capable and well-regarded, Wiley and Burstein set out to provide leadership to the lopsided Democratic majorities that had been returned to both the assembly and senate in the 1973 election.

The New Jersey legislature is composed of representatives of communities as diverse as Newark and the fox-hunting suburbs of Morris County, Jersey City and the resort towns of the Atlantic shore, Hoboken and the stunningly attractive rural areas around the Delaware River Water Gap, and the representatives of these communities can be as diverse as the communities themselves. The legislative chambers in Trenton have made room for gentle, patrician reformers, such as Congresswoman Millicent Fenwick, and the huge barrel-chested owner of a karate school who, other legislators swear, once assisted a motorist change a tire by lifting up the rear of the car. Policy preferences among lawmakers differ as much as their physical appearance, but it was the task of Wiley and Burstein to bring them together.

Not content to accept a passive role for the legislature in responding to the *Robinson* decision, Wiley met with Burstein to consider possible ways to fashion a school finance program. Considered first was the creation of a forum to be chaired by the governor and composed of legislative officers and members of the executive branch, but both legislative and executive officials were reluctant to intermingle their activities so closely.[3] Wiley and Burstein then agreed to combine their separate committees into a Joint Education Committee, so that they could pool their resources and not duplicate each other's work. With Wiley as chairperson and Burstein as vice chairperson, the Joint Education Committee was formally established in mid-April 1974 and promptly became the focal point of the legislature's efforts to respond to the educational aspects of the *Robinson* decision.

The *Robinson* v. *Cahill* decision was a complex one, and some legislators were no more certain of its meaning than other citizens. Unlike other citizens, however, legislators were charged with the responsibility of fashioning a response to a court ruling some candidly admitted they did not understand. After reviewing the court's reasoning, one lawyer-legislator commented:

> The court opinion itself left us with very little in the way of guideposts. The only thing that represented any sense of direction was that they wanted an educated person who could function in society, but beyond that, beyond these generalities, they did not tell us very much about how to go about doing our work. . . . The court had launched us into an uncharted sea.

Some members of the senate and assembly were frustrated by their inability to decide precisely what was being asked of them. An appropriate legislative program would undoubtedly affect school operations, school finance, and the state's revenue system, but no one knew precisely how. In fact, the men and women of the legislature were faced with three discrete tasks: (1) revamping the governance of education in the state; (2) redesigning the state aid system; and (3) raising an uncertain amount of new revenue. Each one of these three aspects of the problem entailed many difficulties, and legislators were obliged to confront all of them at the same time, with few guidelines provided by the court to help them limit their efforts. The court's nebulous declaration of unconstitutionality made legislators reconsider almost every aspect of the state's established educational programs and educational finance system. Before the educational decisions could be made, for example, legislators were asked to consider the role of education in society and to judge the relative importance of creativity, authority, basic skills, and individual fulfillment in the classroom; they were urged to evaluate the claims of liberal arts advocates and career-awareness champions and to appraise professional debates about effective approaches for remediation; and they were forced to balance the benefits of home rule and citizen participation in local schools against the demands of professional employee groups and the imperatives of the state's revitalized constitutional obligation to each student.[4] Judicial involvement in the issue made the legislature reluctant to dispense with topics and quickly impose cloture on debates for fear of denying someone a rightful hearing.

The strenuous efforts of the Joint Education Committee matched the complexity of the issues themselves. The director of a Rutgers University research center was retained to be committee secretary, four full-time legislative aides became available to assist the committee's research, and three dozen consultants were hired to prepare position papers on specific topics under consideration. In the spring of 1974, committee members held dozens of formal meetings and informal conferences and took testimony from more than one hundred people at public hearings throughout the state. Despite its own efforts, however, the greatest resource the committee could draw upon—aside from its leadership—was the personnel of the department of education.

More than a year earlier, the department and the state board of education had assembled a working group to formulate its response to *Robinson* under the direction of the department's Assistant Commissioner for Curriculum and Instruction, William Shine. Shine had ideal qualifications for the job. He had been a classroom teacher and a local school superintendent; his tenure as the department's chief legal officer gave him some background in legal controversies and disputes; and he combined a philosophical bent with a practical understanding of where real decision-making power rested in specific situations. With the department formally headed by an acting commissioner whose health was deteriorating badly, Shine became the leading figure in the department at this time, but it was not a good time to be the leader of the department of education. The department's intramural tensions grew more acute, and unpleasant tasks fell to Shine which otherwise would have been performed by the commissioner. Intradepartmental relationships were strained even more by newspaper articles discussing whether Shine or some other candidate would become the next commissioner of education. Some divisions of the department, with their own candidates, were slow to cooperate in the working group's activities for fear of promoting programs, philosophies, and personalities they did not favor. One top official commented admiringly, "It was only Shine who maintained the stability of the department during this period."

Departmental planning sessions were held to discuss *Robinson*, but division officers responded that their routine assignments would not permit their full participation. When the agencies and divisions of the department were asked how their own activities should be altered to respond to the mandate of *Robinson*, almost every agency urged that it be given more resources. Different parts of the department urged that an appropriate response to the court required more adult education, more testing, more vocational education, more remedial programs, and more school lunches.[5]

Personnel in Shine's Curriculum and Instruction Division would later complain that there was tremendous difficulty getting some parts of the department to act together as a department, and staff members elsewhere would protest that they were excluded from a meaningful role in formulating the department's position. An impartial observer found some validity in both positions:

> Shine probably did prepare the program with his group, but he did it by default for people I suspect never fully cooperated and never submitted helpful materials. . . . Shine probably liked the power that was flowing to him too, what with dealing with the legislature and the associations. This was his program, he was out front and not eager to share this with others. I would have done the same thing myself.

Shine's working group believed that the educational process was a subtle one, which could not be intelligently defined solely in terms of easily measurable items.[6] Education would be destroyed if schools concentrated their attention on topics that could be measured through standardized tests. They further pleaded that it was impossible to define a "thorough and efficient education" in dollar terms and destructive to interpret it to mean mastery of basic skills. The situational variables in learning were too critical, they concluded, to rely on uniform programs for diverse community needs. Arguing that the changing nature of the world made it impossible to prescribe a fixed set of goals and procedures for education, the department discouraged efforts to develop simplistic rubrics for public education. Shine's working group, and in turn the department, advocated the establishment of a comprehensive educational process that envisioned the adoption of diverse educational goals by the state and local school districts and a multidimensional assessment program to determine whether these goals were being achieved. Local communities could adapt the program to their own needs and their own circumstances.

The department seized the rational planning model of the federal Elementary and Secondary Education Act and the Right to Read program and adapted it to satisfy the court's requirements. Educational goals would be established by the state board of education and local districts, curricula would be organized to meet the goals, and periodic evaluations made of the progress each district was making. Continual monitoring and a five-year cycle of formal school approvals would assure that each school was performing at a satisfactory level. The strength of the education community in New Jersey, many have believed, is in the local districts, and this process of goal setting and assessment was designed to tap that strength. Shine's working group had surveyed the professional literature, reviewed educational activities in other states, and concluded that a "process-oriented" reply to *Robinson* was preferable to one based on educational inputs, finance measures, minimum programs, or measurable outputs. Evaluating the group's efforts to formulate a response to the court mandate, one official recalled:

> We came out with a process orientation. But, yes, it is fair to say we began with a process orientation too—a judgment based on our analysis of education: (1) the need to create a long-term process for comprehensive education which would accommodate social change; (2) a judgment reflecting the national dialogue on measurement and acknowledging the inadequacy of testing; and (3) a judgment about the [low level of the] state of the art in education and the importance of what goes on in individual classrooms.

A second characteristic of the formulation of the department's reply to the court was the elaborate provision for external participation. The extent of participation in policy debates determines whether a particular point of view gets expressed or a specific interest gets represented. In New Jersey and elsewhere, inequitable and ill-conceived policies have frequently been traced to the exclusion of groups from meaningful participation in the development of public programs. Thus, widespread participation in the conduct of public policy has become a popular objective in the past decade, and procedures for citizen involvement, freedom of information acts, and sunshine laws have been cast as means to accomplish that goal.

A few years before *Robinson*, the department of education had mounted an extensive process of citizen participation to determine the goals and priorities of the state's schools. Commissioner Marburger believed that confrontation and controversy promoted educational innovation, and his "Our Schools" project, designed to formulate educational goals, had plenty of both.[7] The project sponsored a series of public meetings throughout the state to debate educational philosophies and define school objectives. Despite staff efforts, citizens were often uncomfortable with the format of abstract discussions and distrustful of the department's motivations. At one meeting, Marburger was denounced as a dictator and accused of using the public sessions as a pretext for imposing his own plans on reluctant communities. Educational associations, whose views already carried great weight in policy circles, also had misgivings about the project. They questioned the capacity of citizens to make informed educational decisions, and they feared that the citizen participation process was simply a ploy to undermine their influence. The "Our Schools" project did yield a list of educational goals for the state's schools, but it also renewed bitterness among the state's educational associations.

When the department of education adopted a policy of external participation in formulating its response to *Robinson,* it built on the lessons learned from "Our Schools" activities. The participation exercise under *Robinson* was not designed simply to gather public viewpoints and organizational preferences. Its purposes were more fundamental. As in other states, the education community in New Jersey had been split in the previous decade by contentious labor-management issues. The department saw *Robinson* as an extraordinarily prominent issue that could be used to rebuild the harmony and consensus that had once existed among the state's education groups, and broad external participation was the mechanism to accomplish that. Judicial involvement gave the *Robinson* issues a visibility they otherwise would not have had and presented the department with an opportunity to try to reassemble the state's education community. Thus, external participation under *Robinson* was not intended to generate further controversy in New Jersey, but to rebuild an educational consensus.

Organized groups with educational interests in New Jersey, of course, had their own particular goals, and they all saw the department's program in *Robinson* as a means of securing those goals. The New Jersey Education Association and the New Jersey School Boards Association both saw the decision as a means to increase state support for elementary and secondary education, and increased funding would then permit the two organizations to pursue their respective goals of enhancing the roles of school teachers and school board members.[8] Other associations had their own more specialized objectives. To select only one example from scores, the state association of guidance counselors contended that an adequate response to the judicial ruling would require the state to mandate student/counselor ratios in schools throughout New Jersey.

The department wanted a program that all these groups and others would endorse, and, with remarkable intelligence and diligence, it achieved just that. The department invited representatives from 14 education groups and from other civic, economic, and governmental organizations to a conference to help develop its position on *Robinson*. The participants were asked to formulate specific questions on seven educational topics selected by the department: educational programs, vocational preparation, budgeting, facilities, staff education, organization, and assessment. "Is the State the proper party to develop and administer an assessment program? . . . Should the State mandate courses of study in human relationships? . . . Should large school districts be divided into separate districts? . . . Should teacher certification be for a specific term and renewable?" A list of 659 such questions was sent to each participating organization with a request for responses and reactions.[9] Nine organizations, essentially composed of professional educators, returned completed questionnaires and position papers, and these were then incorporated into the department's proposals and regulations.

The department tried to accommodate whatever suggestions and recommendations it could to build agreement among the groups. The department returned again and again to learn the views of the most concerned associations on a full range of education issues. In reaction to external suggestions from interested groups, for example, the department agreed to specific staffing ratios in local districts for principals, assistant principals, speech correctionists, special education supervisors, school psychologists, school social workers, and learning disability teachers and established regulations for the size of school facilities and school libraries. However desirable such specification may be, it, of course, contradicted the department's philosophy of divergent educational standards. The acceptance of external recommendations, which would not harm the quality of education, was intended to win organizational support for the department's total program.

Educators and other public officials often have difficulty appraising the preferences of nonorganized interests in the operations of the public schools. Sometimes groups with an important stake in public policies—user groups, for example—have no way to express their opinions about the conduct of public policies. The views of schoolchildren and parents about school programs are usually expressed less forcefully than those of teachers' unions. Litigation can prove to the unorganized that they are not alone in their discontent, and it may indicate to them that their desires for change can win support from the courts. Perhaps courts influence the course of public affairs more by stimulating previously quiescent groups to participate in policy debates than by proclaiming innovative notions of constitutional rights.[10]

Nationally, the school finance litigation movement has mobilized some community groups, which once quietly accepted the policy decisions of others, to assert their own objectives. Urban and minority populations have long been notoriously unprepared to champion their own interests in state education circles. With other urgent needs, urban groups have typically devoted less attention to education policy than many suburban areas normally display, and whatever educational activism did emerge was usually directed toward local rather than state officials. The absence of urban educational assertiveness was reinforced by the historic concern of state departments of education for the problems of rural districts. Established when urban areas were centers of educational strength and rural districts had the greatest need for state assistance, many state departments have persisted in their rural orientation, even though the relative situations of urban and rural school districts in recent decades have been reversed.

When court decisions affecting school finance programs were handed down in California and Texas, the National Urban Coalition helped create new groups to champion the interests of urban, minority populations during the preparation of those states' new school aid programs. Four months after the *Robinson* decision, an Urban Coalition staffer was dispatched to Newark, from the organization's offices in Washington, to determine how New Jersey's urban interests were preparing to deal with the ruling. After a week of discussions with minority groups and representatives of big city mayors, the N.U.C. official concluded that few preparations were being made. Data had not been assembled and staff had not been retained to argue for the special needs of urban areas in the upcoming reformulation of the state's school aid program. Recognizing this, the National Urban Coalition decided to establish an organization, patterned after the groups it had assisted in Los Angeles and San Antonio, to press urban, minority viewpoints in New

Jersey. The New Jersey Education Reform Project was never a potent group, never consisted of more than a few professional staff people, but at least it continued to express a concern about the performance of minority students throughout New Jersey's protracted policy debates.

The notoriety that the supreme court bestowed on *Robinson* encouraged groups to become involved in the department's process for responding to the decision, and the department eagerly threw open the doors for such participation. Rather than hiding the formulation of proposals in its bureaucratic corridors, the department created a set of genuine events that permitted almost universal involvement. Voluminous background materials were assembled, countless meetings held, and dozens of policy proposals were subjected to almost continual revision. To keep abreast of all these exhausting activities eventually required the assistance of a full-time professional staff. With the costs of full participation so high, many groups, especially urban-based minority groups, dropped by the wayside. They simply did not have the personnel or the expertise to consider each of the issues that came along. Organizations that did have the resources and intense interest to remain involved in the tiring process, however, did find that their concerns were reflected in the department's positions. Since the most active groups were composed of professional educators, the participation process helped the department rebuild the consensus among New Jersey's active educational associations that it sought.

Procedures for citizen participation in the conduct of public policy are designed to focus attention on issues that might otherwise be ignored, to bring nonconventional views into policy discussions, and to develop leadership among previously unrepresented community groups. Consequences, however, do not always follow intent. Since citizens usually lack the time and energy to master the details of intricate policy debates, procedures for citizen participation often end up expanding the influence of the organized groups most concerned about a public service—usually the groups' professional staff members.[11] While the department maintains that it never lost sight of the needs of minority groups and the inner cities and while the Education Reform Project was frequently present, the department's procedures for external participation in the formulation of its response to *Robinson* became primarily a means of influence and consensus building for the established professional associations.

The third objective of the Shine working group in responding to *Robinson* was to enhance the stature of the department of education in New Jersey educational circles. The department had long been regarded by many political figures as a sleepy institution, the activities of which were guided more by folklore than professionalism. When faced with the *Robinson* issues, departmental leaders had to decide what would be the best vehicle for defining the state's revitalized constitutional obligation to provide a thorough and efficient education. The new education program could be expressed by comprehensively revising the statutes that governed education in New Jersey or by requesting broad new legislation and then preparing a detailed chapter in the department's administrative code to implement it.

The department chose the second alternative, seeking a broad legislative mandate and then concentrating its policy activities on developing a new chapter in the administrative code. Literally hundreds of meetings were held by the department and other members of the state's educational community to debate the issues in the proposed document. As the code went through at least seven drafts, the state board of education and the appropriate legislative committee devoted countless hours to line-by-line reviews of the changing document. The new chapter in the code somewhat clarified the state's educational obligation, but the process of formulation itself could have been as significant as the content of the code. While the department depended on the legislature to enact education statutes, the administrative code was a vehicle of the department itself. The lengthy debate and controversy that swirled around a document of the department established the department in a leadership position it had never previously been granted. The preparation of a chapter in the administrative code placed the state board of education at the center of the political stage and forced it to act in a quasi-legislative way. The board became the subject of ongoing media coverage, the focus of interest group concern, and the object of local school board attention. The board began to exercise a policy capacity which had previously been latent.[12] The process of formulating the new chapter enhanced the leadership role of the board in New Jersey education circles and provided it an opportunity to use that role to improve the quality of education in the years ahead. Regardless of what the department did, however, regardless of what interest groups wanted, regardless even of the preferences of legislative committees, the most important single factor determining the outcome of the *Robinson* controversy would be the position of New Jersey's new governor.

Brendan T. Byrne was chosen the state's new governor, in November 1973, by the greatest electoral margin in New Jersey history. Byrne was a superior court judge who had held a series of appointive posts but had never before run for elective office. His campaign was a skillfully managed affair. A clean profile of honesty was projected and reinforced by the somewhat unsavory image of his opponent. In a campaign that stressed few concrete issues, Byrne's most prominent position was probably that on the adoption of an income tax: "I have said loud and clear that I do not think we need an income tax in the foreseeable future." [13] After issueless campaigns, it is often difficult to predict how public officials will behave once in office. Sometimes the actions of public officials are best understood by exploring their background. Clues to the meaning of politicians' behavior in particular situations can often be found by examining their previous experience, studying the features of the districts that elected them, or discovering who their backers have been.[14] At other times, it is more useful to appraise official actions, not by analyzing politicians' backgrounds but by gauging future ambitions: To what office does an official aspire and what should the official do to get there?

Recent New Jersey governors have been mentioned, not too secretly, as potential vice presidential nominees. They have been political moderates, elected by large majorities in a state that contains farms, rural areas, suburbs, and central cities typical of those found throughout the nation. They have usually been Catholics, governing a state that is not too industrial and not too liberal, but which is, according to the Census Bureau, the country's most suburban. Such "credentials" are widely believed to add electoral strength to a national ticket. Most governors' offices in the United

States are staffed by veterans of the gubernatorial election campaigns, and the Byrne Administration in New Jersey was no different.[15] The governor's office in New Jersey was staffed by people who had displayed ingenuity on the campaign trail and then moved into the State House to grapple with the problems of running the government they had won in November. They were unlikely to shrink from the challenges of ambition.

January is a dreary month in Trenton. The dampness makes the lawn sloping to the east of the State House soggy and forbidding, and the flower beds on the other side of the building are empty. The days are short, but it hardly ever gets cold enough for more than a trace of snow. Even when it does snow, the result is more messy than attractive. As the Byrne Administration assumed office at noon on the third Tuesday of January 1974, the major problem confronting the new regime was what to do about the *Robinson* decision. Some administration officials believed that how the administration handled the *Robinson* situation would serve as the hallmark of the governor's term in office and determine the fate of any future ambitions. With a sense of urgency, the administration wanted action by summer.

The task of developing the administration program was assigned to an official who was both an assistant to the governor and the deputy state treasurer. Since the administration wanted to announce a program by May, to capitalize on the momentum of the electoral victory and to pay the political costs for a tax increase as early in its term as possible, a task force of bureaucrats from seven state departments was assembled to wrestle with the job. Previous tax programs in New Jersey had been prepared by blue ribbon commissions of notables associated with the state's major organizations, but, in this instance, a group of bureaucrats rather than bigwigs was summoned.[16] Deadlines were pressing, the time for study had passed, and the task was seen essentially as the technical one of formulating the correct program—public support would be arranged later. The deputy state treasurer had participated in a similar staff group that had readied the successful legislation for the development of New Jersey's Hackensack Meadowlands, so that model of policy formulation was repeated here.

The task force held a couple of large meetings in Trenton and then went up the road to Princeton for a seminar at the comfortable headquarters facilities of the Educational Testing Service. From outside the state, numerous offers of technical assistance arrived, and the task force listened to the presentations about school finance developments in other areas. Unimpressed by circuit-riding national consultants, the task force concluded that it understood the issues in New Jersey more clearly than outsiders. As attention began to shift to specific aspects of the response to *Robinson,* full meetings of the task force gave way to smaller conferences of selected individuals with detailed expertise. One participant recalls the process:

> To speak of a task force bestows a greater structure on the activity than it really had. . . . People did not sit down in February with a list of activities and make assignments. It was not that at all. It was mostly reactive. People moved in and out as issues followed issues and as events and public needs appeared. [The deputy treasurer] would call up and need something in ten minutes and we would try to assemble it. . . . As the thing developed it was focused very much within the administration inner circle.

As the program was taking shape, the deputy treasurer would clear important concepts with the governor and top officials around the executive office. The administration knew that, whatever else it proposed, it wanted its response to the supreme court decision to be comprehensive and substantial. The Byrne Administration prepared significant recommendations for reshaping the state's policies in each of the three areas mentioned in the supreme court decision: education, school aid, and taxation.

Education. The sensible place to begin was with education. *Robinson* rested on the education clause of the state constitution, so the task force logically asked the department of education how much money was necessary to guarantee a thorough and efficient education throughout the state. The question, however, contradicted the department's belief in the subtlety of the educational process. The request for a pricetag for a thorough and efficient program implied that the state's obligation could be defined by a paragraph or a test. The administration task force was grasping for some definite figures to anchor its total program, but the departmental working group was reluctant to provide them.

The task force listened to Shine's working group and then heard from reformers who argued that the state should frame its constitutional obligation in terms of student performance of basic skills. The major education problem in the state was the ineffectiveness of urban schools, reformers argued, and this would only be addressed when fully documented. Once the failure was precisely verified, they assumed, the inadequacies of urban schools would command greater technical assistance from the state department and greater school aid from the state's purse. No, the department replied. Public support for education is really quite fragile, and the documentation of educational failure in New Jersey's cities would not generate more money for Newark, but less money for everyone in the system. For a time, the decision hung in the balance—to go to the process route recommended by the department or adopt the minimum statewide standards advocated by the reformers.

The task force soon recognized how impressively Assistant Commissioner Shine performed in the meetings with national figures and realized how little it knew about education. The task force chose to defer to the educator. The decision to rely on the expertise and judgment of the department reflected a deep respect for Shine and an admiration for his persuasive abilities. The education community in New Jersey had been plagued by dissension and bitterness in previous years, the task force knew, but Shine had prepared an approach that all the groups backed. Shine had a remarkable capacity for holding people together in an ability to discuss divisive issues without highlighting the points of conflict. The task force concluded that it would have enough problems in the taxation and school aid areas, without inciting the controversies about home rule and educational programs that Shine had apparently tamed. The task force agreed to defer to the recommendations of the department's working group and the state's educational associations.

Throughout their deliberations, Senator Wiley, Assemblyman Burstein, and the members of the Joint Education Committee maintained close relations with the administration's task force and the department's working group. In dozens of meetings and conferences, the committee debated, amended, and finally accepted the basic thrust of Shine's proposal. Adopting the administration's indeterminant view of the educational process, the Joint Education Committee reported:

> It must be borne in mind that education is not an end in itself, but a means to an end—namely, to provide each student upon leaving public school with a reasonable set of skills to function effectively in our economy and society and thus help equalize opportunities in later life. As social and economic conditions change, so must the schools adjust accordingly. The goals of the schools must reflect the needs of a complex and changing world. Given this steady development, it is impossible to prescribe a fixed set of goals and procedures.[17]

The Joint Education Committee recommended that the legislature outline a generalized set of statewide goals for the educational system and then establish a series of administrative routines to be used by state and local agencies in defining specific objectives and standards. Local districts would be responsible for creating their own school programs, but if these programs were found to be deficient after extensive evaluation, the commissioner would then be empowered to order remedial action.

This procedure acknowledged the tensions between New Jersey's traditions of local control of education and the supreme court's assertion of direct state responsibility, while, at the same time, it attempted to avoid as many controversies as possible by relying on the state's established educational structure. In its own words, the administration

> opted for the fullest possible exercise of local discretion and control consistent with the Court decision. We have done this because we believe that concern and the involvement of parents is the ultimate force for a continuous improvement of the educational system. . . . In relying on the diversity of local school districts for the attainment of a thorough and efficient system . . . The State must assume ultimate responsibility for school performance. . . . the minimum components of a thorough and efficient school program [are]—a system for discerning and applying educational standards,

> a procedure for monitoring and evaluation [*sic*] local schools
> in light of these standards, and authorization for state action
> to correct deficiencies in local school operations.[18]

The obligations of the state were sketched in broad terms, and the administrative procedures of each local school district were to be specified in great detail. This indeterminant view of state educational obligations, however, would make it impossible to determine, before legislation had been implemented, objectives clarified, and school programs evaluated, which districts required additional state funds. State aid distributions would have to rest on some criterion other than educational need.

School Aid. State policy proposals are usually presented on behalf of a governor or an administration. Citizens often assume that hundreds—or at least dozens—of people in oversized buildings in the state capital have devoted all their efforts to formulating, refining, and testing each detail of any recommendation for change. Even though there usually are massive buildings and thousands of employees in state capitals, sometimes surprisingly few resources stand behind new policy recommendations. The routine activities of government agencies usually consume all of the time and energy of almost all of the employees, so that the burdens of reform often fall on only a handful of people. This was the case with the formulation of the Byrne Administration school aid proposals in New Jersey.

Herbert Starkey's role in the development of the administration's school aid program is sometimes compared to a point which supports an inverted pyramid: An enormous weight of controversy and activity ultimately rested on only one person. The "money wizard," as he was occasionally called, was not even a regular employee of the state government. Starkey had resigned as the research director of the New Jersey Education Association in 1972, when he reached the minimum retirement age, because he suspected that the organization had become more concerned about the welfare of teachers than the education of children. Shortly after the *Robinson* decision was rendered in April 1973, Starkey was asked by the acting commissioner to become a consultant to the state department of education to help prepare background material for responding to the court's judgment. For almost a year, he put in no more than two or three days a week in developing alternative school aid formulas and working on the department's computerization program. When the Byrne Administration took office in January 1974, Herb Starkey, part-time consultant in the department of education, was practically the only person with detailed knowledge of school finance programs in the executive branch of the state government. As a task force member, Starkey would soon be laboring more than five days a week on school finance plans, but throughout the *Robinson* controversy Starkey—the point of the inverted pyramid— remained a consultant rather than a regular state employee. He ran a shoestring operation on which the administration's whole school finance program was based.

Starkey began his efforts by acknowledging two traditional characteristics of school finance in New Jersey: its heavy reliance on local property taxes and the proliferation of categoric state aid programs to assist specific types of local educational expenditures.[19] From the 1940s to the 1960s, the New Jersey legislature had enacted a series of foundation aid programs that required the state to guarantee to each school district a given amount of money for the education of each student, on the condition that the district impose a property tax at a specific rate. In addition, each district that levied the required tax would receive a minimum grant per pupil, regardless of its own wealth or its own needs. This state program and others, which helped pay for local pensions, transportation costs, special education needs, and the like, together contributed about 28 percent of the money needed to run local schools in New Jersey in 1970.

In 1970, the foundation program was replaced by a guaranteed-value school aid plan designed to equalize revenues among local districts and to encourage communities to improve the quality of their own educational offerings. Under this program, students were not counted equally, but assigned a weighting related to the estimated cost of their schooling. For example, on the assumption that children from disadvantaged families require more costly education, each child whose parent received Aid to Families with Dependent Children (AFDC) was counted as 1.75 children in determining the number of students in a local district. The program then specified a fixed property value per weighted pupil, and guaranteed to each community at least the educational revenue it would have received if the property values in that community had actually reached the stipulated level. The stipulated value was approximately equal to the average statewide property value per pupil. The community could select its own tax rate, and the state was then obliged to contribute its share of the costs, whatever that might be. The program also made minimum aid payments to local districts for each weighted pupil and aimed eventually to cover 40 percent of the total educational expenditures in the state. This program failed to satisfy the requirements of the New Jersey Supreme Court in April 1973, and was declared unconstitutional before it was fully implemented.

When the Byrne Administration task force began to meet, Herb Starkey gathered up the material he had prepared for the state board of education and headed down the street to the State House. He had one plan for the full state funding of education and another that established a district power equalizing scheme. Even though both of these plans were quickly discarded by the task force because of their cost and their incompatability with home rule principles, they did contribute to the eventual program the administration proposed. The administration endorsed a guaranteed-value aid program similar in concept to the one that had been invalidated by the court. It was different from the earlier plan, however, in important details. First, the Byrne Administration proposal guaranteed the revenues to each community from a property value that was twice the existing statewide average, not approximately equal to the state average as in the 1970 program. This meant that almost all the school districts in the state were encompassed within the provisions of the guaranteed-value formula, so that the effective fiscal backing for each pupil was to be roughly equal no matter where in the state the student lived. The establishment of a guaranteed value at twice the statewide average value transformed this plan into a district power equalizing scheme for 95 percent of the school districts in the state. The proposal also departed from the program enacted in 1970 in that it provided no minimum aid to wealthy districts and no extra AFDC weighting for urban communities.

The administration task force had originally considered ending all categorical aid programs and distributing all state aid within the provisions of the equalization formula, but that idea was soon set aside for two reasons. First, the group concluded that it was desirable to target funds to specific educational needs, and, second, they had to consider potential opposition to their proposal from affected groups. As one participant explained:

> If you wipe out the categoricals you are going to have pressure groups all over the state on you. We had problems you had to face up to from a realistic standpoint. The people who put the Beadleston [special education] Act through and expanded it to a point where I think it is the best in the nation are very vocal and they have a very strong influence with your legislators.

The final proposal maintained some categorical assistance to local school districts and also provided extra payments to help cover the excess costs for educating handicapped, vocational, and other specialized groups of pupils.

One of the categorical programs that was maintained—and even expanded—assisted local communities to pay the costs of transportation. Under the 1970 program, the state reimbursed communities for 75 percent of the costs of transporting students to and from school. The Byrne Administration proposal envisioned the state's paying all of the approved transportation costs of local districts in the years ahead. Transportation assistance, however, went most heavily to specific types of communities:

> When you started out, you would have reduced state aid to almost twenty percent of the districts in the state, and the transportation . . . aid was a sop so that they would not be wiped out entirely. So somewhere along there, the notion was that you should compensate for the reduction in formula aid by increasing their transportation aid to one hundred percent. After all, it is not an education cost and it was true that the suburbs would have been hit pretty hard by their new law and most of the transportation aid goes into suburbs and rural areas. This was a way of helping them a little bit. The transportation and categorical was a device to make sure that everybody would get something; they would have been cut in half but not wiped out.

Others supported full assumption of transportation costs by the state because they believed that there was widespread waste and abuse in the current school transportation programs, and total state involvement would eventually lead to greater local discipline and significant financial savings.

In total, the program envisioned almost $550 million in new state aid for local school districts. There was concern, however, about how effectively such a large infusion of money could be used in a single year. One official commented:

> If you had the big infusion of . . . state money, [we wanted] . . . to guarantee tax relief . . . rather than [have it] all go for increased spending. We had some districts where state aid would double and there was no way you could profitably use that money. It would be wasted. There was a realization that increases of that magnitude if all devoted to new spending would really cause repercussions from the taxpayers.

The administration proposed limitations, or "caps," on annual budget increases that would be permitted in local school districts. Low-spending school districts would be allowed to increase their expenditures more rapidly than high-spending districts, so that disparities in per pupil spending among local school districts would be narrowed. Limitations on local expenditure increases also restrained the potential growth in the magnitude of the state's obligation to local school districts in future years. In the past, many believed, large doses of new state aid had accomplished nothing except pushing up the costs of the existing educational system, and they did not want that to happen again.

The total effect of the proposed plan was to raise the state's share of the total education budget in New Jersey from 30 percent to approximately 50 percent by increasing state aid and partially substituting it for revenues raised from local property taxation. According to the task force, places like Newark would realize some increase in state aid, but such districts had already gained significant new revenues under the 1970 program. The largest proportional increases in aid would flow to poor suburban school districts and districts located in rural areas.[20] Despite his meager resources to formulate and define the school aid proposal, Starkey looked over the recommendations with quiet satisfaction. He was pleased with both the strong push toward equalization of resources among rich and poor districts and with the expanded role of the state in educational finance. The proposal had both power and equalization, but Herb Starkey had been around school finance circles in New Jersey for decades. He knew that the real problems would not be in distributing the aid among local districts but in raising the revenues to fund that aid.

Taxation. New Jersey has a long history of dramatic battles to reshape its system for raising tax revenues.[21] In past decades, countless governors, study commissions, and legislative proposals have all advocated fundamental changes in the techniques used by the state and local governments in New Jersey to gather revenue. In 1935, a Republican governor advocated the adoption of a retail sales tax and a state income tax to help support local schools and to pay the escalating costs of public relief caused by the ongoing depression. The recommendation for an income tax was soundly rebuffed, but a sales tax was enacted by the legislature after extraordinary party pressures on both Republicans and Democrats. But that did not conclude the story. Organizations, which were dedicated to the repeal of the sales tax, soon appeared throughout the state and they concentrated their efforts on electing a legislature composed of members committed to their goal. When the primary election was held, it was clear that their efforts were successful. Regardless of which party's candidates won the general election, a majority of the members of the new assembly and senate were committed to the repeal of the sales tax. Quickly acknowledging the tides of public opinion, the legislature rescinded the tax before the general election was even held, and the school aid program it was designed to support foundered.

In 1966 and 1972, Governors Hughes and Cahill respectively urged the legislature to end New Jersey's extraordinary reliance on property taxation, to increase state support for local schools, and to adopt a personal income tax. Despite the fact that both houses of the legislature were organized by the governor's party, first Hughes and then Cahill failed to persuade the necessary number of legislators to follow his lead. Both of their tax programs were rejected. In fact, soon after Cahill's proposal was defeated by the legislature, he lost his bid for renomination in his own party's primary election. These events contributed to the conventional belief that elected officials in New Jersey who advocated tax increases in general and income taxes in specific would face voter retribution at the polls.

This belief was countered, however, by changes that had already begun to appear in New Jersey's revenue and expenditure policies in the decade before *Robinson*. The state's first permanent sales tax was finally adopted in 1966 and was increased almost without protest in 1970. This supplied resources that enabled the state government to play a more prominent role in the provision of public services and tended to dilute the local orientation of the state's politics. While income tax proposals had been defeated in the past, the recent trends in public finance pointed toward increased state taxes and a greater state role in the delivery of public services.

In this uncertain climate, the Byrne Administration seized upon the *Robinson* decision as a justification for proposing a program to raise more than $1 billion in new state revenue, truly a mammoth recommendation for a government whose expenditures at that time were in the neighborhood of $2½ billion. As with the proposals of the two previous governors, the Byrne task force program combined some elements of reform in the tax structure with other aspects that would increase taxes. First, the legislature was urged to raise $550 million in new state revenues to help support elementary and secondary schools by replacing existing funds then raised from local property taxation. Second, the administration requested an additional $200 million to finance the state's assumption of certain social, judicial, and welfare costs then being borne by counties and municipalities. The extraordinarily high property tax rates imposed on New Jersey's cities were not so much the product of educational costs as of noneducational needs, including police, fire service, sanitation, social and welfare expenditures. State assumption of the costs of certain service functions that consumed a significant share of urban budgets would reduce the high tax burdens in those areas, compensate some urban areas that would not realize great benefits under the school aid revisions, and assist Democratic bastions that had made major contributions to Byrne's election as governor. Finally, a tax increase of $300 million was proposed to cover items in the state budget that could not be funded through existing state revenue sources. The price for the ambitious package exceeded $1 billion.

The Byrne Administration's solution for raising the revenue was simple: "The only equitable way to raise the revenue needed for this program of educational reform and property tax relief is an income tax." [22] Briskly, without commenting on campaign promises, the task force recommended a personal income tax, with the rates graduated from a 1.5 percent tax on federal taxable incomes below $1000 to an 8 percent rate on taxable incomes over $25,000. To be sure that wealthy taxpayers would be unable to take complete advantage of the incentives offered in the federal tax law, a minimum tax of 3 percent on incomes in excess of $50,000 was proposed as well. This program was designed to yield approximately $1 billion in the upcoming year and continue to generate additional revenues in future years. The graduated rate structure meant that receipts for the state would increase more rapidly than increases in personal income, thus allowing officials to escape politically unpopular, annual upward adjustments in the rates of other taxes.

The education component of the administration proposal was shaped by Assistant Commissioner Shine, refined by the Joint Education Committee, and accepted by the Byrne task force. The school aid provisions were fashioned by Herb Starkey, the somewhat detached consultant of the department of education, with continual clearances through the Byrne task force. The taxation program was very much the product of the task force leadership and the administration inner circle. With these proposals, the Byrne Administration went to the legislature and the public.

The *Robinson* decision triggered the formation of major Byrne Administration proposals to reshape New Jersey policies governing local education programs, state aid to school districts, and the contours of the statewide tax system. While the supreme court certainly did not participate directly in the preparation of these proposals, the court's presence in the controversy did cast a persistent shadow over the nature and meaning of the daily actions of others. The New Jersey Supreme Court had used *Robinson* to place the issues of tax reform, school finance, and educational quality on the agendas of the other policy-making institutions of government, and the fact that these issues were raised by a formal court decision affected how the governor, the legislature, and the department of education reacted to them.

The *Robinson* decision itself had been written with a greater view to legal considerations than policy development. For philosophical and practical reasons, the supreme court refused to accept the clear-cut trial court rationale requiring equal treatment of taxpayers and fashioned instead an intricate constitutional justification not susceptible to easy legislative action. Unlike court decisions in other states, which were essentially financial judgments, the supreme court's *Robinson* v. *Cahill* ruling ordered New Jersey officials to review the state's total educational program on the way to revamping its school aid scheme and altering its taxation system. The court's participation in *Robinson* multiplied the number of topics that had to be examined, prolonged the time needed for legislative consideration, and robbed legislators of their ability to shape and control the legislative process. Collective decision-making institutions frequently resolve a controversy by including certain aspects of an issue and deleting others, until a policy emerges that is acceptable to the requisite groups and majorities. Court participation in *Robinson* left officials unsure of their ability to restrict examination of the issues before them, and thus rendered the process of policy consideration extraordinarily time consuming.

In addition to its ambiguity, the court's initiative in *Robinson* also had great visibility, not just for the public, but, more importantly, for the state's governing institutions. The governor, the legislature, and the department of education all had to deal with the issues raised by the court, but because the decision was so visible it became entwined with the other concerns of these institutions. While preparing a constructive program, each institution also tried to promote some other objective it espoused. The new Byrne Administration could exhibit the virtuosity of its own policy formation capacity, the assistant education commissioner could advance his philosophy of education and demonstrate his qualifications to become commissioner, and legislative reformers could illustrate the value of their model of legislative operations, which holds that the legislature should contribute meaningfully to the formation of important public policies. The New Jersey Supreme Court required the state's governing institutions to participate in a "process of collective decision" in reply to *Robinson*, but differing premises and institutional motivations made that an uneasy collaboration. Judicial participation in *Robinson* did not sweep aside the disagreements that had existed before the court's ruling. To the contrary, the decision's prominence and ambiguity compounded those disputes and complicated the state's task of responding to the judgment.

The court also bestowed on *Robinson* a compelling quality that other policy topics do not have. No matter the preference of legislators and officials, the *Robinson* issues would not go away without concrete action. They possessed a permanence that both required that they be faced and, at the same time, made them an attractive vehicle for other extraneous policy objectives of other groups. Any policy goal would be secured, if it could be persuasively argued that the goal was a necessary component of the state's response to the court mandate. The Byrne task force foresaw an administration plagued by continuing, politically destructive budget gaps, unless it could devise a program to gain significant new revenues for the next year and for future years.[23] An income tax with graduated rates would be an ideal solution, because it would yield an infusion of money in the first year and progressively larger amounts of money in future years, as prices and incomes in the state rose. Using *Robinson* as a vehicle, the Byrne Administration argued that New Jersey must break with long tradition and adopt a personal income tax to comply with the justices' ruling. While this was by far the most prominent example, other groups as well tried to link their policy objectives to the court-sanctioned agenda item. Proponents of higher teachers' salaries, more audiovisual equipment, and much else turned to *Robinson* to achieve their purposes, and this complicated the state's ability to prepare an expeditious response to the court.

Robinson was a symbolic victory for champions of hard-pressed central cities, and the court action encouraged them to galvanize their resources to seize whatever advantage might appear. The decision led to the founding of the New Jersey Education Reform

Project and to the mobilization of other urban-oriented groups that had previously accepted state education policy without protest. The court's involvement in *Robinson* did stimulate participation by some of these groups in the policy formulation process, but, ironically, it also inhibited the activities of other groups. In certain ways, a litigation process both promotes and contradicts the premises of public participation. Adversary proceedings are governed by strict rules, which limit the information that can be presented in a case and determine who will be full parties to the litigation. Generally, it is difficult for a group to become a party to a suit after it has passed from the trial court to the appellate level. After the trial court decision in *Robinson*, and especially after the New Jersey Supreme Court had delivered its first decision, some groups were alerted to the possible consequences of the ruling. Some organizations feared that the decision would simply yield increased expenditures without commensurate benefits. They wanted to become a part of the litigation to oppose some aspects of the judgment, but they found that the rules of adversary proceedings precluded their involvement as full participants. They found no arena where they could oppose the *Robinson* decision without appearing to subvert the supreme court as an institution, and that was something their members did not want to do. Such groups were relegated to the peripheral role of suggesting to the department what program details would be most acceptable to them. Thus, court decisions stimulate some groups to participate in policy discussions, but respect for the court and the arcane rules of the adversary process inhibit other groups from expressing their own deeply held opinions.

Robinson differed from most issues faced by New Jersey officials in that it had emerged from the state supreme court and not from an administration initiative, an interest group proposal, or an outcry of public opinion. This judicial origin blurred the boundaries of the issue while, at the same time, giving it a prominence, staying power, and symbolism that complicated the already cluttered process by which officials would develop their response to the court ruling. The fact that *Robinson* was a court-initiated agenda item compounded official difficulties in promptly resolving the issue, but, in New Jersey, any proposal to adopt an income tax was likely to encounter widespread opposition. The Byrne Administration proposal surely did.

Elected officials usually enter the State House from a parking lot entrance on the west side of the building. The governor's car is parked parallel to a passageway that leads past the windows of the assembly caucus rooms into the State House. The governor and legislators walk the thirty paces of the passageway, go up nine steps into the building, pass the public phone booths, and then part company, with the governor turning to the right toward the suite of executive offices and the legislators heading left to the senate and assembly chambers. May 15, 1974, was the day on which that parting would be only temporary, for later the governor was to speak to a joint session of the legislature on *Robinson*. When in joint session, the legislature convenes in the assembly chamber. Assemblymen and assemblywomen take their normal places, senators sit on folding chairs installed in the aisles for the occasion, legislative and executive aides crowd the rear of the spacious room, and the governor's cabinet settles in a front row of the overhanging balcony. Behind the assembly rostrum are the legislature's administrative facilities and a spiral staircase, which leads up to the airy corner office of the speaker of the assembly.

Brendan Byrne mounted the rostrum that Wednesday and described to the assembled legislators his administration's plans to reshape New Jersey's education, school aid, and taxation systems. He spoke in detail of the need to guarantee to each child in the state an opportunity to get a good education regardless of the location or social composition of the child's school. He outlined the basic features of the goal-setting and assessment process soon to be proposed by the Joint Education Committee and sketched the contours of the school aid program Herb Starkey and his task force had formulated. Then, without specifying the details, he urged the legislature to adopt a personal income tax to satisfy the court's mandate and to relieve local property taxes. While the large Democratic majorities gave the newly elected Democratic governor much support, many legislators were not persuaded.

Some legislators were unwilling to accept the argument that the court decision required the enactment of a personal income tax.

The chairman of the legislature's Joint Education Funding Committee (which was distinct from the Joint Education Committee) denounced the goal-setting process and its accompanying school aid recommendation as nothing but an expensive pretext to impose an income tax levy. "The decision in the *Robinson* case should not serve as a vehicle for massive changes in the tax structure without the necessity being clearly studied and demonstrated. . . . We neither need nor desire a State income tax. . . ." [24] The chairman urged that additional state aid be granted only to those school districts currently spending less per pupil than the statewide average and to other districts whose educational programs and staffing ratios were demonstrably deficient. This two-part program, the chairman argued, would respond to "the sentiment of the vast majority of our people, who desire a fair but not overly ambitious compliance with the court's mandate." [25] From this perspective, there was no need to enact an income tax or any other major new taxes.

Other legislators accepted the supreme court's mandate for school finance reform, but objected to the administration's revenue proposals. While *Robinson* struck specifically at the heavy use of local property taxation to support education, some lawmakers believed that the court's logic would eventually preclude the use of any local taxation to fund education, for that would become an abdication of the state's constitutional responsibility. At the same time, however, property taxation was too lucrative a source of revenue to abandon entirely. The only realistic, long-term response to *Robinson*, these legislators believed, was to replace local property taxation for the support of schools with a statewide property tax. A statewide property tax at a uniform rate would generate sufficient funds to permit the state to reduce and eventually eliminate dependence on local property taxation to finance education, without the need to impose a personal income tax. At the same time, the use of property rather than income taxation would restrain the growth of future public expenditures and reassure those concerned about seemingly inevitable increases in the costs of government. Furthermore, the regressive impact of property taxation could be partially offset by exempting the first few thousand dollars of value of each person's private residence.[26] Statewide property taxation, these lawmakers argued, could become an equitable, sufficient, and restrained source of revenue for the needs of education.

Finally, there were other legislators who would not publicly oppose an income tax in principle, but who objected to selected aspects of the Byrne recommendations. Some argued that New Jersey should impose a surtax on the federal income tax rather than create an income tax structure of its own. Others wanted to guarantee that newly collected funds would go to schools and localities rather than to state operations, and still others complained that their own localities were not treated well enough under the Byrne Administration proposal.

Voting in the New Jersey legislature is usually done through an electronic machine, with the members throwing a switch on their desk one way for a yes vote, or the other to register their opposition. On the assembly speaker's rostrum is a display of the seating arrangement in the chamber, which lights up to indicate whether and how each member has voted on the measure before the house. Often members hesitate before casting their vote to determine which of their colleagues are in favor of the bill and which opposed. Occasionally, the leadership may put up a bill for consideration without being sure that there are enough votes to ensure passage. On important measures, on rare occasions, the voting machine has remained open as long as an hour while leaders of the partisan majority scoured the floor for elusive votes.

On July 15, 1974, two months to the day after Governor Byrne had addressed the legislature, the assembly speaker looked down at the voting pattern before him and closed the machine, thus recording the assembly's decision on the Byrne Administration's income tax proposal.[27] The final tally recorded that, by a margin of 41 to 38, the Byrne income tax program had passed. It had won the support of legislators from major Democratic party organizations, liberals, and almost all of the assembly leadership, and had been opposed by the small band of Republicans and Democratic traditionalists. Since there were probably a few more votes available for the tax, passage in the assembly had been surprisingly easy, but everyone expected the course in the senate to be much more difficult.

The senate chamber is a more intimate place than the assembly and somewhat more splendid. While the assembly's character accentuates its representative nature, the senate is slightly more clubby and self-assured. The senate's majority caucus meets in a recently refurbished conference room, outside the back entrance of the State House, known as the Bid Room. When the caucus convened on Thursday, July 18, 1974, to discuss the Byrne tax plan, the votes to assure passage were not in hand.[28] The senate president, installed with Byrne's support, adopted a neutral stance, moderating the debate between tax champions and opponents. Another senator, who had been selected by Byrne to be state party chairman, indicated his support of the administration tax plan and then distributed a tax proposal of his own, in case the administration plan could not win sufficient votes. Antitax forces wanted a formal vote in the senate as soon as possible to kill off the Byrne proposal, while supporters wanted to delay action to provide time to round up the needed votes. The caucus compromised by scheduling the vote for the upcoming Wednesday, almost a week away, but, in fact, the administration had no real chance to secure wavering votes. Immediately after the caucus meeting broke up, the senate president called a press conference. The administration program called for the wrong tax at the wrong time, he explained, and he was opposed to it. The outright opposition of a key figure was so devastating that a formal vote was not even taken. So as not to jeopardize loyal supporters by making them cast a futile vote for a lost cause, the administration agreed to withdraw the income tax measure from consideration and not to reintroduce it.

Throughout the fall and winter of 1974, tax plan after tax plan emerged for consideration in the senate—and eventual rejection.[29] Statewide property taxes and a payroll tax proposal were carefully evaluated, but the plan that came closest to adoption was one calling for the enactment of a state surcharge on the federal income tax. Last-minute confusion about the rate of the surcharge that would be necessary and about the distribution of funds among localities eroded support for this program, too. No proposal appeared able to gather the 21 votes needed to enact legislation in the senate.

One of the most insightful students of the New Jersey Senate argues that the best way to understand the senate's actions is to recognize that, when each senator looks in the mirror each morning, the senator says, "Good morning, Governor—I mean, Senator." In 1974 and 1975, many senators had few incentives to help the Byrne Administration succeed, and the administration responded with an antilegislative tone that hampered constructive cooperation. Many senators had their own ambitions and their own policy perspectives, which the Byrne task force had ignored in formulating the administration's program. The governor's ambitious program came down to the senators from on high, with little consultation and little demonstration that the public really supported it. Some senators also opposed the formula for distributing school aid backed by the administration, and were unconvinced of the need to provide a financial cushion for state operations for the balance of Byrne's term. Some lawmakers simply did not like income taxes and saw no reason they should support them. Legislative constituencies represented by some senators would receive new support for their schools under the Byrne proposal, but some of these legislators believed that they would do every bit as well, or better, under some solution to the problem fashioned by the court system, without their having to vote for unpopular tax increases.

The 1974 legislative session ended with the legislature still unable to enact a new tax program or a new education bill. As the end of the year approached, there was a flurry of activity, as executive and legislative leaders tried to construct a tax plan that could be adopted before the supreme court's deadline of December 31, 1974, passed. They failed. New Jersey began 1975 with its legislature in violation of an order of its supreme court. The constitutional confrontation that many had sought to avoid lay ahead. The next move was up to the supreme court.

NOTES

1. Minutes, Permanent Commission on State School Support, 23 November, 1971, New Jersey State Archives.

2. *Robinson* v.*Cahill* II, 63, N.J. 196 (1973).

3. See the files of the Joint Education Committee.

4. See consultant papers assembled by Joint Education Committee, New Jersey Legislature, July 1974.

5. See New Jersey Department of Education, "Draft for T and E Discussion Only," 19 November 1973.

6. See "Report of the Joint Education Committee to the New Jersey Legislature," 13 June 1974, pp. 3–4; and William A. Shine and Susan Kinsey, "Creativity of the School and School Finance Reform: The New Jersey Experience," New Jersey Department of Education, July 1974.

7. Alexander Plante and Michael Usdan, "Evaluation of the 'Our Schools' Project" (12 October 1971), mimeo.

8. See position papers of the New Jersey School Boards Association, 12 December 1973 and 8 December 1975; and of the Education Committee of the New Jersey Manufacturers Association, 19 December 1973 and 25 June 1975.

9. New Jersey Department of Education, "Towards a Definition of 'Thorough and Efficient': A Report to the State Board of Education" (Trenton: mimeo, November 1973).

10. Stuart A. Scheingold, *The Politics of Rights: Lawyers, Public Policy and Political Change* (New Haven: Yale University Press, 1974), chap. 4.

11. Dale Rogers Marshall, *The Politics of Participation in Poverty: A Case Study of the Board of the Economic and Youth Opportunities Agency of Greater Los Angeles* (Berkeley: University of California Press, 1971).

12. Roald F. Campbell and Tim L. Mazzoni, eds., *State Policy Making for the Public Schools: A Comparative Analysis* (Columbus: Education Governance Project of the Ohio State University, 1974).

13. (Trenton) *Times*, 5 October 1973.

14. Joseph Schlesinger, *Ambition and Politics: Political Careers in the United States* (Chicago: Rand McNally, 1966).

15. Donald R. Sprengel, *Gubernatorial Staffs: Functional and Political Profiles* (Iowa City: Institute of Public Affairs, 1969).

16. See, for contrast, the New Jersey Tax Policy Committee, *Summary of the Report* (Trenton: The Committee, 1972).

17. "Report of the Joint Education Committee," p. 3.

18. Byrne Administration Task Force, "Proposed Education Reform—Property Tax Relief Program," May 1974, Part I, pp. 11–13.

19. The passage is based on David Listokin, *Educational Financing Reform: A Guide to Legislative Action* (New Brunswick: Rutgers University, 1974), pp. 8–10.

20. Byrne Task Force, Part I, p. 8.

21. For background, see Richard Lehne, "Revenue and Expenditure Policies," in Alan Rosenthal, ed., *Politics in New Jersey* (New Brunswick: Eagleton Institute, Rutgers University, 1975).

22. Byrne Task Force, Part II, p. 2.

23. Ibid.

24. Raymond Garramone, "Memorandum to the Legislature" (mimeo, undated), p. 2.

25. Ibid., passim.

26. John Russo et al., "Tax Restructuring in New Jersey—An Alternative Plan" (mimeo, undated).

27. See A1875, A1665, A1984, and A3115 of the 1974 Session of the New Jersey General Assembly.

28. Robert DeWitt Gilbert, "Waiting for the Governor: Tax Reform: Summer, 1974" (Seminar paper, Princeton University, 9 January 1975).

29. See the Minutes of the Educational Finance Forum of the New Jersey Legislature, Fall 1974.

5

Justices in the Legislative Process

Mail addressed to the New Jersey Supreme Court is usually opened by one of the aides in the clerk's office. The clerical personnel first recognized the proliferating complexity of the *Robinson* case, as the December 31, 1974, deadline for legislative action approached and then passed. *Robinson* v. *Cahill* had been assigned docket number 8618, and the files for the case began to bulge. Dozens of petitions addressed to the court arrived from towns and school districts throughout New Jersey, from interest groups and associations, from public officials and individual legislators. The impending constitutional confrontation had returned *Robinson* to the front pages of the state's newspapers, and hundreds of New Jersey citizens took the opportunity to communicate their personal views on the case directly to the justices of the court.[1] One letter to the court came from a former marine, of Butler, New Jersey, complaining that the court had become too deeply involved in political issues:

My blaming the Governor for all our ills is wrong. It is actually you men on the Court that are giving us our problems. . . . You bunch of appointed Gods do only what you want to do. You don't give a damn about the masses of people, just the powerful groups who holler the loudest. . . . I wouldn't hire you men to judge a dog show because the dog that barked the loudest, that's the one you would give the prize.

In contrast, a woman from Lanoka Harbor, New Jersey, wished the court well in its efforts and suggested that perhaps the court should play an even more assertive role in education policy:

Frankly, the court should be examining the fraud perpetrated on the taxpayers for failing to deliver a reasonable product— a literate student. If the Court intends to enter an area of legislation maybe in its wisdom it can devise a method to assure that the taxpayer will get what he pays for.

Twenty-one months had passed since the supreme court's first decision, in April 1973, which had declared the state's school finance program to be unconstitutional, and the Byrne Administration and the legislature had not yet been able to enact a replacement. With the legislature in violation of its order, the supreme court had to do something. As the two letters cited indicate, individual citizens disagreed about what should be done, and that disagreement accurately reflected divisions of opinion among legislators, educators, and interest group leaders. The supreme court's situation was a perilous one. As an institution, it had announced that New Jersey had to have a new school finance program, but it was unclear whether the court had either the authority or the will to compel the legislature to act. How the legislature would respond to a new initiative by the court was even more uncertain. As the year 1975 began, Trenton observers foresaw a major battle developing between the legislature and the supreme court, and no one was sure of the victor.

Two hundred years earlier, another battle had been fought in Trenton. George Washington had lost half his Continental Army in a futile effort to defend New York City from the British, and then had retreated across New Jersey looking for new recruits and new supplies. By the time the army reached Trenton, only small bands of militia had appeared to join the forlorn cause, and Washington was forced to slip across the Delaware River and take refuge in Pennsylvania. Thankful that General Sir William Howe lacked the initiative to press the attack in New Jersey and the boats to pursue him into Pennsylvania, Washington received reports that the British had settled in for the winter at Trenton. The Continental Army was ragged, starved, defeated, and demoralized. With as much desperation as hope, Washington led his troops back across the Delaware on Christmas night, 1776, and, in an unexpected reversal, routed the large Hessian encampment at Trenton on the morning of December 26. The Battle of Trenton yielded almost one thousand prisoners, but, more important, it restored flagging confidence in the cause of national independence, revived enlistments, and became a turning point in the revolutionary struggle. Two hundred years later, the Old Barracks, where the Hessian troops were quartered, can still be seen from the windows of the general assembly chamber, and they stand as a reminder to contemporary pundits of the difficulty of predicting the outcome of battles that rage around Trenton.

One person who had given a great deal of thought to struggles between New Jersey's supreme court and its legislature was the former chief justice, Joseph Weintraub. He had presided over New Jersey's highest court for fifteen years, and he had guided the court's strategy during the stormy legislative apportionment controversy in the mid-1960s. The Weintraub Court had been philosophically opposed to the careless imposition of judicial policy preferences and had been quite aware of the ultimate vulnerability of judges in the policy arena. Therefore, its characteristic response to legislative inaction was not to indulge in confrontation, but to devise an indirect strategy for prodding members of the senate and assembly into action. After he had left the bench, Weintraub sat in the sunny, California-style garden room of his home in Orange and explained his general rules for encouraging reluctant legislators to act.

First, there was a matter of reputation. Weintraub explained—with a hint of satisfaction—that he had maintained a reputation for being "bull-headed and arrogant." A reputation for unpredictable assertiveness meant that legislators could neglect judicial pronouncements only at their peril. They could never be wholly sure that the justices would not do something truly horrendous that would jeopardize the legislators' electoral standing. If the court had been perceived to be accommodating and understanding, conscious of the difficulties of legislative action, and unlikely to impose a genuinely disruptive order, reactions to its rulings might have been slower and less comprehensive. Bluff and bombast, Weintraub argued, could sometimes be an alternative to assertive action.

If the court was forced to act, however, certain types of orders were more useful than others. The Weintraub Court believed that any interim remedy imposed by the court in a situation where the legislature refused to act should have one essential characteristic —it should be roundly disliked by everyone.[2] If a program formulated by the court granted new benefits to some groups, it might become counterproductive. The court-bestowed benefits might be so attractive that the recipient groups would work to impede rather than facilitate the enactment of a nonjudicial solution to the problem. In the mid-1960s, for example, the New Jersey court did not impose its own legislative districting plan on the state because it feared that legislators and counties that won increased representation under its plan would cease their own search for a nonjudicial remedy. Instead, the court refused to sanction further elections held under the previous apportionment scheme, a move that upset all the legislators. In this way, the court maintained pressure for legislative action without giving some legislators an additional incentive to oppose its order and its purpose.

Weintraub's third general rule acknowledged that court orders themselves could not command legislative action in heated controversies. Since traditional respect for judicial rulings had declined in the past decade, legislators no longer had to fear voter retribution for ignoring court orders. Even though courts had lost some of their direct power to compel legislators to act, the justices could still initiate activities whose secondary consequences would concentrate pressure on elected officials. Weintraub believed that this could be done most effectively by withholding benefits that resourceful groups derived from ongoing government programs. The suspension of benefits could transform these resourceful groups into lobbyists who demanded action from reluctant legislators in their own right. Compensation for lawyers defending public clients could be jeopardized, for example, so that the legislature would be petitioned to create a public defender system; or the distribution of state aid to municipalities could be enjoined, so that local officials would storm the legislative chambers demanding that something be done. In these ways, numerous independent groups in society could be impressed into the judicial ranks to help overcome a lethargic or resistant legislature.

Weintraub had formulated general guidelines for prodding the legislature into action, but the court was not to have the benefit of his leadership and experience during the *Robinson* struggle. The supreme court that faced the legislature throughout 1975 was a totally different group from the court that had served for more than a decade under Chief Justice Weintraub. Weintraub had retired from the bench shortly after the court had rendered the original *Robinson* decision, and the six associate justices had departed at roughly the same time.[3] While the judicial deadline for the enactment of a new school finance program was passing without legislative action, a new state supreme court was taking shape, led by a new chief justice and composed of new associate justices.

The nomination of the new chief justice was confirmed by the state senate by a vote of 36 to 0.[4] Richard Hughes had been a popular two-term governor during the 1960s, and still retained an enormous reservoir of respect and affection. More an intuitive than a cerebral politician, Hughes established the vigorous tone of his gubernatorial administration by throwing the full resources of the state into efforts to help New Jersey shore communities recover from a severe storm that struck shortly after he came into office. His tenure is remembered as one in which the state began to face up to the problems of urbanization and to its unmet social service needs. This activism was tempered, however, by a compromising practicality, which had earlier won Hughes the nickname "Two Buckets," for someone who typically carried water on both shoulders. As a trial court judge in the decade before he became governor, Hughes had become a specialist in juvenile justice and the operations of the state's probation system, displaying a compassion that would also typify his subsequent activities. Commenting on the three major governmental positions he had held in his career,

Hughes would later conclude: "I believe that governors, chief justices, and judges alike all should have a restlessness, a kind of impatience for the doing of more justice, for the satisfying of more decent human needs." [5] In sharp contrast to Chief Justice Weintraub, Hughes was amiable and compromising rather than intellectually impatient, but, like his predecessor, Hughes was also pragmatic and policy oriented. The Hughes Court was expected to differ from the Weintraub Court in style but not in substance.

The associate justices appointed to serve with Hughes were a more disparate group than the members of the Weintraub panel. Almost all of the Weintraub justices of the 1960s had been elevated to their supreme court positions after lengthy service on the state superior court, where most had sat for more than a decade. Despite the decade of judicial service, these justices were normally in their late forties or early fifties when appointed to the supreme court. The judges appointed to the Hughes panel were an older group with slightly more diverse professional backgrounds. While all were lawyers, a number had no explicit judicial experience prior to joining the supreme court. The Hughes Court justices were just learning their jobs, just learning to work with each other, and just learning how to exercise their power when they ran up against a legacy from the Weintraub years: *Robinson* and a deadlocked legislature.

The task of inspiring a meaningful legislative response to *Robinson* was likely to be even more challenging than the problems the supreme court had encountered in earlier controversies. When the Weintraub Court had acted in the reapportionment cases, for example, its authority was reinforced by the presence of federal courts in the issue. State legislators knew that if they ignored the state court, they would still have to contend with federal judges. While the state supreme court and the state legislature are coordinate branches of the same government, each dependent on the other, the federal court system is an entirely different matter. If genuinely provoked, state legislatures can impeach state supreme court justices, refuse to appropriate funds needed for ongoing operations, fail to raise judicial salaries, and generally make life unpleasant for court personnel. Federal judges, however, are beyond the reach of state legislators. Their authority rests on the United

States Constitution, the supreme law of the land, and their administrative activities are supported by the national government, not by state legislatures. In *Robinson,* the New Jersey Supreme Court was operating very much on its own authority, without the legal or moral support of either the federal Constitution or the federal court system.

Not only was the New Jersey court's authority less compelling in *Robinson* than it had been in other policy areas, but the nature of the issue itself was also less responsive to judicial mandate. *Robinson* affected people's lives much more immediately than did such remote concepts as legislative apportionment. Schools and taxes rank at the top of the public issues that concern citizens, and the supreme court decision promised to have a direct impact on both. When the Byrne Administration pinned a price tag on *Robinson,* requiring the state to raise vast amounts of new revenue, the moral power of the supreme court to inspire a constructive response from the legislature was weakened even further.

The legislature had failed to meet the court's December 31, 1974, deadline for the enactment of a new school finance plan, and the parties to the case turned to the Hughes Court requesting action. Brendan Byrne was now a defendant in the case, as a successor to Governor Cahill, and joining him as defendants were the New Jersey Senate and Assembly, the state treasurer, the commissioner of education, and the state board of education. Even though all the defendants had originally been represented by New Jersey's attorney general, they now discovered that their legal positions began to conflict. As the supreme court considered what to do about the missed deadline, different institutions of the state government recommended different courses of action. Once a defendant, the governor now chose to ally himself with the plaintiffs. Fresh from a series of defeats at the hands of the legislature, Byrne personally and directly wanted the court to take aggressive action to resolve *Robinson.* His motion urged the justices to appoint a special master to define the state's educational obligation and then to redistribute approximately $640 million in state school aid from richer to poorer communities.[6] From Jersey City, Harold Ruvoldt, Jr., presented three alternate motions for the plaintiffs. They petitioned the court either to redistribute state school aid, establish an entirely new state program for the support of education, or arrange a series of conferences and timetables designed to yield a judicial solution to the school finance dilemma in time for implementation by July 1975.[7] The governor and his administration were now leading the plaintiffs' forces, while only the legislature, especially a narrow majority of the senate, remained to advocate restraint.

The senate and the senate president appealed for the court to go slowly. They wanted the court to return the case to a trial court to rehear arguments on the merits of the original questions before taking any further action on its own. Judicial meddling, it was argued, was more likely to confuse the process of the legislative response than facilitate it.[8] Another well-placed citizen, close to the legislature, also wrote a personal letter to former governor and Chief Justice Hughes counseling delay:

> Realistically, I don't believe the present time deadline is fair to Governor Byrne and his legislature. In no way can they build public confidence and understanding in a plan-by-shotgun. To force an educational plan that is not ready will undermine the system. . . . the present T&E bill is loaded with problems and is not nearly ready to be law. . . . [In the legislative district where I live] the two wealthiest school districts get the most money! . . . it takes a great deal of time to develop the right kind of solution—and any deadline will produce not gains but misunderstanding and setbacks. . . . I have a suggestion. To take away aid, at this late moment . . . would be to create educational havoc. . . . The court could fund '75–'76 under the [existing] . . . formula at the same levels of '74–'75 just because it's the only fair alternative left. . . . The court could, at the same time, instruct the legislature to develop a new formula by the *middle* of next year. . . .

The two options before the court were clear: either to secure the constitutional rights of citizens by imposing a judicial solution to *Robinson* or to continue efforts to persuade the legislature, the formal policy-making branch of government, to devise its own, popularly based program to respond to the issues that had been raised by the decision.

For one of the justices, it was not much of a debate. Described by the press as a "vigorous intellect of forceful character," Morris

Pashman had once been mayor and finance director of the city of Passaic.[9] After graduation from law school, Pashman had clerked for a supreme court justice and then served for more than a decade on the state superior court. Graying and bespectacled, Pashman has all the physical characteristics of a judge from central casting. In recent years, his sharp questioning of lawyers, his quotable style, and his exuberant personality have won for Pashman a reputation for what passes as flamboyance in judicial circles. In *Robinson*, he pleaded for affirmative action from the court itself. Two years ago, he wrote:

> we publicly declared our intention to obtain implementation of a plan for [state] compliance . . . with the requirements of the education clause of the Constitution. . . . [We must not] abandon that goal. . . . [Some] fear that the grant of any affirmative relief for this school year would create chaos in the budgetary process in local school districts. . . . A certain amount of confusion and a great deal of dissatisfaction would undoubtedly result. . . . [That] should play no part in our decision. . . . It is no ground for judicial inaction that some measures proposed may be unpopular. . . . It is no ground that there may be resistance to the orders of the Court, whether in local government or in the halls of the Legislature. . . . The real question is: Can this Court, consistently with its obligations to uphold and to enforce the Constitution, trade the constitutionally guaranteed rights of hundreds of thousands of children . . . for the possibility of avoiding some difficulties in meeting local budget-making deadlines. I do not see how this question can be answered in any way but in the negative. . . . To fail [to act] . . . at this late date is to become a party to the perpetuation of the very wrongs which the Court denounced two years ago.[10]

Some complained that Pashman was exaggerating judicial power and usurping legislative prerogatives. One lawyer quipped, "Pashman does not know what legislatures are for except to raise judicial salaries, and, since they do not do that fast enough, he would really like to take that function away from them too." Others pointed to constitutional rights unmet. The state's school finance system did not fulfill the guarantees of the plain provisions of the constitution, they argued, and thus it became the court's obligation, with much hesitance and reluctance, to enforce its own will. The best course of action was not to prod the legislature endlessly to do its duty, but for the court itself to implement its own plan to secure the rights of citizens. Pashman was vigorous and forceful, but he was also a minority of one.

Chief Justice Hughes and the court's majority decided to continue the prodding strategy and granted the legislature additional time to prepare its own plan. The majority asserted that it would be "chaotic . . . [for] many school districts to effect financial changes for the . . . [upcoming] school year at this late date and on such short notice." [11] Therefore, the justices decided to allow the plan that had been declared unconstitutional in 1973 to remain in effect for the school year beginning July 1, 1975, and to schedule new hearings on a reformed state school aid plan to take effect during the school year 1976–1977. Still coming together, perhaps lacking in self-confidence, certainly unsure of the full ramifications of aggressive action, the court majority chose to wait another year for a legislatively sanctioned program rather than impose a solution of their own to the *Robinson* issues. The Hughes Court did adopt the characteristic strategy of the Weintraub Court in preferring to rely on the legislature to formulate specific policy proposals, but its order granting the legislature a year's delay flatly violated one of Weintraub's generalized tactics.

Regardless of intent, many officials interpreted the year's delay as a sign of retreat and indecision. The Hughes Court, they concluded, would temporize and retire when faced with difficult issues rather than push forthrightly ahead. Governor Byrne was bitterly disappointed in the court's procrastination, and his top aides began to tell newspaper reporters that the "court no longer has the prestige or the leadership that made it a powerful force in the state's affairs for the past quarter century." [12] Gone was the "aura of intellectual power and forceful leadership." For some, the order was a sign of surrender; for others, a sign of prudence; but, for most, it meant that the court's influence on the situation declined markedly. One legislator lamented this alleged judicial indecision: "This never would have happened under Vanderbilt or Weintraub.

. . . Weintraub would have firmly told us what to do and we would have done it. . . . we have all discovered now that the court does not mean what it says." Perhaps an earlier court would have instructed the legislature more resolutely, or perhaps not, but the order allowing another year's delay indicated to many legislators that the Hughes Court would be compliant and accommodating rather than truculent and assertive.[13] Once the image of a pliable court had been fixed in the legislative mind, the justices would have to work hard to dislodge it. The Hughes Court had begun to wrestle with the intricate political issues of Robinson, but its first efforts lacked subtlety and finesse.

Stung by the criticism of its order granting the legislature a year's delay, the supreme court kept the Robinson case before it. When the court had allowed the use of the old school finance formula for another year, it had also scheduled hearings on the details of a new state aid plan. It now moved ahead quickly to explore the intricacies of alternative school finance programs. When courts litigate public policy questions, they often conclude that the legal materials submitted during the adversary proceedings do not adequately discuss all the topics that are important to them. Policy oriented courts, which are concerned about the wider social implications of their decisions, often develop their own mechanisms for securing information about the nonlegal aspects of the cases before them.[14]

One common device for gathering nondoctrinal information is the Brandeis brief, a regular brief submitted by one of the parties to a case that explicitly discusses the social, economic, or political dimensions of an issue. According to one well-placed source, "The Brandeis brief is very, very highly thought of in New Jersey." A recent suit in New Jersey tested the constitutionality of restrictions imposed on the political activities of the wife of a sitting judge. One lawyer with an authoritative view commented:

> When asked to make any changes in the law, the [New Jersey Supreme] Court wants to know the impact on society. A case recently arose about the political activities of judges' spouses. The attorney included a survey describing the restrictions and practices in other jurisdictions. That was probably the most persuasive element on which the case turned.

Systematic reading of law review articles and scholarly publications can also supplement the information and perspectives presented to a court by the parties in a specific case. The best legal thinking finds expression in legal periodicals, and the relevant authorities are comprehensively catalogued and carefully analyzed. Evidence indicates that law journals are cited with growing frequency in the decisions of the United States Supreme Court, and courts do, of course, consult articles which are not cited in the written opinions.[15] In fact, some justices comment that the quality of briefs in major cases is not particularly important, because the issues in such cases are widely discussed in easily accessible law journals. Others, however, have become increasingly reluctant to rely on law review articles, because they have come to doubt the objectivity and neutrality of some of the authors.[16] Sometimes, also, it is difficult to find written materials on technical or specialized questions that are pivotal in a specific case.

The New Jersey Supreme Court has been quite direct in assembling the information it thinks it needs to decide a case. Occasionally, the administrative office of the court is instructed to gather the information the justices want, and quite commonly executive departments, municipalities, and associations are asked to provide information to assist the court's deliberations. Sometimes the justices will formulate specific questions, sometimes requests will be presented by the court's clerk, and sometimes the court will request all relevant information on a certain issue. New Jersey's justices have often lamented the fact that they do not have a larger staff to evaluate data on technical issues, so that they can better appraise the societal impact of legal options proposed to them.

The *Robinson* case immersed the New Jersey Supreme Court in the details of the state's school finance formula, and the justices, not being trained in education finance, needed help in understanding the formula's complexities. To help it evaluate the impact of alternative school finance proposals, the court requested the state department of education to provide it with extensive financial data about New Jersey's school districts. The department alone had the ability to estimate how much money individual school districts would receive under various finance proposals, and the justices believed that they needed this information to help them make their legal judgments. The court addressed specific questions to the department.

> If minimum support aid . . . were to be enjoined from distribution for the fiscal year beginning July 1, 1976, please estimate the dollar impact upon each of the State's school districts, as well as the total amount so involved.

> Set forth the total amount of all school expenditures . . . on a district-by-district basis. Indicate the amount and percentage contributed to each district's projected expenditures from State and local sources.

> If the total amount of minimum support aid . . . were to be made available for redistribution under . . . the . . . equalization aid formula . . . Indicate the change from the present aid distributions that would occur, district-by-district.[17]

These questions and others were posed by a court entwined in the details of state school aid formulas and concerned about the consequences of any direct action on individual school districts. Addressing questions to the state education department did produce vast financial data for the court to analyze, but the procedure was not without its pitfalls.

The questions posed by the court focused on important dimensions of the school finance issues that had been raised, but occasionally the inquiries were not framed in precisely the right ways. Department technicians were not always sure whether they should supply the information actually requested by the court or the information they thought the court wanted. Often, as well, there was room for judgment and interpretation in structuring the responses, so that particular aid alternatives would look more or less attractive to the justices. Whose policy preferences were to guide such determinations? Those of the Byrne Administration as expressed by the commissioner, or those of the technicians? The conflict that occasionally appeared over this issue within the department was compounded by the fact that the commissioner and the state board of education were also parties to the *Robinson* litigation itself, with their own interests and objectives, yet the department alone had the data the justices wanted to reach their decisions.[18] Furthermore, when the necessary fiscal data were compiled and transmitted to the court, their implications were not always clear-cut. Ambiguity and uncertainty remained, and department technicians feared that the justices might misconstrue the financial material and impose a school finance order that was not administratively feasible.

Regardless of these problems, the justices wanted to act. They knew that their delaying order had been seen as an abandonment of the constitutional principles of the original decision, and they wanted to remedy that.[19] In addition, Governor Byrne had dramatically come across the way from the State House to appear before them in person to argue for aggressive judicial action to resolve the legislative deadlock. No one could recall the last time the head of the executive branch had appeared before the state supreme court. Brendan Byrne had stood at their podium and argued that the situation was theirs alone to redeem. The court understood a public relations gesture when it saw one, but Byrne had been nurtured in bar association circles that viewed the legislature with contempt and the supreme court with esteem, and the court had its reputation to protect. The justices decided that they would no longer accept renewed pleas from the state senate for postponement and inaction.

In May 1975, the New Jersey Supreme Court delivered its fourth decision in *Robinson*. The court ordered that, for the school year 1976–1977, $300 million in state minimum support aid to local school districts be redistributed, so that more money would go to poorer areas and less to affluent districts.[20] Funds were to be taken from well-to-do suburbs and granted to hard-pressed urban and rural communities. To those who claimed that the court was exceeding its authority, the court responded that the legislature's inaction violated the state constitution.[21] To those who argued that appropriating funds was exclusively a legislative prerogative, the court pointed to "emerging modern concepts as to judicial responsibility to enforce constitutional rights," and then claimed that it was not really appropriating funds at all.[22] The funds would still be appropriated by the legislature and would still be used for educational purposes as the legislature desired. The only difference was that the funds would merely be spent in a slightly different manner from the one the legislature anticipated. Besides, the court held, if any conflict remained between the legislature's peculiar authority to appropriate funds and the court's obligation to realize its interpretation of the state constitution, the court's mandate took precedence.[23] Of course, this order would quickly be set aside, the court promised, if the legislature took timely and appropriate action to remedy constitutional deficiencies in the state's existing education finance program.

Few claims of judicial authority have been more aggressive. No precedents were cited by the court or any of the parties to justify the judicial redirection of expenditures of this magnitude. None could be found. So enterprising was the claim of judicial power that two justices refused to have anything to do with it. Denouncing the "diaphanous thread" of logic used to justify the majority's order, the two dissenting justices argued that there would be no way to restrain judicial appropriations if they were once begun. The result, they pleaded, would destroy the integrity of the established institutions of government.[24]

Justice Morris Pashman took a different view. While acknowledging that the majority's order "will carry the Court into hitherto unexplored territories in the realms of constitutional law and equitable remedies," Pashman wanted the court to be even more assertive.[25] He would have moved more aggressively, Pashman wrote, to establish statewide standards of educational quality as a necessary first step to remedy failures in the performance of the state's school system.[26] In addition, he wanted more state aid to be redistributed to assist the urban areas, which were bearing extraordinarily heavy tax burdens for municipal services.[27] Pashman would simply not accept the majority's contention that a larger redistribution would cause "administrative confusion." "One might expect," he lamented, "that this argument, which has been dusted off, polished up, and put on display by the advocates of the *status quo* at every stage of this all too prolonged litigation . . . would have begun to lose its allure."[28] Less aggressive action than he proposed, Pashman warned, would deny New Jersey's school children their constitutionally guaranteed rights and would sink New Jersey's cities even deeper in their social and financial difficulties.

The Hughes Court had finally acted—perhaps as aggressively

and as quickly as its personality had permitted. *Robinson,* however, was its first major challenge, and it had not had a decade of experience to guide its actions. Since the court's reputation still suffered from the temporizing order it had issued a few months before, many legislators had trouble taking this threat to redistribute state aid very seriously. After all, if the court had split five to two on the simple threat to redistribute aid more than a year in the future, it probably would not be able hold itself together to deliver on that threat when the deadline finally arrived. Furthermore, it was unlikely that the legislature would appropriate money for minimum support aid—or anything else—if it knew that the court would order its use for purposes the legislature did not intend. When July 1, 1976, did arrive, the court might discover there was no money in the categories that it planned to redistribute.

The most serious defect in the court's order, however, was that it became counterproductive. As Justice Weintraub had foreseen, the judicial threat to redistribute state school aid was the alternative that some legislators preferred. Their districts would receive a windfall in state assistance, which they had never been able to secure through the legislative process. These fortunate legislators would not even have to pay the price of voting for the taxes to fund the new aid. The court order had given these elected officials the best of two worlds: greater support for public services within their districts and the continued ability to oppose increases in taxes. Contrary to the court's expectation, the threat to take state aid away from certain school districts did not strongly impel their representatives in Trenton to labor vigorously for a legislative compromise. The districts whose aid was imperiled were, typically, wealthy districts that relied almost exclusively on their own resources to fund their public schools, and to them the threatened loss of state aid was of minimal consequence. "The schools in my district spend $2100 per student," one legislator explained. "How much difference will the loss of $132 make? They will hardly miss it." Even if skeptical legislators took the threat of the judicial redistribution of state aid seriously, it would not hurt the rich, minimum-aid districts badly enough to get excited about it. The Hughes Court had threatened to withhold the benefits that resourceful groups derived from ongoing government programs, but the groups were too resourceful and the endangered benefits too meager to alter significantly the behavior of the affected citizens and their legislators.

The Hughes Court had the unappealing task of cleaning up the problems raised by Chief Justice Weintraub and his colleagues in *Robinson.* The first *Robinson* decision had been a subtle and imaginative one that presupposed a very sensitive judicial role. The events of the Weintraub years had provided a series of suggestions to guide subsequent court performances, but the inexperienced Hughes Court had not been able to integrate these cues into a successful plan of action. Judicial involvement in the legislative process requires a set of skills that cannot be learned in other governmental posts, and the Hughes Court was still developing these talents. Its restraint was interpreted as a lack of will, and its order to redistribute aid failed to propel legislators toward their own resolution of the problem. *Robinson* remained an unresolved issue on the legislative agenda, but the Hughes Court had again surrendered the initiative to the legislature for devising a solution to the problem.

The Byrne Administration had tried without success to persuade the legislature to enact education, school finance, and taxation reforms to respond to *Robinson,* and then the Hughes Court had tried its hand at prodding the legislature into fulfilling the guarantees of the constitution with the same lack of results. Soon the Byrne Administration task force would apparently lose interest in the *Robinson* issues and turn elsewhere, and the supreme court, too, would have many other troublesome controversies before it, but concerned legislators such as Senator Wiley, Assemblyman Burstein, and the members of the Joint Education Committee continued to focus on the educational dimensions of the *Robinson* case.

Early in 1974, the members of the Joint Education Committee had hired a capable staff and had worked late into the night to prepare the *Robinson* legislation, but, when their program emerged, it was clear that these activities reflected the trappings of legislative initiative without its substance. The disparate members of the committee had immersed themselves in the administration's recommendations and had persuaded themselves almost unanimously of their validity, but they had not prepared a program of their own. Despite the committee's long hours, its report became the vehicle for introducing the executive branch proposal rather than a mechanism for explaining a genuinely legislative package. Later in 1974, however, the executive branch education program was set aside, when the administration's companion proposal for the adoption of a personal income tax was rejected by the state senate. It was back to the educational drawing boards for Wiley, Burstein, and the Joint Education Committee.

Even though the administration's program had been set aside, it was soon clear that the committee's long efforts over it were not wasted. During its deliberations, members and staff became familiar with the detailed education issues involved in the proposal, the important concerns of the relevant professional associations, and the viewpoints of the interested legislators. On its own, the committee's talented leadership began to discuss the educational governance and school aid provisions of the original program with the legislators and groups involved, and they had soon assembled a catalog of objections people had to the original Byrne Administration proposal. The committee then drafted a new bill, reflecting the policy positions, organizational pressures, and constituency perspectives of a broad spectrum of legislators.

Some legislators had objected to the strong terms used to define the major elements of the state's new thorough and efficient educational system envisioned in the administration legislation. There was, they contended, no way that the state could "assure" that all students in each and every school throughout New Jersey could read or do anything else, and to promise that, in a statute, would soon involve the state in endless lawsuits for punitive damages. Comparisons of similar provisions from the administration bill and the newly drafted committee substitute illustrate the strategic retreat that the committee made in specifying the characteristics of a constitutional educational system. According to the administration bill, one element of that system would be:

> Sufficient instruction to assure the attainment of reasonable levels of proficiency in the basic communications and computational skills. . . .[29]

After the committee's editing, this read:

> Instruction intended to produce the attainment of reasonable
> levels of proficiency in the basic communications and com-
> putational skills. . . .[30]

When the administration discussed staff, it specified:

> Sufficient qualified personnel to enable all pupils to develop
> to the best of their abilities. . . .[31]

This standard was amended by the committee's pen to require:

> Qualified instructional and other personnel. . . .[32]

In response to complaints of legislators, the committee went through
the administration bill qualifying and diluting numerous absolute
statements that appeared in the original draft. The committee's
handiwork produced a new bill, which was more conservative than
the administration's effort, less likely to inspire new litigation, and
more consonant with what could reasonably be expected from the
state's schools. While the administration's standards would realis-
tically be honored only in the breach, the committee draft could
actually be used to upgrade local educational activities.

Another major objection legislators had to the administration's
education program was its cost: a price tag of $550 million in new
state revenue. Soon after the administration tax program was first
rejected by the state senate, the Joint Education Committee began
efforts to devise a proposal which would be less costly.[33] While the
original administration proposal had envisioned the state's paying
one-half of New Jersey's bill for elementary and secondary education, the committee scaled this down, requiring the state to pay only
40 percent of the costs of education in the state. Even this modest
increase in state support would be phased in over two years. The
new committee plan was still a guaranteed-valuation plan, like its
administration predecessor, but this element was scaled down, too.
Instead of guaranteeing to each community in the state the revenues from a tax base worth twice that of the statewide average,
the committee's version offered to local districts the revenues from

a tax base which was 1.43 times the statewide average. While these amendments reduced the costs of the entire education program from $550 million to approximately $325 million, they also reduced the number of school districts in the state that would receive assistance. Of the state's school districts, 95 percent would have been aided by the administration's equalization formula, but less than 80 percent were to be assisted by the scaled-down committee version. Legislators representing the districts that received no aid under the equalization formula appeared unwilling to support the committee's proposal without further amendments.

The committee set to work to formulate a new program that would provide aid to more school districts without reducing the allotments expected by the districts already covered. More votes were thought to be needed from legislators representing suburban Bergen County, where the excluded districts were concentrated. In addition, the commissioner of education argued that it was educationally desirable for the department to maintain some financial contact, under the equalization formula, with all the school districts in the state regardless of their wealth. For these reasons, the committee soon devised a "mandated cost" program, which granted to each school district in the state a minimum amount of state assistance. The rationale was that, since the state by statute required local school districts to keep records and maintain other services, the state should also contribute to financing the mandated costs. Herb Starkey and other members of the administration task force became increasingly unhappy as their school finance program continued to lose both its power and its equalizing potential, but its amended details continued to attract wavering legislators.

The third set of legislative objections to the administration's education program centered on the features of the "thorough and efficient" process of goals, curriculum, and evaluation. Many legislators feared that the department of education would administer the statute in precisely the wrong way, being rigid where it should be flexible and being permissive where it should insist on clear standards. When the committee first examined the department's proposed regulations for implementing the new education legislation, it appeared that these fears were well grounded.[34] The committee saw detailed standards for the size of school buildings, the number of assistant principals, and the procedures of local record keeping, but it could discover little in the department's implementation program that would promise improved student performance. The department's progress in preparing regulations to implement the new education program had been presented to the supreme court as evidence of the executive's responsiveness, but close examination made many legislators uneasy.[35] For wearisome months and countless conferences, the committee worked with the department to build legislative support by ever so gradually shifting the regulatory focus from inputs and procedures to student performance. While not fully successful, as would later become apparent, the committee did relieve the worst fears of many lawmakers who believed that the new program would concentrate energy and resources on administrative routines rather than on educational deficiencies. To reassure those legislators further, separate legislation was introduced and passed creating a permanent legislative committee to oversee the implementation of the new education program and to evaluate its impact.[36]

The Joint Education Committee was responsible for the education and school finance components of the state's response to *Robinson,* but not for the revenue elements. Even though the legislature remained deadlocked over various revenue proposals—and perhaps to contribute to the pressures to resolve that deadlock—the committee moved for consideration of its new education bill. Prospects looked brightest in the senate, so it was presented there first. The last-minute changes made to attract undecided senators brought unexpected votes into the affirmative column, and the commitee's program passed with a few votes to spare. Administration supporters and representatives of traditional party organizations lined up solidly for the bill, and they were joined by a few suburban lawmakers attracted by the minimum aid provisions and the Republican senator on the Joint Education Committee, whose rural constituency stood to receive more state assistance under the new legislation than any other legislative constituency in the state.[37]

The extra time for study and examination complicated consideration of the issue once it moved to the assembly. One key senate supporter of the bill commented, "The bill would never pass in the senate now that people understand it better." For weeks, legislative and departmental aides lugged around computer printouts describing the financial impact of the proposed legislation on each school district and each legislative constituency in the state, and circulated drafts of administrative regulations explaining how the department and county superintendents of education planned to implement the new program. Every lawmaker who sought to learn how the proposal would affect his own constituency had ample materials to work with. There was initial acceptance of the proposal, since the authorization of more than $375 million in new state aid meant that every legislative constituency in the state would receive additional assistance. The early enthusiasm waned, however, as some members of the assembly recognized that their constituents would pay more in new taxes than they would get back in new state aid, and as others discovered that districts that they regarded as less needy than their own would receive a greater increment in state assistance. Furthermore, the latent skepticism about the performance of school systems in urban areas began to be expressed, as some lawmakers asserted that the new education program would simply raise teachers' salaries and still leave too many youngsters unable to read. During a long and tiresome day, assembly leaders, and then the governor, called in individual legislators to try to persuade them to contribute their votes to the 41 needed for enactment of the senate-passed program. Late in the day, when Senate Bill 1516 was finally put up on the assembly board for a vote, and the assembly speaker looked down at the electronic display embedded in the rostrum to see how the members were dividing, it was clear that the coalition that had passed the measure in the senate was holding together in the assembly as well. Liberals, administration supporters, organizational Democrats, and a few other strays combined to provide the votes needed for passage, while most Republicans joined with Democrats from unstable constituencies to cast dissenting votes.[38]

On September 29, 1975, New Jersey finally had a reformed education and school finance plan to respond to the state supreme court's *Robinson* v. *Cahill* decision, which had been delivered on April 3, 1973. Some shook their heads in despair at the two and one-half years that had elapsed since the justices had first spoken and lamented the destructive controversy that had centered on the state's schools during this period. Others responded that to prepare and build support for a significant revision of the state's major public service, which would reorient the activities of more than one and one-half million students and teachers in so short a time was no small accomplishment. Certainly, a new program had been devised, passed by both chambers, and signed into law by the governor, but the controversy remained unresolved in its most critical aspect. There was still no revenue plan to fund New Jersey's new school finance program, and agreement on one appeared every bit as remote as it had been when the court had first rendered its decision more than two and one-half years earlier.

From 1973 to 1976, reluctant Trenton legislators had seized every conceivable justification to postpone action on the state's revenue problems. Whenever there was an excuse to put off action for another week or another month, the legislature took it. After the assembly passed the new education bill, in September 1975, the involvement of the court in the *Robinson* controversy gave legislators yet another reason to postpone consideration of a new tax plan. A legislative aide met with the press to explain that "most senators are not willing to act on any taxes 'until they see what the Supreme Court is going to do.' " [39] Since the new education plan was passed in response to the court's declaration that the previous plan was unconstitutional, many legislators wanted a guarantee that the new plan would satisfy the court before they endured the anguish of voting for substantial new taxes.

The complaint of the legislative aide was certainly a rationalization for procrastination, but it also expressed a general consequence of judicial action. "One of the difficulties with the resort to litigation to solve such problems" as *Robinson,* one scholar has written, "is that we thereby tend to absolve others from responsibility." [40] Judicial participation in the *Robinson* issues meant that the justices had assumed some of the responsibility that traditionally belonged to the legislature and the governor for devising a program to help the state meet emerging social needs. Responsibility, once assumed, is not easily shed or delimited, especially when that responsibility is for making unpopular decisions. The problem of the diffusion of responsibility is compounded when courts choose to initiate issues rather than enforce policies. Widely shared responsibility for unpopular decisions necessitates careful coordination among all the participants if a conclusion is to be reached, and it allows each participant the capacity to frustrate the entire process by inaction. Once the justices had assumed some responsibility for *Robinson*, their responsibility had to be persistently exercised, or the process they had set in motion would come to a halt.

The state senate stood idle while its lawyer asked the supreme court to declare the thorough and efficient program constitutional and to lift its threat to redistribute state school aid. Governor Byrne also went to court to petition the justices to approve the new education program, but, in addition, he urged the court to allow its redistribution order to remain in effect until the new school finance plan had been funded. The urban reformers objected strenuously to the program the legislature had just enacted. They complained that the state had not defined its constitutional obligation in any discernible way in the new legislation; they pointed out that the new financial provisions were unrelated to the educational need of students; and they protested that the hard-pressed urban areas, which had brought the suit in the first place, were not notably better off under this plan than under the one that had been declared unconstitutional in 1973.[41]

The hearing on the constitutionality of the new legislation was held in the fourth-floor courtroom of the supreme court building. On November 24, 1975, the assembled litigants and the crowded spectators heard the justices question the various attorneys, acknowledge the need for a quick decision, and mention that a ruling could be expected by the middle of December. As the middle of December came and went, and then the end of December gave way to the new year, rumors circulated in Trenton that the court was badly split over the decision. On January 30, 1976, the justices' decision was finally distributed, but the usual checklist inscribed with the name of each justice, which provides room to indicate whether each had voted "For the Order," "Dissent," or "Concur in Result," was not attached. Instead a complex score card was clipped to the bulky decision, allowing the justices five voting options. An explanatory "Vote Sheet" recorded the numerous judicial variations:

> Chief Justice Hughes joins in the opinion of the court and files a concurring opinion. Justice Mountain joins in the opinion of the court except as to Part IV. Justice Sullivan joins in the opinion of the Court. Justice Pashman dissents. Justice Clifford joins in the opinion of the Court. Justice Schreiber joins in the opinion of the Court and files a concurring opinion. Judge Conford joins in the opinion of the Court only as to Part IV; he files a partially concurring and partially dissenting opinion.

The court's per curiam decision began by asserting that only the facial constitutionality of the new legislation was being judged, because no trial court record had examined the specific provisions of the new law. The court then emphasized the powers that the legislature had delegated to the commissioner of education to ensure that local school districts provided a constitutionally adequate education and concluded that the commissioner was empowered to take all steps necessary to correct any educational or financial deficiencies in local school operations. The court turned to the state aid formula embedded in the new legislation and commented, "The fiscal provisions of the Act are to be judged as adequate or inadequate depending upon whether they do or do not afford sufficient financial support for the system of public education. . . ." [42] With a noticeable lack of enthusiasm, the court held,

> We cannot say that under these circumstances the dollar input per pupil, keeping in mind that there may be and probably are legitimate differences between and among districts and students, will not be sufficient to offer each pupil an equal educational opportunity as required by the Constitution.[43]

For these reasons, the court found that the new act was constitutional in all respects—assuming that it was fully and promptly funded. Chief Justice Hughes wrote eloquently of his "personal doubts" about the constitutionality of the Public School Act of 1975, and then agreed to concur in the court's decision out of respect for the separation of powers, judicial restraint, and the absence of a clear record of the impact of the new legislation.

Justice Pashman was less trusting. He detailed his personal, legal, and educational doubts about the "constitutional buoyancy" of the new law, and concluded that he would not accept it as an adequate response to *Robinson* until a trial court had assembled a fuller record.[45] Together with Judge Canford, Pashman then carefully described his objections to the state aid provisions of the Public School Act and its failure to remedy the problems of municipal overburden.[46] The January 30, 1976, decision was a sprawling one, with justices going their own way on almost every issue. To one point alone, however, each of the seven did subscribe: "the 1975 Act, absent funding, could never be considered a constitutional compliance with . . . the New Jersey Constitution. . . ."[47] Yet the Act remained unfunded, and the legislature appeared no closer to solving the revenue riddle than it had been months or years before. Despair settled in on the legislators who had championed the earlier efforts; and some believed that only the court could impose a solution to the state's revenue needs.

In New Jersey, revenue bills originate in the state assembly. In January 1976, a new assembly, elected the previous November, moved into the chambers in the east wing of the State House, with no record of its own on previous taxation programs. A new Democratic speaker was elected for the assembly, Joseph LaFante of Bayonne, and a new majority leader, Assemblyman William Hamilton of Middlesex County. The new leadership team recognized the failure of the administration and the court to resolve the *Robinson* issues, but it believed that it had its own obligation to try to devise a tax package that could pass the legislature's treacherous course. The speaker and the majority leader began meeting with small groups of two or four legislators in their districts to discover the combination of proposals which would be acceptable to "the folks at home." Breakfasting in Howard Johnson's or spending Saturday mornings at Hamilton's law office, the leadership soon recognized that property tax relief was every bit as important to the legislators as funding the state's schools, and increased financial support for the operations of the state government was far down on almost everyone's list of attractive elements for a new revenue program.

Departing from traditional practice, the leadership turned to the assembly taxation committee, rather than the executive branch, to put together its legislative package, and it was certainly a complicated program.[48] The package included homestead rebates to reduce residential property taxes and tax credits and rebates for citizens who rented. Other elements created a state program to share tax revenues with localities on a per capita basis and authorized the state to pay the full costs of the extraordinary tax breaks given senior citizens and veterans. To guarantee that new revenues would not simply go to increasing the costs of existing government services, percentage limitations were placed on the permissible increases in expenditures by municipalities, counties, and the state itself. A number of specialized taxes were repealed under the program, and tax deductions were authorized for college or private school tuition. All new revenues would go either to reduce local property taxes or pay the $375-million tab now attached to the Public School Act of 1975, and no funds would be used to help support the activities of the state government itself.

The assembly leadership and the assembly taxation committee first worked on the details of the property tax relief schemes, because they wanted the press to concentrate its early coverage on the attractive aspects of the program, not on the unpopular taxation dimensions. Eventually, however, the price would have to be paid and taxation proposals formulated. The assembly leadership needed approximately $700 million in new revenue to increase school funding, reduce local property taxes, and repeal the specialized levies for the first year, and $800 million for the same purposes in the second year. An increase in the state retail sales tax from 5 percent to 7 percent would come close to providing the funds needed for the first year, but it would fall approximately $100 million short in subsequent years. The most reasonable alternative was to recommend the adoption of a personal income tax, and the leadership's version had a graduated rate from 2 percent to 4 percent of gross income. While rounding up support for the program, it was agreed that the tax would be only a temporary measure, which would "self-destruct" on June 30, 1978, unless reenacted by a subsequent legislature. In addition, another element of the tax package that was accepted to win needed support authorized the calling of a tax convention in the spring of 1978 to reconsider the full range of taxation alternatives available to the state. Finally, for the many legislators who doubted that the thorough and efficient educational program of goals, curriculum, and assessment would improve the quality of instruction in the state's schools, an amendment to the Public School Act of 1975 was accepted that directed the department of education to establish statewide minimum standards for the performance of basic skills.

The fifteen-part legislative package prepared by the assembly leadership was a complicated one, with some details still requiring refinement, but it did possess some coherence. It stressed to "the folks at home" that every possible safeguard would be provided so that the adoption of a personal income tax would not be used to increase the size of the public sector. Instead, the funds were to be used only to reduce local property taxes, repeal specialized taxes, and support public schools. No funds were to pay for new state government activities. A 2 to 4 percent income tax embedded in such a program should have been able to win support from a variety of legislators, and it did. Both the Republican and Democratic leaders in the assembly joined in a bipartisan effort to enact the numerous pieces of legislation in a late-night session, which began on Monday afternoon, March 15, 1976, and extended many hours into Tuesday morning.

There was relief in the assembly—almost a sense of euphoria—that they had finally formulated and passed a complicated program which they believed responded capably both to the mandate of the supreme court and to the wishes of the general public. The package was not one devised by the governor or imposed by the court. It was a genuinely legislative package, developed to fit the expressed sentiments of the people's representatives in the assembly. With a sense of pride, the assembly leadership knew that the tax package was one of the first instances in which the legislature itself had initiated a comprehensive program in a major policy area, and, even if people disagreed with the content of the proposals, at least they would have to respect the accomplishment. Whatever its fate, the assembly tax program of March 1976 would be a landmark in the institutional development of the New Jersey legislature.

The fate of the program, however, now passed into the hands of the senate, which had rejected the Byrne income tax legislation two years before and which had subsequently shown few signs of changing its position. Unhappy that the program did not provide additional funds for state operations, the administration still agreed to back it vigorously. Administration supporters in the senate tried to coordinate the efforts of the executive branch with those of resourceful interest groups to persuade wavering legislators to endorse the assembly program.

Most of the money from the new tax would go into schools and thus inevitably into teachers' salaries, so the New Jersey Education Association threw its full energies into the fray. In the office of the NJEA's top political strategist stood a large chart listing the state's 40 senators with their likely positions on the new tax program. Some were sure votes and others were as surely lost, so attention was concentrated on those whose positions were not firmly defined. Some senators wanted an indication of public support for the tax package. The association's local chapters and its automated mailing lists were organized by legislative district, and requests were directed to these areas to deluge certain senators with supportive letters. If certain other senators should have received numerous letters from schoolteachers endorsing the tax program, they would have been likely to stand up in party caucus and display the appeals as evidence of the selfish motives of people behind the tax package. Word went out not to approach these lawmakers. Despite these efforts and others, senators were not easily swayed. Their positions had become well established during the preceding two years, and it would be politically embarrassing for them to reverse themselves at such a late date. Each senator had carefully examined the issues many times and long ago decided what was the best course. Early reading of senate attitudes indicated that that body would again refuse to pass a tax bill and that the legislative deadlock would continue for yet another school year.

Finally, the patience of the New Jersey Supreme Court ran out, as the all-too-prolonged litigation threatened to drag on even further. The justices accelerated their timetable for action and called the parties to still another hearing to discuss how the court should proceed. Governor Byrne's counsel set the tone of the hearing by predicting that "arguments will today get back to practicality rather than legality, politics rather than law." [49] Most of the attorneys addressing the court dispensed with precedent and spent their allotted time discussing which course of judicial action would most likely prompt a responsible reply from the legislature. Should the court redistribute school aid to assist poorer communities, take money from noneducation areas of the state budget to fund the Public School Act fully, impose a statewide property tax on its own authority to raise the additional moneys needed for the schools, or enjoin the distribution of all state school aid until the legislature had acted? Each lawyer who stood at the podium before the impressive panel of justices began with the traditional phrase, "May it please the court," but the situation clearly did not please the court. Chief Justice Hughes repeatedly explained, with visible discomfort, how reluctant the court was to be considering the questions now debated before it. Almost plaintively, he appealed for some way the court could satisfy its constitutional obligations without impinging on the prerogatives of the legislature. Hughes the chief justice, like Hughes the governor, had carefully counted his votes, however, and he knew that he now had the support he needed to act.

The New Jersey Supreme Court's seventh decision in *Robinson*, delivered on May 13, 1976, was testimony to how complex the litigation had become. The list of lawyers participating in the case had grown so long that it was now almost as lengthy as the court's decision. A lawyer in the attorney general's office read an early copy of the justices' new ruling to a colleague who had called from the attorney general's office in Kansas, and then heard only laughter over the line. The Kansas attorney assumed that what he had been read was a fabrication left over from April Fool's Day. But the justices' order was no joke. It was simple, and its thrust clear: "On and after July 1, 1976, every public officer, state, county or municipal, is hereby enjoined from expending any funds for the support of any free public school." [50] The legislature had not established a constitutional plan to finance the state's schools after July 1, and the court decided that it would not tolerate the use of an unconstitutional fiscal scheme for yet another year. After July 1,

1976, New Jersey's elementary and secondary schools would close unless the legislature acted.

The impact of the court's order was not so momentous in July as it would have been in September, but it was still significant.[51] One hundred thousand students normally enroll in academic programs throughout the summer in New Jersey, and handicapped youngsters participate in educational activities the year-round. In addition, administrative personnel use July and August to prepare the schools and develop the curricula for the 1.4 million children who attend the state's educational institutions during the regular academic year. To all of these groups and others, New Jersey's schools would be closed on July 1, if the legislature did not act, and no one could foresee how long they would remain closed.

Wednesday, June 30, 1976, was a sultry day in Trenton and also a dramatic one. Dozens of state officials were crowded into another courtroom trying to grapple with the events that Harold Ruvoldt's argument had set in motion. This time, however, the scene was a federal courtroom rather than a state one. New Jersey's silver-haired attorney general, William Hyland, was there, along with the governor's counsel, Lewis Kaden. Mark Hurwitz, executive director of the New Jersey School Boards Association, watched from the right of the room, and Ruth Mancuso, president of the New Jersey State Board of Education, sat on the left near a staff member of the New Jersey Education Association. A dozen state legislators and legislative aides were scattered throughout the courtroom competing with law clerks for chairs. New York media personalities jostled with income tax opponents for a good view of the proceedings, while a good many federal marshals stood about the room to keep order. Ruvoldt sat quietly at the front of the room to the right.

Today, the officials had not assembled to argue the merits of the *Robinson* decision itself. This day, the attorneys were gathered in the federal courtroom to contest only the remedy that the New Jersey Supreme Court had imposed. Local school districts pleaded that the New Jersey court order closing the state's schools would violate the provisions of the federal Constitution. They asked the federal judges to protect their federal rights against the actions of state judges. At 10:45 A.M., the court aide turned on the bronze lamps at each end of the judicial bench and straightened the judicial chairs. At 11:08, another judicial aide distributed legal materials at the judges' places and then announced in a high pitched voice: "Oyez, Oyez, Oyez. All persons having business before the honorable, the United States district court for the district of New Jersey, give now your attention and you shall be heard. God save these United States and this honorable Court."

Eleven federal district judges then filed into the courtroom and took their places in two rows behind the elevated bench, five in the front row and six in the back. The chief judge explained that the federal district court was sitting en banc, bringing together all the district's judges, because of the importance of the issues being brought to it.[52] Three separate civil actions, filed on behalf of local school boards, had petitioned the federal court to overturn the New Jersey State Supreme Court order scheduled to close New Jersey's schools at midnight. If the state court order stood, the petitioners claimed, federally guaranteed rights would be blatantly violated.[53] A decade of student-conduct cases, it was alleged, had concluded that individual students could not be expelled from school and denied an education without due process of law, and here all the students throughout the state were being denied an education without the opportunity to express any position whatsoever. Furthermore, the effect of the state court order would be to create two classifications of students in New Jersey, those who could afford to attend a private summer school and those who could not, and then to deny an education to those who were less resourceful. Finally, the petitioners argued, there was a federal right to a minimal education, and closing the state's schools patently violated that right. The petitioners did not protest the *Robinson* decision itself, only the remedy selected by the state supreme court to implement the ruling.

Procedural questions were occasionally addressed to the chief judge, who then gathered his ten benchmates into a very unjudgelike huddle to determine the response. In its turn, the Byrne Administration argued that the federal court should stay out of *Robinson*.[54] It believed that the state school closing order had focused such pressure on the legislature that the likelihood of concrete action was substantial. The governor's counsel claimed that the possibility of federal action was creating a new set of uncertainties over the distribution of state school aid and giving the legislature yet another excuse for evading the choices necessitated by *Robinson*. Only if the court quickly and conclusively refused to intervene in the case, the administration contended, was the legislature likely to act.

Sitting in the back row of judges were two former United States attorneys who had collaborated in the past as federal prosecutors. Now, they combined to pose the sharpest and most challenging questions to the Byrne Administration lawyers. If the legislature is in violation of the constitution, why are you supporting an order directed against an innocent party, the state's children? Does anyone represent the state's children? Yes, the Byrne Administration conceded, the children were in an extremely unfortunate position. Is there any legally rational nexus between the court order and the result it is intended to achieve? Is it not incredible, beyond belief, that the administration could sanction the closing of the state's schools? The tense severity of the judicial questioning was accentuated by recent journalistic speculation that one of the federal judges planned to resign from the bench and oppose Brendan Byrne in the upcoming gubernatorial election.[55] The two former prosecutors asked barbed questions forcefully, but it soon became clear that no one was marching behind them.

Late that Wednesday afternoon, the panel of federal judges decided, by a vote of nine to two, not to grant the petition overturning the state supreme court order. Meeting throughout the day, the legislative leadership failed to devise a tax package that could win the support of a majority of both the assembly and the senate. At the department of education, an emergency unit had been established to explain to local officials which activities would be prohibited by the state court order and which permitted. Meanwhile the state supreme court justices conferred by phone, but since the legislature had not acted, they allowed their order closing all New Jersey public schools to go into effect at midnight.

The dramatic twelfth-hour appeal to the federal judges was clearly designed to skirt the authority of the New Jersey Supreme

Court. On three other occasions as well, different parties tried to take *Robinson* to the United States Supreme Court in equally unsuccessful attempts to escape the reach of New Jersey's justices.[56] Despite these legal maneuvers, *Robinson*'s three-year domination of New Jersey politics was never challenged by a direct political assault. For almost forty months, for more than one thousand days, the justices provoked New Jersey legislators with *Robinson,* yet no one had mapped a serious campaign of retaliation. A few curmudgeons in the senate made intemperate remarks, a resolution was introduced to impeach all of the court's justices, and there was desultory talk of deleting "thorough and efficient" from the state constitution, yet no one mounted an assiduous effort to take on the court or reverse its decision.[57] In the national arena, legislative attempts to curb Supreme Court decisions have become almost commonplace. One recent five-year period saw Congress consider 44 proposals to reverse high court rulings and adopt 40 of them.[58] Yet no such effort materialized in New Jersey.

Judicial involvement in policy disputes has often made courts—and especially their specific decisions—the objects of legislative attack. In most instances, however, a single decision, no matter how repugnant to lawmakers, is not enough to trigger legislative reaction. To crystallize antagonism, courts usually have to set a particularly unpopular course in one ruling and then persist in it in subsequent decisions despite the signals of opposition.[59] *Robinson* was only a single case, albeit a protracted one, and the justices had used it to support causes which few legislators wanted to oppose publicly, fair treatment for school children and property tax reform. If *Robinson*'s standard had stood explicitly to benefit people accused of crimes or even adults entrapped in poverty, a legislative counterattack would have been more likely.

Traditional prestige probably shielded the New Jersey Supreme Court from legislative attack as well, but not in a direct or immediate way.[60] New Jersey legislators generally believe that the courts are unpopular with their constituents, and they themselves normally feel few inhibitions in dealing with the judiciary. Yet, legislators are political persons who do not ordinarily undertake projects which have little chance of success. When legislators surveyed potential allies for a campaign against the court, they discerned few reputable colleagues. Unlike strategists for national organizations, who in recent decades have become accustomed to attempts to manipulate the judiciary, responsible leaders of state groups and associations still retain the customary respect for judicial institutions. They remain unwilling to lend their organizations to a campaign apparently designed to undermine the court system, despite personal misgivings about *Robinson*'s wisdom and consequences. Since interest groups normally play an important role in attacks on courts, the reverent or inexperienced attitudes of group leaders in New Jersey probably forestalled frontal opposition to the supreme court before it took shape.[61]

Probably the most important reason that *Robinson* did not stimulate a legislative assault on the judiciary was that the lawmakers would have had to take on not only the justices, but also the governor. The executive and the judiciary had joined in a common effort to compel the legislature to fund *Robinson,* and defiance of the court would also have meant heightened conflict with the executive branch. Furthermore, a legislature is not a homogeneous group, with all members listening to the cadence of the same drummer. From the start, some lawmakers had championed the principles of *Robinson* and recommended its full funding. Therefore, only a narrow and undependable legislative majority would have been available to fight the court.[62] Finally, state legislatures are still not so resourceful or assertive as the national Congress. The same deficiencies of staff and the same inattentiveness of part-time leadership that combine to make state legislatures unreliable policy-making institutions also preclude them from mounting a coherent assault on the judiciary. The legal strategists for the New Jersey legislature, for example, were also practicing attorneys, who were personally reluctant to mention, let alone recommend, direct opposition to the court.[63] If state legislatures continue to develop in the years ahead, and if state organizational elites experience more encounters with judicial participation in the conduct of public policy, notable instances of legislative reversals of state supreme court decisions may become more frequent. In 1976, the New Jersey legislature was not yet up to such outright defiance.

The supreme court order closing New Jersey's schools produced the first signs of movement among the members of the state senate. A court order, alone, was simply a piece of paper, irrelevant and unperceived by almost all of their constituents, but a closed school disrupted the daily lives of average citizens. Employed parents, who depended on the schools to tend their children while they were at work, had to make other arrangements. Thousands of education employees at the state and local level were laid off, and, most disturbingly, handicapped children would go without the continuous instruction they needed. For a few days, people could adjust to the demands of the situation, but, if the days turned into weeks and the novelty wore off, legislators knew that the public would demand that something be done. Those demands would not be primarily directed at justices, protected by black robes and lengthy terms of office, but at elected members of the senate and assembly. The Hughes Court had successfully employed Weintraub's third rule for activating a reluctant legislature.

The threatened closing of schools was sufficient impetus to shift only a few votes in the senate from opposition to support of a state income tax, but a few votes were enough. For the first time in the state's history, the New Jersey Senate passed a bill imposing a personal income tax on the state's citizens. The senate tax plan, however, was not the income tax program that had passed the assembly the previous March. The senate's income tax was set at a flat rate of 1.5 percent, regardless of taxpayer income, and it was designed to yield only about one-half the revenue that the assembly program would produce. The senators were willing to institute an income tax to open the state's schools, but they did not want to fund property tax reductions, revenue sharing, or anything else. When presented with the senate plan, members of the assembly, many of them elected on platforms of reducing local property taxes, rejected it by a resounding vote of 77 to 2.

On Wednesday afternoon, June 30, shortly after the federal judges had decided to let New Jersey's schools close, the assembly came into session for a final attempt to devise an acceptable tax plan. The assembly met all of Wednesday night and all of Thursday night, and finally adjourned at 1 P.M. on Friday after nearly three days of agony. In two straight all-night sessions, the assembly voted down four different tax plans, representing various sales tax and income tax recommendations. The proposal that came closest to success was put for debate at 4:35 A.M. on Friday, July 2. Even at that hour, 14 legislators discussed the merits of a measure, which was a scaled-down version of the March program, to be financed by an income tax at a rate of 2 percent on the first $20,000 of income, and at 2.5 percent on income beyond that. The voting machine was opened at 6:20 A.M., as the morning light began to stream in the assembly windows. Soon the tally board indicated that the measure had won 37 of the needed 41 votes, and the leadership went to work trying to round up 4 additional voters. Different members had specific and sometimes inconsistent requests: one wanted more money for the homestead exemptions, another wanted sponsorship of a companion bill, and still another demanded that the bills be considered in a different order. Slowly, painfully, the leadership won 2 more votes to push the total to 39, but it became clear that they could go no further. At 7:16 A.M., 56 minutes after it had been opened, the electronic voting machine was closed, with the count registering 40 votes in opposition to the proposal, and 37 votes in favor. With tempers frayed and bodies weary, the legislators went off for breakfast and more meetings. After a few more futile hours of effort, exhaustion and fears for the health of certain members put an end to any more attempts to resolve the stalemate.

As the rest of the country celebrated the nation's Bicentennial, saw the armada of tall sailing ships in New York Harbor, attended festivities in their own communities, or watched network television's panorama of events, New Jersey legislators mulled over the condition of the state's schools. On Tuesday, July 6, the members of the assembly returned to Trenton, and the speaker spent the morning discussing the tax program, which had been voted down on Friday, with recalcitrant legislators. Some legislators found merits in the plan that they had previously overlooked, but others discovered defects that had not been apparent to them earlier. The leadership was within one vote of the necessary majority, but, when the session was adjourned shortly before midnight, the elusive votes still had not been assembled.

The next day, Wednesday, July 7, New Jersey's schools remained closed, and the state assembly returned again to the State House to search for the perfect combination of bills that could win 41 votes. Again, the leadership put up the restricted version of the

March package. The homestead property tax reduction was there, the revenue-sharing program, tax credits for renters, senior citizens, and parents of private school and college students, limitations on expenditure increases, a tax convention, and a 2 to 2.5 percent income tax, which would expire in two years unless renewed. It was the third time that essentially the same program had been presented to the assembly. At 8:05 P.M., all eyes in the assembly chamber were on the tally board, where, after agonizing minutes, the forty-first vote for the tax program was finally recorded. Continuous contact had been maintained with the senate leadership, which promised that the senate would accept the new tax package, and it did so on July 9, 1976.

NOTES

1. The court received approximately two hundred letters on *Robinson* that are publicly available. The letters presented here have been edited for grammar, but not for content.

2. Dominick A. Mazzagetti, "Chief Justice Joseph Weintraub: The New Jersey Supreme Court 1957–1973," *Cornell Law Review* 59 (January 1974): 215.

3. The associate justices who served with Weintraub during the 1960s were: Vincent S. Haneman, 28 November 1960 to 1 March 1971; John J. Francis, 20 August 1957 to 2 September 1972; C. Thomas Schettino, 20 March 1959 to 9 September 1972; Haydn Proctor, 28 October 1957 to 16 June 1973; Nathan L. Jacobs, 17 March 1952 to 28 February 1975; and Frederick W. Hall, 24 February 1959 to 31 March 1975.

4. Richard J. Hughes was nominated by Governor Cahill, confirmed by the state senate on 19 November 1973, and sworn in as chief justice on 18 December 1973.

5. (Bergen) *Record*, 16 June 1975.

6. Brendan T. Byrne, Motion for an Order in Aid of Judgment, 2 January 1975.

7. Harold J. Ruvoldt, Jr., Motion for Relief, Alternate Motion for Relief, and Second Alternate Motion for Relief, 3 December 1974.

8. David Goldberg, Brief of the President of the New Jersey Senate and the New Jersey Senate.

9. (Trenton) *Sunday Times-Advertiser*, 18 May 1975.

10. 67 N.J. at 40–44.

11. 67 N.J. at 37.

12. (Trenton) *Sunday Times-Advertiser*, 18 May 1975.

13. For an account of a compliant Weintraub Court, see Thomas Julius Anton, "The Politics of State Taxation: A Case Study of Decision-Making in New Jersey Legislature" (Ph.D. dissertation, Princeton University, 1961).

14. Adolf A. Berle, *The Three Faces of Power: The Supreme Court's New Revolution* (New York: Harcourt, Brace & World, 1967); and Philip B. Kurland, *Politics, the Constitution, and the Warren Court* (Chicago: University of Chicago Press, 1973), chap. 5; Richard S. Wells and Joel B. Grossman, "The Concept of Judicial Policy-Making: A Critique," *Journal of Public Law* 15 (1966): 305–6.

15. Chester A. Newland, "Legal Periodicals and the United States Supreme Court," *Midwest Journal of Political Science* 3 (February 1959): 58–74.

16. Wright Patman, "Lobbying Through Law Reviews," in Walter F. Murphy and C. Herman Pritchett, eds., *Courts, Judges, and Politics* (New York: Random House, 1961), pp. 309–10.

17. Letter from Florence R. Peskoe, Clerk of the Supreme Court of New Jersey, to Dr. Fred G. Burke, Commissioner of Education, 2 May 1975; see also communication of 21 October 1975.

18. The New Jersey Education Association and the Educational Testing Service had partial data on New Jersey school districts, but the data were not complete.

19. 67 N.J. at 356.

20. 67 N.J. at 350.

21. 67 N.J. at 347.

22. 67 N.J. at 352.

23. 67 N.J. at 354.

24. 67 N.J. at 375, 384.

25. 67 N.J. at 357.

26. 67 N.J. at 360–63.

27. 67 N.J. at 371–74.

28. 67 N.J. at 367.

29. New Jersey Legislature, 1974–1975 session, S1256, Section 9.

30. S1516, Section 9.

31. S1256, Section 19.

32. S1516, Section 19.

33. See minutes of 24 September 1974 meeting.

34. Meeting of the Joint Committee on the Public Schools, 21 February 1975.

35. See letter of Senator Raymond H. Bateman to Senator Stephen B. Wiley, 5 November 1975.

36. New Jersey Statutes of 1975, chap. 16.

37. See analysis prepared by the Joint Committee on the Public Schools, 13 April 1975.

38. S1516 was passed in the assembly on 22 September 1975 by a margin of 42 to 32.

39. (Trenton) *Evening Times,* 25 November 1975, p. 1.

40. Philip B. Kurland, "Equal Educational Opportunity: The Limits of Constitutional Jurisprudence Undefined," *University of Chicago Law Review* 35 (Summer 1968): 600.

41. "Brief of the New Jersey Education Reform Project of the Greater Newark Urban Coalition, Amicus Curiae, Regarding the Public School Education Act of 1975," 4 November 1975.

42. *"Robinson V,"* per curiam, 30 January 1976, slip opinion, p. 21.

43. Ibid., pp. 22–23.

44. Hughes, C. J., concurring, 30 January 1976, slip opinion, p. 4.

45. Pashman, J., dissenting, 30 January 1976, slip opinion.

46. Conford, P. J. A. D., temporarily assigned, concurring and dissenting, 30 January 1976, slip opinion.

47. Per curiam, 30 January 1976, p. 5.

48. The 1976 bills in the final package were A1330 AcsAca, A1513, A1663 Acs, A1736 Aca, A1738 AcaAca, A1739 Aca, A1745, A1761, A1762 Aa, A1763 Aa, A1764, A1765, A1766, A1777, and A1809.

49. *"Robinson VI,"* Order of the court to show cause of 19 February 1976.

50. *"Robinson VII,"* per curiam, 13 May 1976, slip opinion, p. 6.

51. Citizens Task Force on the July 1 School Crisis, "Report to Governor Brendan Byrne" (Trenton: mimeo, 17 June 1976).

52. For the institutional impact of this type of proceeding, see Burton M. Atkins, "Decision-Making Rules and Judicial Strategy on the United States Courts of Appeals," *Western Political Quarterly* 25 (December 1972): 626–42.

53. United States District Court for the District of New Jersey, Civil Action Nos. 76–1176, 76–1187, and 76–1188.

54. Lewis B. Kaden, "Supplemental Memorandum in Support of Motions

to Dismiss," 29 June 1976.

55. *New York Times*, 2 July 1976, p. B-2.

56. *Dickey* v. *Robinson*, 414 U.S. 976 (1973); *Klein* v. *Robinson*, 423 U.S. 913 (1975); and denial of application to stay New Jersey Supreme Court Order of 13 May 1976 on 10 June 1976.

57. See Assembly Resolution No. 30, introduced 14 June 1976 by Assemblyman Kenneth Gewertz, "providing for the impeachment of the members of the Supreme Court of the State of New Jersey. . . ."

58. Harry Stumpf, "The Political Efficacy of Judicial Symbolism," *Western Political Quarterly* 19 (June 1966): 1.

59. Adam C. Breckenridge, *Congress Against the Court* (Lincoln: University of Nebraska Press, 1971), pp. 85 ff.

60. C. Herman Pritchett, *Congress versus the Supreme Court* (Minneapolis: University of Minnesota Press, 1961), p. 19; John R. Schmidhauser and Larry L. Berg, *The Supreme Court and Congress: Conflict and Interaction, 1945–1968* (New York: The Free Press, 1972); Stuart S. Nagel, "Court-Curbing Periods in American History," *Vanderbilt Law Review* 18 (June 1965): 926–27.

61. Walter F. Murphy, *Congress and the Court: A Case Study in the American Political Process* (Chicago: University of Chicago Press, 1962), p. 251.

62. See legislative opposition to *Dickey* v. *Robinson*. The Democratic senate caucus reportedly considered a direct challenge to the supreme court in 1974, but decided against it by a narrow majority.

63. Others have suggested that the legal profession's support for the court system is multifaceted: Michael W. Giles, "Lawyers and the Supreme Court: A Comparative Look at Some Attitudinal Linkages," *Journal of Politics* 35 (May 1973): 480–86.

6

Impact and Aftermath

The residents of New Jersey had lived through three years of turmoil since the state supreme court had issued its first decision in *Robinson,* in April 1973. After six more state court rulings and five additional federal court opinions, *Robinson* had finally been settled. Weary reporters had lost count of the number of tax plans that had been proposed to the legislature before the senate and assembly had finally agreed to enact a new tax plan for New Jersey, a new school aid system, and a new program to guide local education. Many New Jersey citizens first recognized a consequence of the new *Robinson*-induced legislation on Friday, September 3, 1976: Listed on the stubs of paychecks, distributed by employers throughout the state that day, was an additional withholding item, one labeled deduction for the state's new income tax. Sidney Glaser, Director of the Division of Taxation in the Treasury Department, had spent much of the previous week explaining to groups, officials, and the press how the new tax system would work, but many citizens still did not like what they heard. Soon a noisy crowd of demonstrators deposited a crate of tea on the doorstep of "Morven," the governor's mansion in Princeton, to echo the city of Boston's protest against the enactment of an earlier tax, and then five thousand tax opponents rallied at the State House to denounce the "oppressions visited upon us by runaway officialdom." [1] As part of a legislative compromise, the new tax was scheduled to expire on June 30, 1978, unless it was renewed. Altogether, the *Robinson* issues would dominate public policy discussions in New Jersey for more than half a decade.

The years of controversy between April 1973 and July 1976 affected not only residents' tax bills but also the state's school finance system, its program for supervising local education, the activities of interest groups in New Jersey, the contours of the state's policy process, and the well-being of its court system. Citizens and officials trying to appraise the impact of the *Robinson* events on these facets of state politics face two challenges. The first is to determine how *Robinson* actually changed the behavior of the institutions, and the second is to decide whether these changes would have occurred for other reasons, even if the supreme court had never ruled in the *Robinson* case. This effort is partially speculative, but it is important for our understanding of how courts are involved in the conduct of public policy.

School Aid. The first school year affected by the state aid program passed by the legislature in response to *Robinson* was 1976–1977. The new plan replaced the State School Incentive Equalization Aid Law of 1970, which had been passed when William Cahill was governor and which had been declared unconstitutional by the state supreme court. [2] The Cahill program had been phased in over a number of years and was not fully funded until 1974–1975. The supreme court allowed the Cahill program to be used for the 1975–1976 school year, and it then required the legislature to pass a new program for 1976–1977 to satisfy its *Robinson* decision.

The New Jersey legislature appropriated $1103 million to aid local school districts in 1976–1977, the first year of the *Robinson* program, which equaled $771 in state aid for each pupil enrolled in the state's public schools. In 1974–1975, the last year before the *Robinson* controversy froze the state's school aid budget, the legislature had granted $782 million to local school districts, or approximately $537 for each pupil. Therefore, as table 1 indicates, state school aid appropriations increased by $321 million between 1974–

TABLE 1

NEW JERSEY STATE AID TO LOCAL SCHOOL DISTRICTS
1966–1977

Fiscal Year	Total (in millions)	Per Pupil
1965–1966	$179	$139
1966–1967	293	221
1967–1968	313	228
1968–1969	342	242
1969–1970	409	282
1970–1971	433	294
1971–1972	450	302
1972–1973	522	352
1973–1974	593	404
1974–1975	782	537
Mean annual increase	14.7%	
Projected 1975–1976	$897	$622
Projected 1976–1977	1030	720
Actual 1975–1976	777	544
Actual 1976–1977	1103	771

Notes and Sources:
State aid includes all revenues received from the state by local school districts as reported in Commissioner of Education, *Annual Report: Financial Statistics of School Districts,* plus expended state appropriations for the Teachers' Pension and Annuity Fund, as reported in the annual *State of New Jersey Budget.* (Due to delayed publication, the adjusted appropriations in the 1977–1978 *Budget* were the basis of the state aid figure for 1976–1977.) For the years 1965–1966 through 1975–1976, per pupil aid was computed on the basis of average district enrollment, as reported in the Commissioner's *Annual Report;* the average enrollment for 1976–1977 was estimated to be 1,430,000. The mean annual percentage increase in state aid was calculated after *excluding* the years with the highest and lowest increases; without excluding those two years, the mean annual increase for the decade would have been 18.9 percent. The mean annual percentage increase was used to project 1974–1975 state aid to 1975–1976 and 1976–1977.

1975 and 1976–1977, a sum which amounted to $234 per pupil. From one perspective, this increase in state school aid, and the continuing appropriation in subsequent years, can be attributed to the impact of the *Robinson* litigation on New Jersey's public policies. On this basis, some argue, *Robinson* increased state school spending by $321 million, or 41 percent, over 1974–1975.

A closer assessment would not be so ready to attribute the full increase in state school spending between 1974–1975 and 1976–1977 to *Robinson*. Table 1 shows that state aid to local school districts doubled in the half-decade before the *Robinson* suit was filed, between 1965–1966 and 1969–1970, and it doubled again in the half-decade after the suit was filed but before the new state legislation was implemented, between 1970–1971 and 1974–1975. Altogether, the dynamics of state politics were increasing state aid to local schools at an annual rate of 14.7 percent in the decade before the *Robinson* program. There is no reason to believe that this trend would have come to an abrupt halt in 1974–1975 without *Robinson*. Assuming that the increase in state assistance to local districts would have continued to increase at the same rate in 1975–1976 and 1976–1977 as it had in the previous decade, the total projected state aid for local school districts would have equaled $897 million in 1975–1976 and $1030 million in 1976–1977 without *Robinson*. Comparisons of the projected aid for 1975–1976 and 1976–1977 with the *actual* aid for those years yield a more informed estimate of the impact of *Robinson* on state school aid appropriations. For this two-year period, the *Robinson* controversy reduced total state spending for local schools by about $47 million. The comparisons reveal that *Robinson* held down state aid to local districts by approximately $120 million in 1975–1976 and increased total state aid in 1976–1977 by approximately $73 million. In the years after 1976–1977, credit for a modest increase of about 7 percent in state assistance to local school districts can be attributed to *Robinson*. With the enactment of the *Robinson* program, state aid to equalize resources among local districts increased at the rate that would have been projected from the experience of the previous decade, state assistance for special education and teachers pensions increased more slowly than would have been anticipated, and state expenditures for local pupil transportation increased more rapidly than would have been expected from the trend of the years between 1965–1966 and 1974–1975.

State school aid programs contain two elements: one component determines how much money will be appropriated for state support of local schools, and a second component specifies how the money will be distributed among the local districts. Jersey City and Harold Ruvoldt, Jr., originally challenged the constitutionality of New Jersey's school finance program, not simply because they wanted to increase state support for education in general, but because they wanted to increase state aid to places like Jersey City. The Cahill equalization formula had distributed state funds among school districts by guaranteeing each district an average property tax base per pupil, by providing an extra allowance for children from AFDC families, and by granting a minimum amount of state aid to each local school district regardless of its own wealth. The *Robinson* program guaranteed each local district the revenues from an above-average property tax base, ended the special assistance for children from AFDC families, and maintained the minimum aid program. How did Jersey City's fortunes compare under the two programs?

The *Robinson* suit was originally filed in the Hudson County Superior Court during the 1969–1970 school year. During that year, the Jersey City School District received 20 percent of its total revenues, or about $7 million, from the state government. As table 2 records, Jersey City received slightly more state aid per pupil than the typical municipality in 1969–1970, but its per pupil expenditures reached only 86 percent of the expenditures of the average school district in the state. In the years after *Robinson* was filed, the amount of state aid received by the Jersey City School District increased dramatically. By 1974–1975, the last year before court action, Jersey City's aid receipts had grown to $26 million, and they reached $39 million in 1976–1977, when the new *Robinson* program was implemented. The state government paid 20 percent of Jersey City's school costs in 1969–1970, 44 percent in 1974–1975, and a full 58 percent in 1976–1977. Jersey City received 5 percent more aid per pupil than the typical municipality in 1969–1970, 69 percent more in 1974–1975, and 73 percent more in 1976–1977. During the years from 1969–1970 to 1976–1977, Jersey City's per pupil expenditure increased from 86 percent of the average school district expenditure to 97 percent. In each of these four categories —total state aid receipts, state aid as a percentage of total revenue, per pupil aid in comparison to statewide aid receipts, and per pupil expenditures in comparison to statewide expenditures—Jersey City

TABLE 2

JERSEY CITY SCHOOL DISTRICT FISCAL ITEMS
1970–1977

Fiscal Year	State Aid (in millions)	Percentage of Total Revenue from State	Per Pupil Aid Jersey City/ State Ratio	Per Pupil Expenditures Jersey City/ State Ratio
1969–1970	$ 7.8	20%	1.05	.86
1970–1971	8.4	22	1.07	.90
1971–1972	9.4	19	1.06	.90
1972–1973	12.5	26	1.22	.90
1973–1974	15.6	30	1.37	.90
1974–1975	26.2	44	1.69	.92
1975–1976	28.5	43	1.94	.94
1976–1977	38.7	58	1.73	.97

Notes and Sources:
Aid and expenditure totals in this table *exclude* appropriations for the Teachers' Pension and Annuity Fund. Per pupil expenditures are for day school students including transportation. All data for the years 1969–1970 through 1975–1976 are drawn from Commissioner of Education, *Annual Report: Financial Statistics of School Districts.* Data for 1976–1977 are estimates provided by the Jersey City School District and the New Jersey Department of Education; average state enrollment for 1976–1977 was estimated to be 1,430,000, and average enrollment for Jersey City was estimated to be 36,000 students.

made impressive gains in the years after *Robinson* was filed. Did the *Robinson* litigation itself produce these gains for Jersey City or were they the product of some other forces?

Jersey City realized the greatest increase in aid receipts, not under the *Robinson* plan, but under the plan enacted during the Cahill Administration. By 1974–1975, aid receipts exceeded $26 million, Jersey City was receiving 69 percent more aid per pupil than the average school district, and the state was paying 44 percent of the city's school district budget. Further increases in aid were realized when the plan the legislature adopted in response to the court was implemented, but those gains under the *Robinson* program were produced by the increase in state funds used to aid all local school districts, not by favorable changes in the formula which distributed the aid among local districts. In fact, the Cahill Administration formula itself was even more favorable to Jersey City than the *Robinson* formula. According to data submitted by the department of education to the state supreme court, if the funds distributed under the *Robinson* formula had been distributed under the Cahill formula, Jersey City would have received $43 million in state aid in 1976–1977 rather than the $39 million it did receive.[3] The previous pages have demonstrated that almost all the money appropriated to support the *Robinson* program would have been appropriated even if the litigation had never taken place.

The worth of the *Robinson* aid formula should not be measured simply by its impact on the Jersey City school system, however. Increased state contributions to the school district's budget reduced the burden shouldered by Jersey City property taxpayers, and that was one of the objectives the judges had in mind. In 1969–1970, Jersey City property taxpayers contributed $27 million to run the city's schools, while in 1976–77 they paid only $22 million, despite the virulent inflation that had characterized the intervening years.[4] Furthermore, other communities in New Jersey with characteristics unlike those of Jersey City had their own severe school finance problems that merited attention. The Cahill formula, with its heavy weighting of children from welfare families, served the needs of the state's largest urban centers, while the *Robinson* formula favored communities with low property values per pupil, and these were sometimes different areas. Other areas without any concentration of valuable business properties and with few students from welfare families reaped the greatest benefits under the *Robinson* program, and the needs of these communities were as genuine as those of places like Jersey City. *Robinson* did not bestow disproportionate new benefits on the state's biggest cities beyond what had been foreshadowed in the Cahill Administration program, but it did grant additional funds to other areas of clear economic need. The eventual impact of the *Robinson* formula will only be determined in the years ahead by real estate values in individual communities and by the financial choices made by local school districts. It is clear now, however, that substantial disparities remain in the funds available to support the education of children in different parts of New Jersey.

Education. The *Robinson* legislation affected New Jersey's schools in ways that had nothing to do with their financing. On July 1, 1976, the Public School Act of 1975 became the guiding statute for the state's education system, and this required each school district in New Jersey to adhere to the procedures of the new "thorough and efficient" process. This process required local districts to define specific educational goals, to shape their programs to meet these goals, to assess their accomplishments, and to take whatever corrective actions were necessary. The New Jersey State Department of Education prepared administrative regulations to implement the new legislation and reorganized its own structure to conform to its new duties. Over the years, the department had built an organizational strategy based on the value of subject matter specialists who assisted with art, history, or English programs, but now that strategy was replaced by one in which departmental personnel served as planners and evaluators. Local pilot districts were designated, in a number of counties throughout the state, to experiment with the new thorough and efficient process before it officially became law. Soon citizen groups and professional assemblies met in individual districts to discuss the goals of their school systems as the first step in the newly mandated educational process.[5]

The "T & E" process, as it is dubbed now, has the potential for revitalizing local education in New Jersey, refocusing attention, away from financial and labor-management issues and toward curriculum questions and overcoming citizen alienation from schools, but it is not yet clear whether its potential will ever be realized. The process is patterned after the procedures of formalized rationality that appeared in federal social programs half a century ago and that have characterized most new federal programs authorized since the mid-1960s. Ritualized planning requirements are now a part of federal programs for highway and hospital construction, health care and criminal justice activities, community development and transportation services, as well as federal programs to aid education. Federal planning requirements assume that poor program performance is caused by uninformed policy judgments and that this performance will be improved by the explicit, publicized consideration of program objectives, alternative policy techniques, and differential programmatic consequences. Despite the widespread imposition of federal planning requirements, however, both physical planning and social service planning have been criticized on a number of grounds.

Physical and social planning is often a weak tool, which has little independent impact on the quality of life or provision of service it pretends to guide. Land use planners have great difficulty demonstrating that physical planning routines have shaped the course of metropolitan development in areas where they have been active. Typically, planning documents are elaborately prepared, colorfully illustrated, appropriately distributed, and then generally ignored. A careful analysis of educational planning activities in selected state departments arrives at the same conclusion. Jerome Murphy has reviewed numerous cases of educational planning for special education, early childhood programs, library services, and the like in South Carolina, New York, Massachusetts, and other states. He concludes that most planning routines have no impact on the educational services that the states eventually provide.[6] In one case, the educational planners recommended the creation of a state kindergarten system, which was subsequently implemented, but, even in this case, the motivating recommendation originated with the governor who was unaware of the departmental study. The work of educational planners served as a rationalization for the governor's proposal, but it did not initiate or reform the program in any significant way. In most cases, planning is a feeble instrument, which barely affects the market forces, institutional dynamics, and patterns of public preference that shape the provision of human services.

Planning's questionable impact on service provision contributes to the second set of complaints that are raised most often—the bureaucratic complaints. Planning, it is said, is simply another administrative requirement that does not improve service to the public. Extensive planning requirements consume valuable administrative resources, demand widespread citizen participation, and necessitate multiple official clearances, all of which take time from delivering public services to citizens. New employees must be retained, clerical staff assembled, and office space arranged—not to improve educational quality but to satisfy bureaucratic requirements. Planning routines also entail a subtle transfer of authority from localities to the state and from the people who provide services to the people who administer institutions. Professionals actually involved in delivering services often feel degraded by the planning process. They believe that they no longer have the authority to provide the services expected of them, and some confess to a sapping of personal initiative.[7]

In New Jersey, bureaucratic objections to the T & E process were expressed vociferously by local teacher groups and administrators. The new administrative code required school districts to submit more budgetary information than the staff of the state department could conceivably look at, they protested, much less evaluate. Some of the data required under the T & E program were already submitted to the department on other forms, and the department made no use of them; why send more data to Trenton which could not be examined, local educators wondered. Some objected to the comprehensiveness of the data collection procedures. No matter how the state's constitutional requirement of a "thorough and efficient education" was defined, some districts argued, a large fraction of the state's schools would exceed it. If one can be sure that many school districts in the state are already meeting constitutional requirements, why subject them to the costly routines of departmental approval? The costs of bureaucratic procedures will outweigh any conceivable benefits. The department's scarce administrative resources ought to be concentrated on those schools whose needs cried out for assistance, rather than dissipated in feeble efforts to monitor all the activities of all the schools in all parts of New Jersey. The administrative regulations of the new program might be intelligently implemented today, some local officials conceded, but what about in future years? Departmental regulations are normally administered with increasing rigidity as the years pass. The most likely prospect for the future of the T & E process, from the perspective of many local officials, would be ever-more-strict enforcement of an ever-growing number of detailed regulations. When innovators pass from the governmental scene, their imaginative proposals may well be transformed into the bureaucratic redtape of thoughtless administration.

The T & E process *could* improve the quality of education in

New Jersey schools in the years ahead, but today there is no way to be sure. To realize its full potential, the program requires the kind of skillful implementation that does not characterize either state or federal agencies. Like most educational innovations, the ultimate success of the T & E program will be determined in individual classrooms and registered in the academic performance and the fruitful lives of students years or decades in the future.

Robinson gave more than the T & E process to the education community in New Jersey. The years of controversy ventilated the state's education problems at a time when there was more fundamental censure and castigation of schools than there had been for decades. *Robinson* crystallized a host of tangential school issues, which might not have been faced if New Jersey had not lived with its unsettled education program for years on end. Traditional schoolpeople were not pleased, but *Robinson* focused attention on a number of education topics that they would have preferred to have left undisturbed. Most publicized was the minimum standards issue. A strange coalition of urban reformers and comfortable suburbanites teamed up against the educators to demand the establishment of statewide minimum educational standards for student performance in New Jersey. Urban reformers believed that the schools in their communities were not working for their children, and something had to be done to improve them. The T & E process, which envisioned the same teachers and the same administrators doing pretty much the same things that they were already doing, simply was not adequate. The definition of statewide minimum education standards would demonstrate unequivocally that their schools required improvement, and the recent litigation would constitutionally compel the state to guarantee that improvement. With minimum standards, additional technical assistance would flow to their hard-pressed schools, the urban reformers believed, and additional millions in state aid would follow as well.

Many suburbanites joined the call for minimum standards, because they too wanted the state department of education to concentrate its administrative expertise on the needs of central city schools. Motivated by both altruism and self-interest, they agreed that urban schools were producing illiterate and unproductive adolescents who would grow into an unruly and dependent adult population. They wanted the department to do whatever was necessary to guarantee that the urban schools worked, and, if this required them to pay slightly higher taxes, they were willing. The cost today for education would be cheaper than the bill they would have to pay in the future for welfare and unemployment. Other suburbanites favored minimum statewide performance standards, because they were convinced that their schools would exceed them comfortably. State officials would direct their attention to schools elsewhere and leave them to run the schools in their communities as they desired.

Traditional educators cried out that minimum standards reflected an elitist colonialism on the part of the affluent toward urban minorities. These educators protested that the imposition of minimum standards would simply be used to threaten and evaluate teachers. Furthermore, public documentation of the educational deficiencies of urban schools would compound their problems by heightening a sense of futility among both the teachers and the students. Traditional educators protested, but to no avail. When the assembly leadership sought votes to enact its tax package in March 1976, it carefully canvassed legislator attitudes on a variety of issues. One group of legislators believed that the education program that would consume most of the new funds, the Public School Act of 1975, required amendment. Neither students nor citizens would get their money's worth unless the program were altered to provide for minimum educational standards, the lawmakers argued. Needing additional votes and generally agreeing with the sentiment, first the assembly leadership and then the Byrne Administration agreed to legislation instructing the department of education to define minimum educational standards for student performance.

Minimum standards were not the only issue brought into focus in New Jersey by *Robinson*. Other measures designed to make educators more accountable to the general public and to the legislature were also proposed during these years. The Public School Act limited the size of expenditure increases by local school districts, and the commissioner announced that these "caps" would not be lifted to facilitate teacher salary negotiations. The issues of teacher training and recertification were debated during the *Robinson* years, and legislative hearings were held on the question of teacher tenure in local school districts, even though no final solution was reached.

Robinson gave to New Jersey a new organizational structure for its department of education, the T & E educational governance process, and the consideration and enactment of other measures promoting educational accountability. How many of these developments would have occurred without *Robinson*? The reorganization of the New Jersey State Department of Education was engineered by a new commissioner, and political administrators frequently choose to symbolize the innovativeness of their tenure through bureaucratic reorganization. New Jersey's new education commissioner displayed his break from the department's historic tensions and animosities by replacing the leadership structure of the department with his own people. The litigation controversy probably shaped and guided the departmental reorganization, but, with or without *Robinson,* it is likely that structural alterations would have been made in the department of education during these years.

Accountability was a fad in educational circles throughout the nation in the mid-1970s, but school finance reform litigation contributed to its persistence. A number of states imposed limitations on school expenditure increases during these years, but in each case these provisions were part of a larger program reforming state school aid legislation.[8] The scrutiny generated by litigation in a hostile climate accentuated the skeptical attitudes many public officials were developing about educational performance. Minimum standards and teacher recertification were issues that arose in states other than New Jersey during these years, but the issues probably would not have been so well defined and carefully considered, and, in some instances, acted upon without the attention attracted to them by the school finance reform litigation.

Robinson bequeathed the T & E process to New Jersey's education community, but would something very similar have emerged in the state if the suit had never occurred? The process of goal definition, curriculum development, and periodic assessment was strikingly similar to the proposals advocated in New Jersey during the Marburger years. Those recommendations had encountered opposition in the past, but they had been partially implemented. The T & E process was a more coherent version of the Marburger approach, and it contained a clearer statement of the commissioner's obligation to order corrective action when unconstitutional deficiencies were revealed in local schools, but the continuities with earlier programs were unmistakably apparent. Judicial participation in Robinson certainly strengthened the hand of the commissioner of education in implementing his new program, but the eventual success of the department's administrative efforts to improve the quality of education in New Jersey can not yet be appraised.

Even more difficult to appraise are the opportunities that were lost because of the energy and effort consumed by *Robinson*. The court required the legislature to address the complex thorough-and-efficient issues during the 1973–1976 period, and the attention devoted to this problem effectively preempted thoughtful consideration of other controversial education topics. By defining the state's educational problems in comprehensive terms and by implying that their nature was essentially fiscal, the court reduced the possibility of achieving piecemeal reforms on other educational fronts during these years. Collective decision-making institutions responsible for a wide range of policy areas normally concentrate on each governmental function only occasionally, and the New Jersey legislature's opportunity to review education in the mid-1970s was expended on *Robinson*. A few legislators lamented this development. They believed that something had been happening to the state's educational institutions in the past half-decade, which they did not understand and which their constituents did not like, yet consideration of these unformed issues had been overwhelmed by the dynamics of the taxation and school aid debate. Legislative action proceeded on some education topics in these years, but the opportunity had been lost in the mid-1970s to examine profound questions in the state's most consuming policy area, and another opportunity might not come along for another half-decade. Public schools in the state might well have worked better for rich and poor alike, if the extraordinary effort devoted to *Robinson* had been invested in other education debates or other policy areas.

Interest Groups. The educational interest groups in New Jersey had lived with *Robinson* since April 1973. They had debated its provisions, argued about its impact on the state's public schools, and lived with its uncertainty for more than three years. Most examinations of interest groups and public policy try to determine how group activity shapes governmental programs. Were resourceful groups able to amend proposed legislation to protect the interests of their members and advance the well-being of their associations? Were the preferences of less important organizations ignored throughout the legislative process? What strategies and tactics characterized interest group efforts to influence the course of events, and to what extent were the final policy decisions based on substantive considerations rather than organizational pleading? As the previous chapters have shown, educational interest groups in New Jersey played an important role in the consideration of the *Robinson* issues and in the formulation of the state's response to the ruling. Our subject here, however, is not how such groups affect the course of events, but rather how the events of *Robinson* affected the educational interest groups involved in the controversy. Were the associations themselves different for having lived with the *Robinson* issues and the *Robinson* certainties for more than three years? Did the turbulent events triggered by the court decision transform the characteristics of groups and group activity in New Jersey educational circles, and if so—in what ways? In sum, what changes in the behavior of the largest associations and the smallest can be attributed to the impact of *Robinson?*

Some New Jersey education associations have multimillion-dollar budgets and scores of professional staff, while others maintain an office in Trenton and hire only a few professional employees. Then, there are groups such as the Association for Adult Education of New Jersey and the New Jersey Personnel Guidance Association. Both of these groups were founded in the early decades of the twentieth century, and today both have about a thousand members. Neither has paid professional staff, elaborate suites of offices, or well-endowed treasuries. The members of both the Personnel Guidance Association and the Association for Adult Education know that traditional educators regard their contributions to the educational enterprise as marginal, and, therefore, they have dedicated their organizations to professionalizing their activities through workshops and in-service training sessions.

These two associations first became involved in deliberations about *Robinson* in 1973, at the request of the state department of education. They believed that the department's invitation for them to participate in policy discussions testified to the department's acceptance of the importance of their contributions to education. The groups wanted counseling and adult education to be an integral part of the thorough and efficient process that was evolving, but, as the debates wore on, the organizations became wary. The department, they felt, wanted them to participate, but evidently did not want to listen to what they had to say. Relevant departmental proposals vaguely left standards for counseling and adult education to the discretion of local school districts. When some legislators referred to courses in exotic dancing as the core of adult education and described counseling as a fringe activity of little value, the two associations suddenly discovered that they had to fight for their goals of certified guidance counselors and mandated adult education programs. In fact, they soon realized that they would have to fight even to prevent drastic reductions in financial support for their existing programs.

The unsettling debates about the *Robinson* program convinced both groups that they had to become directly involved in politics for the first time. In their communications with the department, the associations began to advocate positions rather than simply express professional judgments. Legislators first received protest letters from guidance counselors, and Trenton officials first read newspaper advertisements explaining the importance of adult education. The department of education and the governor's office were submerged in an impressive flood of mail, and adults enrolled in continuing education programs demonstrated for increased funding for their courses. The *Robinson* events led both organizations to reassess their conduct and redirect their energies. Associations that had once been content to hold professional workshops are now building their expertise in public relations and governmental lobbying. The *Robinson* controversy, one organizational official claims, has now made the groups "politically savvy."

The *Robinson* events also politicized the activities of better established education organizations. As New Jersey's policy process has evolved in recent years, legislative committees have become more open, more autonomous, and more important. Policy judgments are now being made in legislative committees, and the lawmakers there are receptive to suggestions made by external groups. Staff members of a principals' association report that they now devote more effort to legislative relations than they once did, because the new openness of the committee system makes their participation more influential. At the School Boards Association, there have been changes in staff assignments that also reflect developments of recent years. Traditionally, relations between the New Jersey School Boards Association and the department of education were maintained by education professionals with expertise in specific programmatic areas; staff members with experience in curriculum planning, assessment, school board law, or teachers' rights would be tapped to represent the association when those issues were discussed. Now, relations with the New Jersey State Board of Education and the leadership of the department have been reassigned to personnel in the School Boards Association responsible for government relations. These activities, once thought to demand educational expertise, are now seen to require lobbying skills. The conduct of education policy throughout the nation has become increasingly political in recent years, and this pattern has appeared in New Jersey as well. New Jersey education associations have entered the political arena with growing frequency, and they have perfected their weapons for doing battle there. Education policy was being politicized in New Jersey before the *Robinson* decision, but the events that followed the court's ruling accelerated that trend and carried it further than it otherwise would have gone.

New Jersey education associations have adopted a more politicized stance not only in relation to the formal institutions of government but in their dealings with their own members as well. Traditionally, education groups in New Jersey had favored increased state aid for local school districts with one voice, but they had been less firm in support of the adoption of a personal income tax to raise the needed revenue. Their members liked income taxes no more than the average New Jersey citizen, and the groups were reluctant to act. During the *Robinson* controversy, the governor's office repeatedly asserted that increased state aid could only be provided if the legislature enacted an income tax. The administration planned to disrupt local budgeting, jeopardize existing aid receipts, and withhold contributions to teacher pension funds until the legislature acted. As the *Robinson* dispute evolved, most organizations explained the close relationship between state support for education and the adoption of an income tax to their members. In its communications to its members, for example, the New Jersey Education Association transformed the thorough and efficient process from an education issue to a bread-and-butter issue, and the association warned the state's teachers that their own well-being could only be secured if they supported the adoption of an income tax.[9] The positions of other education associations were not so strident, but *Robinson* made them all more committed proponents of the enactment of the state income tax than they once had been.

The *Robinson* controversy and the new state program for supervising local education gave the professional associations a new function and a new importance for their members. During the years of uncertainty while the *Robinson* program was being developed and first implemented, local educators had few reliable sources of information about activities in the state capital. As the new program ominously encountered delay after delay, the teachers, principals, and superintendents were often forced to rely on their membership organizations for information about the provisions of the new legislation, which would directly affect their daily lives. When the new legislation came into effect, the primary orientation of the education department shifted from providing curricular assistance to monitoring and evaluating the conduct of education in the state. Henceforth, local educators had to rely on their own associations for much of the professional assistance that would once have come from the department. In addition, the new legislation envisioned local staff involvement in designing goals, programs, and assessment instruments for local school districts. Staff participation in such activities will probably become part of the collective bargaining process that has now appeared in most New Jersey school districts, and will thus make individual educators further dependent on the membership associations.

All of these developments are deepening the involvement of membership associations in the conduct of education policy in New Jersey. The established education groups have expanded their functions and capabilities, the lesser education groups have redirected their activities, and minority organizations have been welcomed into the pro-education coalitions. *Robinson* has made the politics of education in New Jersey somewhat more group-oriented than it has been in the past, but the decision has also introduced a potentially destabilizing element into the picture. If the urban reformers remain active, their pressures for improved student performance are likely to come into embittering conflict with the interests of the membership of resourceful education associations. Renewed educational conflict will probably integrate education decision making in New Jersey even further into the state's general patterns of policy making.

Policy Process. When the assembly speaker gaveled the exhausted chamber into recess after fruitless all-night sessions in June and July 1976, most regarded the endless meeting as another manifestation of a hopelessly inept legislature. The contempt that many citizens already felt for the legislature was reinforced that summer when New Jersey's public broadcasting system televised the disorderly legislative events throughout the state. Commentators submerged the ambiguities of institutional development in accounts of undignified frustration and grimy inaction, and the result was another portrait of legislative madness. After the telecasts, pollsters reported that the state's citizens rated the performance of the New Jersey legislature about on par with that of a recent President while his impeachment proceedings were in progress.[10]

New Jersey's antilegislative tradition certainly rests on much that is valid, but it also reflects much that was a great deal more valid a decade ago than it is today. In the years before the *Robinson* decision, many national organizations devoted themselves to improving the operations of state legislatures throughout the country. One student has concluded that in the last ten years, "Legislatures have been developing their resources; they have been adding staff; they have been expanding facilities; they have been reorganizing and refashioning their procedures; . . . in short, they have been expanding their capacities to do a better job." [11] As a result, state legislatures may be among the few governmental institutions that are better able to manage their problems today than they were ten years ago. The New Jersey legislature has joined in these developments. Its ability to take independent positions on the important issues that come before it has increased dramatically in the past decade. Its Office of Fiscal Affairs now makes estimates of tax receipts that are often more accurate than those of the executive branch. Senate and assembly committees are now assigned full-time staff from the Legislative Services Agency, and the committees now meet often and prepare statements that inform other legislators of the implications of specific recommendations. Legislative committees are now becoming involved in the appropriations process, and executive domination of that process shows the first signs of accommodating programmatic legislative involvement. The quality of information the legislature can bring to the consideration of selected issues now rivals, and occasionally exceeds, that which is available to the executive. Neither the legislature nor the executive is omniscient, but today they are more on a par than they were a decade ago.

Individual legislators have begun to translate this accumulating institutional capacity into recognized expertise in specific policy areas. One need not applaud their recommendations to acknowledge that certain lawmakers on both sides of the aisle have mastered the details of legislative proposals concerning education, capital punishment, cancer prevention, and coastal protection. Some of the legislative confusion of the mid-1970s reflected the emergence of a new process for fashioning public policy in New Jersey to replace total reliance on the executive and on interest groups. The governor still dominates the formulation and enactment of policy initiatives in New Jersey, but now legislative channels are being created to express perspectives not accepted by the administration, and legislative minds are being devoted to the actual preparation of policy initiatives that are independent of those of the executive.

Increased legislative capacity and enhanced autonomy in the conduct of public policy were already slowly developing in New Jersey politics at the time of the *Robinson* decision, but that ruling highlighted fundamental issues at a critical time and thereby accelerated the transitions that were then occurring. The original program to respond to the education and school aid components of *Robinson* was formulated by the executive branch, but that draft was set aside in the wake of the defeat of the governor's tax proposals in the summer of 1974. On its own, the leadership of the Joint Education Committee then prepared its own version of the legislation after consultation with numerous lawmakers and education association representatives. When the attention of the governor's office turned elsewhere, Senator Wiley and Assemblyman Burstein worked with committee staff to revise the administration recommendations to conform more closely to legislative preferences. After prolonged contention and controversy, the Wiley-Burstein program was finally enacted, and its passage marked one of the first occasions on which the New Jersey legislature displayed significant initiative in the preparation of a comprehensive program affecting the provision of a major public service.

The history of the enactment of the 1976 taxation program was even clearer evidence that institutional development had occurred in the New Jersey legislature. After two years of bitter debate over administration proposals, 1976 dawned with a widespread feeling that the taxation problem was one that could only be resolved by the supreme court. Two years of disputes did not disclose the way out of the situation; it only pointed the way to further legislative stalemate. With grim prospects, the assembly leadership began the lengthy consultations that eventually provided the key to ending the long governmental deadlock. Where administration leaders and administration technicians had failed to devise a package that would win the support of the senate and the assembly, legislative leaders and legislative technicians had succeeded. Whether good or bad, the final solution to the 1976 taxation dilemma was a genuinely legislative solution, developed with the direct advice of the people's representatives. Whatever its faults, the assembly program tried to accommodate popular wishes and tried to respond to public preferences. The actual formulation of the complex tax package became an institutional accomplishment of rare magnitude, and it constituted persuasive evidence of the development that has occurred in the New Jersey legislature over the past decade.

Numerous examples of legislative initiative could be collected from recent sessions of state legislatures in all regions. Throughout the country, renewed legislative energy is being channeled into the formulation of new governmental programs designed to respond to pressing public problems. The political incentives for authoring new programs are attractive to legislators; their efforts win widespread media attention, earn the gratitude of clientele groups, and establish a concrete record that can be displayed to constituents. In many instances, expanded staff resources have made it too easy for lawmakers to reap the benefits that accrue to the sponsors of new legislative programs. The national Congress frequently serves as an implicit model for state legislatures, and some have adopted its prosperity to enact a new program before the dust has setttled from the passage of the last new initiative. Increasingly, legislatures at both the state and national level are being characterized as "bill factories," which pass programs with such bewildering frequency that administrative agencies are scarcely able to establish a structure to implement one program before it is amended or replaced by another. This caricature probably exaggerates the disruption produced by legislative energy at the state level, but it does indicate that policy initiation is not the only standard by which to evaluate legislative performance.

Reviewing the implementation of statutes is a legislative task every bit as important as the initiation of new programs. Without legislative oversight, poorly conceived programs might continue unattended and well-designed policies might be undone by administrative bungling. Legislative surveillance can also serve as an antidote to the normal bureaucratic tendency to become responsive to internal considerations at the expense of program goals and clientele groups. The incentives for monitoring the implementation of programs are usually less attractive to legislators than those for creating new programs. Few newspaper stories are written about the battles waged to improve the performance of existing programs, even though the social consequences of such programs may be far reaching. Furthermore, elected officials may jeopardize their relations with established interest groups when they review the conduct of existing programs and alienate the leaders of major administrative agencies. In addition, it is almost always quicker to create a new organization than to reform an entrenched one, and legislators usually devote their efforts to activities which will have visible results within a relatively short time.

Legislative efforts to respond to *Robinson* were not confined to the formulation of the new statute but extended to the creation of a mechanism for the ongoing review of the implementation of the newly authorized program. A permanent Joint Committee on the Public Schools was established with responsibility to:

> . . . conduct a continuing study of the system of free public schools, its financing, administration, and operations, and to make recommendations for legislative action as it deems practicable and desirable for the maintenance and support of a thorough and efficient system of free public schools.[12]

Some elements of the education community in New Jersey welcomed the new committee, because they believed that it would become an impartial forum where troublesome problems could be candidly discussed. When some expressed fear about the consequences of growing legislative involvement in the conduct of education in the state, others replied that the legislators would soon lose interest in monitoring education and turn to more pressing issues. Whatever the eventual results and achievements of the Joint Committee on the Public Schools, its creation testifies to the concern of New Jersey legislators for the effective implementation of new programs and not just their enactment.

Robinson stimulated the evolution of a reformed policy process in New Jersey politics to replace the patterns that prevailed in the mid-1960s. This process is characterized by more active legislative participation in the conduct of public policy and by a more energetic state presence in the management of traditionally local or private affairs. Organized groups are more deeply involved in policy issues today than a decade ago, and the coherent role played by local party organizations has been disrupted. These developments began to appear long before *Robinson* and will probably continue after it is forgotten, but the prominence of the court's ruling hastened their evolution and contributed to the emergence of a new process for conducting public policy in New Jersey.

Supreme Court. The New Jersey Supreme Court launched the *Robinson* dispute in April 1973, and that court was no more immune to the consequences of the ruling than the state's other governing institutions. The chief justice stated that *Robinson* taught the court a new respect for the limitations of its power and a new willingness to accept the decisions of the legislature.[13] Some attorneys argue that the legislative program that the court approved as an adequate response to the state's constitutional obligations in 1976 would never have satisfied the supreme court of 1973. Numerous deficiencies, these lawyers contend, would have prevented the 1973 court from endorsing the act: 60 percent of school funds were still to be raised from local revenue sources, while the state continued to provide significant aid to New Jersey's richest school districts; no special mechanism was established to compensate urban areas for their extraordinary property tax burden, and no special provision was included to relieve the backlog of capital construction needs that had accumulated in hard-pressed communities; and finally, the total process of goal setting and assessment had a disturbingly ethereal quality, which could become a mere facade for perpetuating the constitutionally inadequate status quo. These lawyers believed that the years of institutionally threatening controversy persuaded the court to lower its aspirations and accept any legislation that promised to put an end to a destructive situation.

Occasional judges and lawyers alike confide that the protracted *Robinson* litigation left the judiciary shellshocked and wary. Judges now want to avoid cases, some believe, that could embroil the court system in new disputes in future years. One court official reports that, in *Robinson*'s aftermath, judges were reluctant to hear cases that even touched on school finance issues. Others detect retreats from an active judicial role on zoning, racial quotas, and a broad range of other cases and attribute this to the lingering impact of *Robinson*.

During the *Robinson* years, the tradition of unanimity on the New Jersey Supreme Court came to an end, and the practice of dissent became more common within the court. The extent of agreement on the Weintraub Court was no greater than on the Hughes Court, one well-placed court observer reports, but the earlier panel submerged its internal differences by emphasizing the points of consensus. The divided opinions in five prominent *Robinson* decisions granted justices a license to dissent on other cases. The dissent rate on the New Jersey Supreme Court rose from 11 percent in 1972, before *Robinson,* to 28 percent in 1976.[14] Traditionalists in legal circles asserted that judicial dissents reflected a lack of intellectual leadership on the court and pointed to Chief Justice Hughes, and Hughes replied rather tartly that the dissents were a product of the "fresh and vigorous" minds that sat on his court. Regardless of the cause, dissent became judicially acceptable during these years, even though it is not now possible to determine whether the change is simply a momentary departure from established practice or a profound reorientation of court conduct.

The *Robinson* years also revealed a growing willingness of elite groups to criticize the judiciary. *Robinson* was only one of a number of court decisions throughout the country that led lawmakers to consider denunciations of judicial activism more seriously. In New Jersey, the case added ammunition to the slowly accumulating stockpile of those who believed that there was too much law in society and too much judicialization of the conduct of public policy. No dramatic incident appeared, but elite criticism of the judiciary became slightly more pronounced. It was always difficult to get the New Jersey legislature to approve a judicial pay raise bill, but the challenge became even more arduous during the mid-1970s. Sensing a possible issue in the gubernatorial election year, campaign staffs discussed the merits of reforming the state's judicial selection procedure. Perhaps appointment by the governor should be scrapped in favor of direct election by the public, some commented. Such opinions were probably temporary, but champions of the judiciary could not be sure.

One victim of aroused antagonism toward the judiciary was Senator Stephen Wiley. Wiley was the sponsor of the Public School Act of 1975, a prominent advocate of the adoption of a state income tax, and a consistent supporter of Byrne Administration proposals.[15] Soon after the Byrne Administration came into office, rumors circulated that Wiley would be appointed to the state supreme court. Years later, after he had voted with the Byrne Administration on the education program, the income tax, and countless other measures, Senator Wiley finally was nominated by Governor Byrne to the state's highest court. Opponents of the Byrne Administration and critics of the actions of the supreme court seized on a legal technicality to argue that the Wiley appointment was unconstitutional, and they eventually persuaded a superior court judge and then a majority of the supreme court itself to agree with them. Despite his overwhelming confirmation by the state senate, Wiley was prohibited from joining the supreme court. Subsequently, he remained a senator from Morris County.

And what about the other players in this drama?

Jersey City Mayor Thomas Whelan was sent to prison in 1971 for accepting kickbacks, and he is still there.

Judge Theodore Botter has been promoted to the appellate division of the New Jersey Superior Court.

Paul Tractenberg took leave from Rutgers Law School to become director of an advocacy law center concentrating on education issues, but he later returned to his teaching post.

Chief Justice Joseph Weintraub became active in civic matters after his retirement from the bench and served as an occasional adviser to the Byrne Administration in its subsequent relations with the supreme court.

Assistant Education Commissioner William Shine was not promoted to the post of commissioner. He is now superintendent in one of New Jersey's largest school districts.

William Hamilton was elected speaker of the New Jersey Assembly in 1977, and *Al Burstein* became assistant majority leader.

Kenneth Robinson, now nineteen, graduated from Dickinson High School in Jersey City and then entered the armed forces. With remarkably good timing, his graduation came only a few days before Governor Byrne signed the income tax bill, closing the final chapter in a story which had started when Robinson was eleven.

NOTES

1. (New Brunswick) *Home News*, 19 September 1976, p. A3.

2. Chapter 234 of the Public Laws of 1970, enacted on 26 October 1970, became effective on 1 July 1971.

3. See material submitted by the New Jersey State Department of Education in a response to a request from the supreme court, dated 2 May 1975.

4. Local revenues of 1969–1970 derived from Commissioner of Education, *Annual Report: Financial Statistics of School Districts, 1969–1970;* and 1976–1977 estimated by Jersey City School District. See also Russell S. Harrison, *Equality in Public School Finance* (Lexington, Mass.: D. C. Heath, 1976).

5. For the New Jersey State Department of Education's perspective on the implementation of the *Robinson* law, see its monthly newsletter, *Interact*.

6. Jerome T. Murphy, *State Education Agencies and Discretionary Funds* (Lexington, Mass.: D. C. Heath, 1974); and Dennis R. Judd and Robert E. Mendelson, *The Politics of Urban Planning: The East St. Louis Experience* (Urbana: University of Illinois Press, 1973).

7. Ernest R. House, *The Politics of Educational Innovation* (Berkeley, Cal.: McCutchan, 1974).

8. Dale Cattanach, Robert Lang, and Lloyd Hooper, "Tax and Expenditure Controls: The Price of School Finance Reform," in John Callahan and William Wilken, eds., *School Finance Reform: A Legislators' Handbook*, (Washington: National Conference of State Legislatures, 1976), p. 60; Illinois and Michigan are exceptions.

9. Raymond Schwartz, "Content Analysis of Interest Group Communications to Members—New Jersey Education Association and New Jersey School Boards Association" (Seminar paper in Department of Political Science, Rutgers University, May 1976); *New York Times*, 15 November 1975, p. 31.

10. New Jersey Poll 23, Eagleton Institute of Politics, Rutgers University, October 1976. The question and responses were: "How good a job do you think the New Jersey Legislature is doing—excellent, good, only fair, or poor?" Excellent—1 percent; good—18 percent; only fair—54 percent; poor —20 percent; and, don't know—8 percent.

11. Alan Rosenthal, "Legislative Control," in *Legislators and the Legislative Process* (Topeka: First Institute for Kansas Legislators, 1976), p. 17.

12. Chapter 16 of the Statutes of 1975.

13. (Newark) *Star Ledger*, 30 May 1977, p. 1.

14. Beth Rivers, "Dissent on the New Jersey Supreme Court, 1972–1976" (Seminar paper in Department of Political Science, Rutgers University, May 1977).

15. (Newark) *Star Ledger*, 12 February 1977, p. 1; *Vreeland v. Byrne*, 72 N.J. 292.

7

Conclusion

The events of the *Robinson* v. *Cahill* litigation comprise a crucial chapter in the history of the nationwide school finance reform movement. The movement seeks nothing less than a fundamental reformulation of the mechanisms for funding elementary and secondary education in the United States. The financial stakes involved in this effort are awesome. In 1977, approximately $65 billion were spent to support local schools in the United States, and the ways in which this amount of money is raised from taxpayers and distributed among local school districts have a larger impact on society than do most other policy topics that command public attention. A great deal more was involved in the movement than simply money, however. The school finance reform movement was stimulated by a concern for the well-being of children who attend many of the nation's urban schools, and the movement strove to guarantee that these students would have the opportunity to develop the skills needed to lead useful and fulfilling lives.

The *Robinson* litigation made two critical contributions to the national school finance reform movement. The movement first attracted public attention in the late 1960s and early 1970s with

194

impressive legal arguments and propitious courtroom victories. It first appeared on the front pages of the country's newspapers when the California Supreme Court delivered its first decision in *Serrano* v. *Priest.* That court handed the reformers a sweeping victory by declaring California's school finance system to be unconstitutional, because it made the quality of a child's education dependent on the wealth of the child's parents and neighbors. The exhilaration of the reformers' victory was soon replaced by the frustration of defeat when the United States Supreme Court ruled in *San Antonio* v. *Rodriguez* that there was no federal right to an education and that the reformers' Fourteenth Amendment arguments were not convincing. Within weeks of the dismaying legal setback in Washington, however, the New Jersey Supreme Court let the reformers know that the rejection of their federal constitutional arguments did not close the courtroom door to further school finance reform litigation. The *Robinson* decision was based on a clause of the New Jersey Constitution, and it demonstrated to the disheartened reformers that successful challenges to existing school finance statutes could well rest on state constitutional grounds. By underlining the vitality of state constitutions and by displaying their relevance for education funding issues, *Robinson* kept the school finance reform movement alive in the discouraging days after *Rodriguez.*

Robinson, in this way, reinforced a trend that Associate Justice William J. Brennan of the United States Supreme Court has called an "important and highly significant development for our constitutional jurisprudence."[1] For more than two decades, United States Supreme Court decisions under the Fourteenth Amendment have been designed to protect the rights of citizens against actions of both the national and the state governments. Recently, Brennan writes, more and more state courts have been unwilling to rely on the federal judiciary alone to provide adequate constitutional safeguards. As the United States Supreme Court has appeared to pull back from its earlier interpretations of the federal Bill of Rights, some state supreme courts have moved in to fill the gap. With increasing frequency, they have begun to rule that state constitutional provisions guarantee greater rights than do the clauses of the federal Bill of Rights. Even when the wording of the counterpart constitutional provisions is identical, state supreme courts have refused to follow the interpretations of the United States Supreme Court. Boldly and forthrightly, they have expanded the meaning of these constitutional provisions beyond what the court in Washington has been willing to accept. The imaginative decision of the New Jersey Supreme Court in *Robinson*, based as it was on the state's constitution, typified the revitalization of the state constitutional law that is occurring in many parts of the country.[2]

The school finance reform movement showed signs of losing its vitality in the years after the *Rodriguez* decision, but then the resolution of the *Robinson* controversy appeared to give it a second life. In New Jersey, reformers had faced extraordinarily difficult circumstances: massive changes in governmental leadership, an incompatible governor's office, disruptive transformations in the state's politics, the nation's highest unemployment rate, and the close association of the school finance issue with the question of the enactment of a personal state income tax. Despite all of these difficulties, the case had finally been closed with some degree of success. Since the *Robinson* litigation had moved further and faster than controversial suits in other states, New Jersey's experiences provided lessons for other people embroiled in similar situations. The conclusion of the protracted fiscal controversy in New Jersey encouraged school finance litigants elsewhere to press on with their suits. In the months after the resolution of *Robinson*, news reports from Long Island discussed the progress of a local suit challenging the constitutionality of New York State's program to fund its elementary and secondary schools.[3] As 1977 began, newspapers announced that the California Supreme Court had delivered another decision that restricted even further that state's ability to rely on local property taxation to finance schools.[4] Immediately thereafter, the Connecticut Supreme Court ruled that the Connecticut system for financing public schools from local property taxes was unconstitutional, because it denied children from poor school districts the opportunity to get an education equal to that received by students in richer areas.[5] In the post-*Rodriguez* despair, *Robinson* had encouraged reformers to explore the versatility of the provisions of state constitutions, and, when the school finance reform movement had lost its momentum in 1976, the conclusion of the *Robinson* controversy had released activists in other states to renew their own efforts. In the decades ahead, the *Robinson* case will be remembered as a landmark in the process of reshaping the nation's school finance system to fit the realities of twentieth-century urban development.

In addition to *Robinson*'s impact on the school finance reform movement and its commentary on the relations between the state and federal courts in the 1970s, the litigation was also significant because it illuminated certain characteristics of judicial involvement in public policy disputes. This account of *Robinson* has differed from most accounts of notable lawsuits in two ways. While most studies rely on the records of one party to a case, this volume has been prepared with the assistance of participants on all sides of the issue. Plaintiffs, defendants, judges, lawmakers, educators, and interest group officials have contributed their insights and their perspectives to this analysis. Furthermore, this volume has examined the public policy responses to the *Robinson* litigation as well as the litigation itself. It has moved beyond the courtroom to explore events in the governor's office, the legislative arena, and the executive departments. With these two advantages, it has been possible to describe commonplace legal happenings as well as a series of events that are inconsistent with the traditional assumptions about civil litigation. In fact, the generally accepted model of litigation would distract us from much that took place in the life of the *Robinson* controversy, and it would confuse us about the significance of much else that occurred.

The traditional purpose of civil court action is to settle disputes between two private parties about private issues.[6] The dynamics of society were classically assumed to flow from the actions of private individuals, and civil litigation was designed to facilitate their initiative. Rules of social conduct were clarified though civil adjudication, and each party was assured that the other could be compelled to comply with those rules in their private transactions. Litigation was begun when one party believed that its interests had been abused in a specific situation. The nature of the opposing legal arguments was determined directly by the two sides. The quality of these arguments did not concern the general public, because the final court ruling would affect only the parties' interests rather than the broader interest of society. Since the outcome of any court proceeding influenced primarily the parties to the litigation, questions of legal standing were easily resolved, the activities of judges were essentially passive, and the thoroughness of the fact-gathering procedure was of limited significance. The court's opinion in a case generally produced a clear resolution of the dispute, and it ended judicial participation in the controversy. This description ignores many subtleties of traditional civil litigation, but, nonetheless, its premises have shaped our understanding of the involvement of courts in the conduct of public policy.

This study demonstrates that numerous events in the *Robinson* controversy simply do not conform to the expectations of the traditional model. First and foremost, the court system in *Robinson* was not examining a private dispute between private parties. Like so much contemporary litigation, the *Robinson* case was designed to contest the validity of established public policies. In such circumstances, the bipolar format of courtroom adjudication made little sense. Time after time in this litigation, groups with a vital interest in the proceedings found themselves voiceless and unrepresented. Even though the original suit was directed against school districts alleged to be too resourceful, homeowners whose property tax bills were said to be too low, and children whose education was argued to be too well funded, these groups never had a meaningful opportunity to participate in the litigation. When all New Jersey schools were closed on July 1, 1976, no one appeared before the justices to represent the children who were locked out of school or the working parents who had to bear the financial burden of providing alternative day care facilities for their children. In this case, the adversary process brought forth two parties who shared many of the same policy preferences. The Cahill Administration dispatched a young attorney to oppose the policy goals of Ruvoldt's suit in the courtroom, yet at the same time it was advocating those same goals before the legislature. The department of education, a defendant throughout the lengthy legal proceedings, cheered Ruvoldt along in his actions and applauded his final victory. In *Robinson*, in fact, there was as much, if not more, conflict among the defendants on one side of the courtroom and among the plaintiffs on the other side than there was between the two supposedly antagonistic camps. When government agencies encourage and facilitate litigation designed to force them to do things they really want to do anyway and then concede important points to the plaintiffs during the course of the trial, the traditional model of civil adjudication is of little analytic assistance.

The judges in this case were anything but neutral, passive arbitrators of issues presented to them. Judge Theodore Botter did much to shape the original litigation in his Hudson County courtroom, circumscribing some issues, rejecting others, and emphasizing a ground in his decision that was of marginal importance to the participants. Contrary to many commentaries, some judges reported that the briefs in this case were of limited significance, because respected outside materials adequately examined the legal and policy questions involved. During its consideration of the case, the New Jersey Supreme Court actively sought nondoctrinal information about the issues involved in the case from some sources and received unsolicited advice from others. The chief justice candidly discussed his generalized tactics for prodding the legislature to do what he could not order it to do, and the court later negotiated indirectly with the legislature to reach the same end. In this litigation, the court, the governor, the executive branch, and the legislature all acted in ways that do not conform to the assumptions of the traditional civil adjudication process.

Some analysts argue that the unexpected behavior of participants in the legal process results from the fact that courts are now dealing explicitly with public policy issues. While it is true that courts are now more intimately involved in policy disputes than they once were, this policy involvement alone does not adequately explain everything that has occurred in this case. Rather than simply concluding that courts participate in the conduct of public policy, it is necessary to examine more closely the nature of judicial policy involvement.

Courts play an assortment of specialized roles in public policy controversies in the United States that are limited only by the imagination of attorneys. The principal function of courts in environmental matters, one student has concluded, is to delay projects until doubts about their environmental consequences can be resolved by administrators.[7] In another context, litigation has been used to challenge the activities of the officials of the United Mine Workers' Union so as to encourage and legitimize internal opposition to the established leadership group.[8]

On a more generalized level, a recent analysis of the functions of state supreme courts contends that "Supreme court decisions often occur at or near the end of the political process. . . . Thus a court decision may end a long and troublesome argument that has developed in the political system. . . ."[9] The bitter, divisive, emotional debate about the propriety of abortion in our society was dampened when a court not only sanctioned the controversial practice but also specified the conditions under which it could be performed.[10] This study of the *Robinson* v. *Cahill* litigation did not see a supreme court resolve a long simmering conflict; to the contrary, in this case a court ignited such a dispute. In New Jersey, the courts were used to bring an important matter before the legislature, which the busy and reluctant members would have preferred to ignore. Much to their displeasure, the supreme court placed the issues of education, school finance, and taxation squarely before the two chambers, and the legislators had no choice but to deal with them. The court raised the issues and then granted the legislature surprising latitude to develop its response. The posture of the New Jersey court was so permissive in this case that it eventually approved a new education program that reinstated many of the constitutional defects that it had previously criticized. In this instance, the New Jersey Supreme Court was not making decisions about the content of public policies, but was raising issues for consideration by other governmental institutions. The court performed here an agenda-setting function rather than a decision-making one.

The distinction between agenda setting and decision making, some claim, is a distinction without much of a difference. After all, some New Jersey justices sought from the beginning to use *Robinson* to promote an income tax, and in the end the New Jersey legislature closed the controversy by enacting just such a tax. The designation of agenda items does influence the tone and direction of public policies, but it does not determine their content. In fact, when a topic is placed before the decision-making institutions of government, there is no guarantee that any significant changes in public policies will result. Most topics considered each year by the policy-making institutions are set aside without formal action. Furthermore, even when new programs are enacted, neither their general orientations nor their detailed provisions are foreordained. A new education program, for example, could benefit either urban or suburban schools, gifted or vocational students, or those in need of remedial work, teachers, administrators, or taxpayers, or even building contractors and equipment manufacturers. The decision to impose specific public policies remains quite distinct from the generalized consideration of those policy topics.

TABLE 3

JUDICIAL POLICY FUNCTIONS

	Decision-Making	Agenda-Setting
Litigant Orientation	Courts	Governor, Legislature, Agency
Litigant Tactic	Define Standards	Highlight Inequity
Rights-Remedies Relationship	Intertwined	Separated
Judicial Edict	Injunctive Relief	Declaratory Judgment
Judicial Orientation	Implementation	Direction
Judicial Opinion	Incremental	Innovative
Research Orientation	Compliance	Judicial Impact on Process

The differences between the agenda-setting and decision-making functions of the courts are reflected in the content of judicial rulings as well as in many other facets of the litigation process. Table 3 isolates specific elements of the litigation process and displays the distinct form given to each of these elements by both the agenda-setting and decision-making orientations. If plaintiffs expect judicial decisions to impose specific policies on society, their litigation strategies will be oriented strictly toward the courts. Their task will be to persuade the judges that their arguments are compelling. If, on the other hand, courts are to be used to raise issues for governmental consideration, plaintiffs' attention should extend beyond the courtroom. Under such conditions, David Kirp explains, "The heart of the reform question is not the lawsuit. . . . The reform or lack of reform depends on what the State Legislature is planning to do." [11] Thus, litigation strategists should consider not only the courts, but also how the legislature, the governor, and the executive agencies will deal with the issues that are placed before them. Legal arguments must not only satisfy judicial requirements, but they should also be designed to facilitate rather than impede action from other governmental institutions. When legal actions become part of a broader campaign to reform public policies, reformers should be sure that the argument presented to a judge reinforces rather than undermines the collateral efforts directed toward other institutions. [12]

The traditional decision-making role of courts encourages litigants to try to devise explicit policy standards that willing judges can then impose on society. Separate but equal schools was one such standard, which gave way to a rule ending segregation with all deliberate speed. One man, one vote was another judicially adopted policy standard fashioned to guide reapportionment litigation, and the fiscal neutrality principle of the school finance reformers was offered to the courts as a judicially manageable criterion that could be used to justify a lengthy series of decisions in that policy area. Reformers usually invest great energy in formulating legal standards, because their judicial acceptance means that the battle is largely won. [13] Once defined, a judicial standard traditionally became both a statement of legal rights as well as the yardstick for measuring the realization of those rights. When courts perform decision-making functions, questions of rights and remedies are intimately intertwined, with one flowing almost automatically from the other. Judge Botter reflected the decision-making orientation when he proposed a policy standard of equal treatment for taxpayers. Both Judge Botter and the New Jersey Supreme Court accepted the agenda function with their undefined order to reform educational governance. Under the newer agenda-setting orientation, the questions of rights and remedies are separated from one another, as court actions become more future-oriented and less retrospective.[14] No explicit policy standards are adopted. Litigants strive to persuade the court, first, that a social inequity exists that will not be remedied without judicial action, and, second, that action can be taken by the court without risking dangerous consequences. Since no self-fulfilling standards of rights are involved, judges know that nothing foolish or unfeasible will be imposed on society solely by their authority. Rights can be examined without evaluating remedial actions.

The judiciary, too, treats agenda-setting litigation with different techniques from those it uses to handle cases that actually decide policy issues. The outcome of traditional litigation is expressed through an edict specifying the relief that the vanquished must surrender to the victor. Injunctive relief is not a possible outcome of agenda-setting litigation, however, because, in these cases, courts typically do not endorse explicit policy standards that can then be enforced on society. The consequences of an agenda-setting decision are not defined by a judge, but are left to the interaction and negotiation of the chief executive, the legislature, and the administrative agencies. To deal with these cases, courts have been authorized in recent decades to issue declaratory judgments, which require that affirmative action be taken to remedy a situation but which do not specify the character of that action.[15] Courts use declaratory judgments to provide direction to the traditional policy-making institutions of government, but they do not use them to implement specific policies. A frequent criticism of the declaratory judgment technique is that it permits courts to decide cases without considering the restraints that are imposed by the need to get a decision implemented. Liberated from the requirement to define and document the availability of relief, judges are freer to hand down imaginative and innovative rulings in agenda-setting cases than they are in suits that directly impose new public policies. A judgment in the latter type of litigation is normally characterized by incremental shifts from established doctrine rather than sweeping departures from precedent.

These two judicial roles influence the activities of researchers as well as those of courtroom litigants and jurists. The assumption that courts function as decision makers in the conduct of public policy has led social scientists to concentrate on certain questions rather than others. Because specialists in the study of public law generally view courts as decision-making institutions, they have devoted great effort to explaining why individual judges vote as they do in particular cases and why the public obeys some judicial rulings and evades others.[16] Emphasis on the agenda-setting functions of courts encourages scholars to explore other issues. The agenda-setting orientation encourages them to examine how the participation of courts in public policy controversies affects the course of those controversies. It directs students of public law to determine what consequences flowed from the fact that an issue was placed before the normal policy institutions of government by the court system rather than by some other agenda-setting mechanism. It leads social scientists to isolate the features of court-raised agenda items and compare them with the characteristics of public issues raised in other ways. Our examination of the events in *Robinson* explores this topic. What are the characteristics of court-raised agenda items, and how did these characteristics shape the course of school finance events in New Jersey?

The first characteristic of the court decision in *Robinson* was its *ambiguity*. The New Jersey Supreme Court had refused to define precise policy standards in its opinion because it consciously sought to fill the agenda-setting role, because it wanted to circumscribe the legal implications of its ruling, and because it did not know itself what policy standards it favored. The court issued a broad order to the state to define its educational obligation and redesign its program for financing local schools. This order launched the legislature and the executive branch on an open-ended review of multi-faceted educational issues and forced them to entertain major changes in the state's tax structure. The number of specific topics within the scope of the court's decision strained the state's policy formation capacity, and the *persistence* of the court's mandate complicated the state's policy formation task even more. Since the court's decision would not go away without concrete action by the legislature, it became the vehicle for many groups in the state in promoting their own goals. Some used the *Robinson* controversy to try to improve the business efficiency of school operations,[17] others sought to enrich specialized educational activities, and still others saw in it the need to enact a personal income tax. Governments usually make major changes in established programs only when the necessity for such changes has been demonstrated unequivocally. The number of topics considered during the *Robinson* debate and the prominence of the fiscal dimensions of the issue distracted the legislature from proposing or even considering basic reforms in New Jersey's educational system. The ambiguity and persistence of the court's rulings led the state to evaluate a wide variety of tangential topics, cluttered the primary policy issues at stake, and predisposed the state to make only minor changes in the existing educational structure.

The *Robinson* debate in New Jersey lasted for more than three years, from April 1973 to July 1976, but, nevertheless, the court's ruling itself had had an *immediacy* about it. The supreme court required the state to deal with the education and finance issues during a period when the patterns of public opinion and the conditions of the relevant institutions were decidedly unfavorable. Policy institutions in the United States usually concentrate on topics when the climate of the times is supportive. The nation's environmental policies, for example, are a heritage from the late 1960s and early 1970s. Those policies would look vastly different if they had been critically reexamined and totally redrafted during the sobering years of the mid-1970s. The New Jersey Supreme Court focused attention on education issues at a time that would not have been selected by the department, the legislature, or the education community in general. During the mid-1970s, negative views of education were ascendant in Trenton, and the department was less prepared to cope with basic issues than it had been in the past or would be in the future. *Robinson* articulated the cares and aspirations of the 1960s, but it suffered from the excesses of those years and from the restraints of the 1970s. By the mid-1970s, organizational concerns about the problems of urban and disadvantaged communities were not as prominent in New Jersey education circles as they once had been, and the funds from federal and state sources did not flow as freely. Citizens and legislators who first examined education policies during the mid-1970s have frequently adopted the critical views of education associated with those years, and they are likely to persist in their evaluations in the decades ahead, even if popular sentiments about education turn more favorable. Reformers who use litigation to help change public policies give up some of their control over the timing of their campaigns.

Judicial involvement in *Robinson* also gave the issue a *legitimacy* and a *visibility* it otherwise would not have had. Newspaper reporters picked up copies of the decision and wrote front-page stories that alerted New Jersey's policy-oriented community that this was a problem that would have to be dealt with. The notoriety of the court action stimulated the creation of one new group and reoriented the activities of many others. It brought some of these organizations closer together than they had been in the past and provided them with a coherent target for their activism. The litigation enhanced the status of some nontraditional groups in education policy circles, and the court's involvement implied some endorsement of their critical protests. The fact that the state supreme court had placed the *Robinson* issues on the agenda of governmental action probably increased the attention that citizens paid to these topics and probably made the department of education somewhat more outward looking. *Robinson*'s prominence also meant that the debate soon encompassed the unrelated concerns of the state's policy institutions: the department of education's leadership struggle, the display of the Byrne Administration's policy capacity, and the development of the legislature's institutional resources.

The final quality of *Robinson* was its *intrusive* character. Quite literally, the opinion intruded into the normal activities of the policy institutions it affected. The ruling's judicial aura rendered the normal determinants of legislative behavior slightly less important than they usually were. The court reduced the salience of partisanship, constituency, and program performance for legislators and heightened sensitivity to the claims of fiscal equity. In addition, the department of education was forced to live for years with the knowledge that the structure and financing of its basic mission had been labeled unconstitutional by the state's highest court and yet without knowing what new governing process would replace it. The uncertainty of administrative life under such conditions promoted an institutional narcissism which contributed little to program operations. All organizational routines were in an unsettled state because of the decision, yet nothing could be done to implement change until the controversy had been resolved. This situation went on for years. The continuing, critical scrutiny of the state's educational system not only enervated the personnel charged with operating the schools, but it also crystallized other issues that were not an essential part of a response to the court. Structural reform of the department, expenditure limitations on local school districts, and greater accountability of educational institutions were all issues that were acted upon during the *Robinson* years partially as a result of the court's involvement in the controversy. Finally, the New Jersey Supreme Court, with its decision, assumed some responsibility for the operations of the state's school system, and this assumption in turn allowed others to escape the full burden of their own duties. The diffusion of responsibility allowed some legislators to avoid confronting unpopular choices, and it gave others the courage to make them.

Judicial participation in *Robinson* made the issue *persistent, ambiguous, immediate, visible, legitimate,* and *intrusive.* These qualities resulted from the nature of judicial action, and issues raised by other agenda-setting techniques would have had other characteristics. A topic placed before the policy institutions of government by an outburst of public opinion, for example, would more likely be transitory than persistent. Political leaders have developed numerous techniques for displacing such topics, including the appointment of study commissions, symbolic action, calculated distraction by other issues, or simple delay. When interest groups struggle to raise their issue to governmental attention, officials are more likely to indict the cause as selfish than to accept it as legitimate. The characteristics of the *Robinson* issue were shaped by the judicial involvement, but the significance of those qualities was determined by the conditions in New Jersey at the time of the decision. The immediacy of the issue, for example, would have had different consequences in the mid-1960s than it had in the mid-1970s. Research attention should be devoted to identifying various agenda-setting techniques, cataloging the specific qualities of each, and predicting the implications of those qualities in different situations.[18]

Courts are seen in most circumstances as resolving conflicts rather than initiating them. Certainly, the *Robinson* case is not typical of most legal actions in the United States. Perhaps the agenda-setting role most prominently characterizes judicial action at a particular point in the evolution of legal doctrine. Federal regulatory agencies, Theodore Lowi argues, were typically created when Congress wanted to deal with a particular problem but did not know precisely what it wanted to do.[19] The establishment of a regulatory agency displayed congressional concern and at the same time initiated action that would, Congress hoped, lead to the development of a satisfactory remedial policy. Analogously, courts, too, may be hesitant and accommodating when they first enter a policy area, willing to let others formulate definitive standards and balance conflicting public priorities.[20] Only when experience has developed legal doctrine and judicial self-confidence, do courts begin to assert more firmly their own policy conclusions. As legal doctrines in a policy area evolve, courts may shift from being agenda-setting mechanisms to becoming decision-making institutions.

Even though the agenda function may be most apparent at an early stage of doctrinal development, few court decisions exclude it entirely. Jack Peltason has pointed out that almost every judicial statement has both agenda-setting and decision-making implications for the conduct of public policy.[21] Courts typically combine these two orientations in each of their rulings, resolving certain aspects of a policy debate themselves and leaving others to the discretion of the traditional policy institutions. "Agenda setting" and "decision making" are ideal analytic types, and in the real world actual decisions fall somewhere on a continuum between the two, sometimes closer to one pole and sometimes closer to the other. Even decisions that appear to erect unambiguous judicial standards often leave important room for imaginative policy response. The New York State Legislature once interpreted the "one man, one vote" reapportionment standard in such a way that it proposed to reduce the already inadequate representation of New York City, while claiming to be in compliance with the letter and spirit of a court's ruling.[22] Students of public law usually concentrate on the policies imposed by court action, while they overlook the politics of settling issues that are newly raised by judicial pronouncement. The agenda-setting implications of a court decision are often significant, and sometimes they are as overridingly important as they were in the school finance reform litigation—and they should not be ignored.

How will the critics of judicial activism react to the assertion of this study that courts sometimes set governmental agendas rather than impose public policy choices? The constitutional critics whose arguments rest on the future well-being of governmental institutions will probably not be mollified. They will still complain that the popular support that is necessary for the successful functioning of the judiciary is undermined by any judicial involvement in public policy disputes, regardless of the nature of that involvement. The traditionalists among them will argue that popular acceptance of court rulings rests on the presumption that judges are doing nothing more than applying generally accepted principles to specific situations; more modern commentators, who endorse less stringent standards, will still contend that decisions must at least appear to flow from "neutral principles." [23] Yet, the public opinion data discussed in chapter three of this study and presented in Appendix B challenge the assumptions on which these arguments rest. These data indicate that even the best publicized court rulings escape the attention of the general public. If this is true, it is difficult to argue that the logic used to justify specific rulings will affect popular evaluations of court performance. Liberals and conservatives, Republicans and Democrats, rich and poor, the educated and the unschooled, old and young, all rate court performance at about the same level. Popular support for the judicial system appears to be quite independent of the legal rationale put forth in written opinions. In fact, courts are so remote from people's lives that popular evaluations appear to be independent even of the policy direction implicit in court judgments. The data suggest that public ratings of the judiciary are based on an appraisal of government in general rather than on any of the activities of sitting judges.

Furthermore, the degree of popular support for the judicial system appears to have little influence on the public's stated willingness to comply with individual decisions. In addition, abstract evaluations that citizens make of their likely compliance often give way to their immediate interests in specific situations. This appears to be true of elite groups as well as of the general public. Our interviews with legislators did unearth some comments on the quality of the *Robinson* decision, but, in all instances, these comments appeared to be rationalizations for the lawmakers' policy preferences. Legislators who approved of the policy consequences of the decision applauded the supreme court, and those who opposed *Robinson*'s policy implications were critical of the ruling. Constitutional critics of judicial activism fear that a series of policy-oriented decisions will alienate a succession of different groups. Eventually, the number of antagonistic groups will become so large that they will constitute a majority. They will withdraw their support from the judicial system and then the country's legal structure will collapse. This forecast assumes that groups that oppose one decision will oppose the entire judicial system and that a group once in opposition will remain in opposition forever. There is no reason to accept either assumption. Almost no conceivable action is sufficiently profound that it would in itself lead to the withdrawal of support from a governmental institution, and it is certainly likely that opponents of one court ruling could have their confidence in the judiciary restored by the next decision. The court system in the United States is granted broad latitude, and its popularity apparently rests more on the generalized success of public policy than on public approval of specific actions. Even though the constitutional critics of judicial activism will not be totally satisfied, they should be less opposed to courts performing agenda-setting tasks than decision-making functions. They should welcome the fact that courts are more insulated from policy controversies in the first role than in the second and, therefore, less likely to squander the public approbation these critics find necessary.

The unique combination of assertiveness and restraint that characterizes the agenda-setting role should please the pragmatic critics of judicial activism. Their fears that courts will impose decisions whose unanticipated consequences will be socially destructive should be relieved. Any policy action that results from the consideration of a court-initiated agenda item will not be authorized by judges alone, but will benefit from whatever wisdom, foresight, and expertise the traditional policy institutions of government possess. The agenda-setting role can be viewed as an expression of judicial humility. It does not claim that judges know best what public policies should guide social conduct, but it does permit judges to direct governmental attention to some festering problems whose consequences they consider to be diluting public rights. This judicial role does not assure the passage of enlightened public policy, but it does guarantee that no policies will be imposed on society that are not at least sanctioned by traditional democratic institutions.

The radical critics of judicial activism have pointed out that the American legal structure was created by established elites to protect their own well-being.[24] They assert that the visionary goals of the Constitution have now been achieved. Legal principles that once may have had a progressive impact on society stand today as an impediment to further reform. Since adherence to precedent imposes something of the past on the present and the future, defenders of established ways are likely to reap the final legal victories when they launch a concentrated counterattack on the principles of reformers. Furthermore, these critics argue, despite apparent success, past court victories have not transformed society so much as their legal architects would like to claim. The radical critics doubt that judicial activism will produce meaningful results, and the events of the *Robinson* controversy may lend some weight to their contention. The protracted New Jersey litigation yielded a mixed set of consequences. Some results were positive and some were negative, while the total impact of most others will not be clear until they are worked out by subsequent litigants, courts, legislatures, governors, bureaucracies, and school districts. Even though the final impact of *Robinson* has not yet been determined, however, events in New Jersey during these years do contain lessons for litigation-oriented reformers elsewhere.

Reformers should select targets for their litigation that correspond to the types of reactions they seek. Legislatures and executive agencies are governmental institutions but their actions are guided by different imperatives and their reactions to judicial rulings are likely to reflect different considerations. In general, bureaucratic activities are based on the procedural aspects of established public policies. Executive agencies have a large permanent staff whose days are devoted to specialized administrative tasks, and, in their daily conduct, these staff members normally respect the standards and pronouncements of the professional groups active in individual program areas. Legislatures, in contrast, are more fluid, less institutionalized, and less specialized organizations. With a popularly elected membership, they are better informed about changing currents of public opinion. Legislatures are less stable and less detached than executive agencies, but more confident of their own authority and more sensitive to developments in their own environment.

The differing foundations of these two institutions yield varying responses to judicial decision. Endowed with their own legitimate policy-making role, legislators examine, appraise, and evaluate court opinions more skeptically than do bureaucrats. Once convinced of the appropriateness of judicially mandated reform, however, legislatures will probably be freer and less committed to established ways than bureaucracies. Even though bureaucracies will probably be quicker to accept court rulings, their policy responses are likely to be more firmly rooted in established procedures than will those of legislatures. In *Robinson*, educators and education-oriented legislators backed a program that preserved existing school district activities, while the proposals for concrete change won support among the majority of legislators who had no special commitment to established ways. When courts are used as decision-making institutions, more faithful responses are likely to be won from bureaucrats than from legislators, but, when reforming litigants want courts to place an issue on the public agenda, legislatures are more likely to approve meaningful departures from existing programs and policies.

Litigants who seek to advance their policy goals through agenda-setting suits need to mount a more elaborate effort than do reformers asking the judiciary to impose policy decisions. Since many institutions contribute to the traditional adoption of new public programs, reformers must be attuned to the likely responses of each. Victories over one institution can be lost in another arena if reformers' resources or attention are lacking. New Jersey's new educational governance and finance plans showed few direct traces of reformers' efforts, because the reform groups lacked the expertise to participate in the comprehensive reformulation of a major program area. Ad hoc reform groups are better able to affect piecemeal change in existing programs than fundamental orientations of total departments.

Agenda-setting litigation also needs to be more carefully integrated into the comprehensive campaign of reform than does litigation that simply asks courts to impose policy decisions. Well-endowed reform movements should develop different strategies for dealing with each governmental institution to become involved in a controversy. The objective, of course, is to lead each institution to reinforce the others in a common drive toward the reformers' objectives, but this is often extraordinarily difficult to orchestrate. Since the operations of governmental institutions are based on different assumptions, the arguments which move one institution may well impede the actions of another. In *Robinson*, Byrne Administration rhetoric, designed to scare the legislature into action, was later quoted in a federal courtroom by opposition lawyers trying to frustrate administration plans. Different institutions of government are likely to get in each other's way if they are compelled to work together too closely for too long a period. Reformers should use courts to jolt policy institutions into action, but they should not ask the judiciary to compel these institutions to endure long periods of forced intimacy. Since incremental change is quicker to accomplish than comprehensive reform, litigation efforts of that type will probably yield greater success.

Courts participate in public policy controversies in a variety of different ways. This study has examined the consequences of one type of judicial involvement in one policy context. Before sweeping assessments of the propriety of judicial participation in the conduct of public policy can satisfactorily be concluded, however, greater effort must be devoted to the development of classifications of judicial policy actions and to the documentation of the consequences of each. When that task has been completed, we shall be in a better position to decide in what ways courts should participate in the conduct of public policy.

NOTES

1. William J. Brennan, Jr., "State Constitutions and the Protection of Individual Rights," *Harvard Law Review* 90 (January 1977): 489–504.

2. A. E. Dick Howard, "State Courts and Constitutional Rights in the Day of the Burger Court," *Virginia Law Review* 62 (June 1976): 873–944.

3. *Board of Education, Levittown* v. *Nyquist*, Index No. 8208/74 (Nassau County Supreme Court).

4. *Serrano* v. *Priest*, 96 Cal. Rptr. 601, 487P2d 1241 (1971); and *New York Times*, 31 December 1976, p. 1.

5. *New York Times*, 19 April 1977, p. 1.

6. See the insightful analysis of Abram Chayes, "The Role of the Judge in Public Law Litigation," *Harvard Law Review* 89 (May 1976): 1281–1316.

7. Joseph L. Sax, *Defending the Environment: A Strategy for Citizen Action* (New York: Alfred A. Knopf, 1971), p. 113.

8. Peter Kalis, "Private Litigation and the UMW," *Yale Review of Law and Social Action* 3 (Winter 1972): 272–79.

9. Kenneth N. Vines, "Political Functions of a State Supreme Court," *Tulane Studies in Political Science* 8 (1962): 56, as quoted in Thomas R. Morris, *The Virginia Supreme Court: An Institutional and Political Analysis* (Charlottesville: University of Virginia Press, 1975), p. 158.

10. *Roe* v. *Wade,* 410 U.S. 113 (1973).

11. David Kirp, in "School Finance Litigation: A Strategy Session of the Lawyers' Committee for Civil Rights Under Law," *Yale Review of Law and Social Action* 2 (Winter 1971): 162.

12. Joel L. Fleishman and Carol S. Greenwald, "Public Interest Litigation and Political Finance Reform," *The Annals of the American Academy of Political and Social Science* 425 (May 1976): 114–23; and Peter R. Kolker, "The Test Case and Law Reform in the Juvenile Justice System," *Yale Review of Law and Social Action* 1 (Winter 1970): 64–71.

13. David K. Cohen and Michael S. Garet, "Reforming Educational Policy with Applied Social Research," *Harvard Education Review* 45 (February 1975): 17–43; Milbrey W. McLaughlin, *Evaluation and Reform* (Cambridge, Mass.: Ballinger, 1975).

14. This discussion benefits from Chayes, "The Role of the Judge," p. 1292.

15. Judiciary Act of June 14, 1934, ch. 512, 48 Stat. 955; E. M. Borchard, *Declaratory Judgments* (New York: Banks-Baldwin, 1941).

16. G. A. Schubert, *The Judicial Mind Revised: Psychometric Analysis of Supreme Court Ideology* (New York: Oxford University Press, 1974); Theodore Becker, *Political Behavioralism and Modern Jurisprudence* (Chicago: Rand McNally, 1965); J. Woodford Howard, Jr., "On the Fluidity of Judicial Choice," *American Political Science Review* 62 (March 1968): 43–56; Stephen L. Wasby, *The Impact of the United States Supreme Court: Some Perspectives* (Homewood, Ill.: Dorsey Press, 1970); Theodore L. Becker and Malcolm M. Feeley, eds., *The Impact of Supreme Court Decisions: Empirical Studies* (New York: Oxford University Press, 1973).

17. See New Jersey Legislature Task Force on the Business Efficiency of the Public Schools, *Interim Report* (February 1977) and chapters 212 of the Public Laws of 1975 and 77 of the Public Laws of 1976.

18. Roger Cobb, Jennie Keith-Ross, and Marc Howard Ross, "Agenda-

Building as a Comparative Political Process," *American Political Science Review* 60 (March 1976): 128.

19. Theodore J. Lowi, *The End of Liberalism* (New York: Norton, 1969).

20. Robert G. Dixon, Jr., *Democratic Representation: Reapportionment in Law and Politics* (New York: Oxford University Press, 1968).

21. Jack W. Peltason, "After the Lawsuit Is Over," in Jack W. Peltason, ed., *Federal Courts in the Political Process* (New York: Random House, 1955).

22. Richard Lehne, *Legislating Reapportionment in New York* (New York: National Municipal League, 1971).

23. Herbert Wechsler, "Toward Neutral Principles of Constitutional Law," *Harvard Law Review* 73 (November 1959): 16.

24. R. Lefcourt, ed., *Law Against the People: Essays to Demystify Law, Order and the Courts* (New York: Alfred A. Knopf, 1971), and E. V. Rostow, ed., *Is Law Dead?* (New York: Simon & Schuster, 1972).

APPENDIX A

Elite Interviews

This book rests heavily on interviews conducted with participants in all facets of the *Robinson* controversy. Most of the interviews were conducted by the author. Some were carried out by two graduate students in the Political Science Department at Rutgers University, Carole Holden and Merle Treusch. Most interviews combined a structured schedule of questions with additional questions that focused on the special activities of the person being interviewed and were conducted on the date and in the community cited. As noted, a few interviews were conducted by telephone. Each person interviewed has been briefly described below by his or her position in the *Robinson* litigation. In dozens of cases, additional discussions with the interviewees occurred at times other than the formal meetings cited here. Numerous interviewees became valued research assistants in the project, saving copies of documents and making notes on meetings, which otherwise would not have been available. Some people interviewed for this project requested that their participation not be acknowledged, and their names have been deleted from the list below.

The interviewees were assured that they would not be directly quoted in ways that could be personally embarrassing to them. These interviews are the sources of the uncited quotations throughout the text. In a few instances, a statement attributed to a "departmental official," a "judge," or a "legislator" may be composed of words from more than one person. I have felt free to quote directly material which has been published elsewhere.

Adubato, Michael, New Jersey Assemblyman; November 25, 1975, Newark.
Armiger, Dr. Mary Lou, Assistant Director of Instruction, New Jersey Education Association; March 31, 1975, Trenton.

Arnold, James A., Chief of Tax Research and Statistics, Department of the Treasury; December 22, 1975, Trenton.

Ascher, Gordon, Director of Assessment and Evaluation, New Jersey State Department of Education; February 25, 1976, Trenton.

Auerbach, James, President, New Jersey Federation of Teachers; February 10, 1976, Union.

Bateman, Raymond H., New Jersey State Senator, Senate President 1970–1972; September 15, 1975, Somerville.

Bedell, Eugene J., New Jersey State Senator; October 9, 1975, Keansburg.

Bills, Harold, Monmouth County Superintendent of Education, Formerly Acting Assistant Commissioner for Administration and Finance, New Jersey State Department of Education; February 9, 1976, Freehold.

Borrus, Jack, Lawyer for General Assembly; June 24, 1976, North Brunswick.

Bothwell, Robert, National Urban Coalition; telephone, September 21, 1976, Washington, D.C.

Botter, Theodore, Judge, New Jersey Superior Court (Appellate Division); March 29, 1976, Hackensack.

Brooks, William, Deputy Assistant Commissioner, New Jersey State Department of Education; October 23, 1975, Trenton.

Buehler, Herbert J., New Jersey State Senator; November 6, 1975, Trenton.

Burstein, Albert, New Jersey Assemblyman, Chairman, Assembly Education Committee 1974–1975, Assistant Majority Leader 1976; August 20, 1975, Jersey City.

Chesner, Walter, Legislative Assistant, New Jersey Association of Secondary School Principals; April 14, 1976, Trenton.

Clayton, Joseph, Former Acting Commissioner of Education of New Jersey; April 29, 1976, Belmar.

Cochran, Thomas, Special Assistant to the Governor; June 25, 1976, Trenton.

Dumont, Wayne, Jr., New Jersey State Senator, Chairman, Senate Education Committee 1972–1973; October 13, 1975, Phillipsburg.

Dyer, Henry, Vice President, Educational Testing Service (retired); March 19, 1976, Princeton.

Esmay, Judith, Advocates for Education; February 24, 1976, Morristown.

Ewing, John H., New Jersey Assemblyman, Chairman, Assembly Education Committee 1970–1973; September 3, 1975, Bernardsville.

Feldman, Matthew, New Jersey State Senator, Senate Majority Leader 1974–1975, Senate President 1976; September 16, 1975, Teaneck.

Foran, Walter E., New Jersey Assemblyman; September 10, 1975; Flemington.

Garramone, Raymond, New Jersey State Senator; October 20, 1975, Westwood.

Garrubbo, Joseph L., New Jersey Assemblyman; September 23, 1975, Union.

Goldberg, David, Lawyer for the Senate; July 8, 1976, Trenton.

Goldman, Clifford, Deputy Treasurer and Special Assistant to the Governor; December 22, 1975, Trenton.

Haines, Frank, Executive Director, New Jersey Taxpayers' Association; February 18, 1976, Trenton.

Hall, Frederick W., Former Justice, New Jersey Supreme Court; June 1, 1976, Somerville.

Hamilton, William J., New Jersey Assemblyman, Majority Leader, New Jersey Assembly 1976, Assistant Majority Leader 1974–1975; October 2, 1975, New Brunswick.

Harris, Dolores, Former President, Adult Education Association; March 18, 1976, Glassboro.

Havrilesky, Katherine, Director of Field Services, New Jersey State Department of Education; December 10, 1975, Trenton.

Higgins, Denise, Assistant Director of Government Relations, New Jersey School Boards Association; January 30, 1976, Trenton.

Hurwitz, Dr. Mark W., Executive Director, New Jersey School Boards Association; March 17, 1976, Trenton.

Jacobs, Nathan L., Former Justice, New Jersey Supreme Court; March 22, 1976, Livingston.

Kaden, Lewis B., Special Counsel to the Governor; June 22, 1976, Trenton.

Karcher, Alan, New Jersey Assemblyman; October 10, 1975, Sayreville.

Kinsey, Sue, Division of Curriculum and Instruction, New Jersey State Department of Education; November 15, 1975, New Brunswick.

Lanning, William, New Jersey Legislative Services Agency; April 28, 1976, Trenton.

LeRoy, Gibson, State Legislative Chairman, New Jersey Congress of Parents and Teachers; March 4, 1976, Trenton.

Lewis, Arthur W., Judge, New Jersey Superior Court (Appellate Division) temporarily assigned to Supreme Court; August 6, 1976, Cherry Hill.

Lipman, Wynona M., New Jersey State Senator; October 29, 1975, Newark.

Long, David C., Lawyers' Committee for Civil Rights Under Law; July 7, 1976, Washington, D.C.

Loos, Peter, Research Director, New Jersey Senate; August 14, 1975, Trenton.

MacInnes, Gordon A., New Jersey Assemblyman; September 2, 1975, Morristown.

McDavit, Dr. H. W., Executive Director, New Jersey Association of Elementary School Principals; March 30, 1976, Trenton.

McDonnell, Estela, Education Co-ordinator, Puerto Rican Congress; March 4, 1976, Trenton.

McDonough, Peter J., New Jersey State Senator; October 2, 1975, Plainfield.

Mancuso, Ruth, President, New Jersey State Board of Education; January 12, 1976, Sewell.

Marburger, Carl, Former Commissioner, New Jersey State Department of Education; telephone, June 28, 1976, Columbia, Maryland.

Martin, Harold, New Jersey Assemblyman; September 5, 1975, Creskill.

Miller, Henry, Executive Director, New Jersey Association of Secondary School Principals; April 14, 1976, Trenton.

Moran, Jim, Executive Director, New Jersey Association of School Administrators; April 13, 1976, Trenton.

Muller, Paul, New Jersey Legislative Services Agency; August 1, 1975, Trenton.

Musto, William V., New Jersey State Senator; Mayor, Union City, New Jersey; October 29, 1975, Union City.

Nash, Mary, New Jersey League of Women Voters; January 28, 1976, Montclair.

Newman, Daniel F., New Jersey Assemblyman, Chairman, Assembly Education Committee 1976; October 1, 1975, Bricktown.

O'Brien, Walter, Director, Government Relations, New Jersey Education Association; March 22, 1976, Trenton.

Ogden, Evelyn, Director of Program Management, New Jersey State Department of Education, December 12, 1975, Trenton.

Perkins, William O., New Jersey Assemblyman; October 3, 1975, Jersey City.

Peskoe, Florence R., Clerk of the New Jersey Supreme Court; July 22, 1976, Trenton.

Ramsay, Dr. William, Former Executive Director, New Jersey Association of School Administrators; April 2, 1976, Trenton.

Reid, Octavius T., Assistant Executive Director, New Jersey School Boards Association; March 24, 1976, Trenton.

Reilly, James, Research Director, New Jersey Education Association; February 23, 1976, Trenton.

Ruane, Robert M., New Jersey Assemblyman; September 29, 1975, Trenton.

Rubin, Larry, Research Director, New Jersey Education Reform Project; June 4, 1976, Newark.

Ruh, Gustav, Gloucester County Superintendent of Education; January 12, 1976, Sewell.

Russo, John F., New Jersey State Senator; October 7, 1975, Toms River.

Ruvoldt, Harold J., Jr., Attorney for Kenneth Robinson et al.; July 28, 1976, Jersey City.

Ryan, James F., Former Corporation Counsel, Jersey City; telephone, July 6, 1976, Jersey City.

Sadat, Deena, New Jersey Legislative Services Agency; July 30, 1975, Trenton.

Scardino, Anthony, Jr., New Jersey State Senator; October 8, 1975, Lyndhurst.

Shine, William, Assistant Commissioner of Curriculum and Instruction, New Jersey State Department of Education; January 12, 1976, Cherry Hill.

Skillman, Stephen, Assistant Attorney General, New Jersey; August 3, 1976, Trenton.

Smith, Irene, President, New Jersey National Association for the Advancement of Colored People; March 18, 1976, Wenonah.

Sommer, Jane, Deputy Attorney General, New Jersey; December 2, 1975, Trenton.

Spizziri, John, New Jersey Assemblyman; September 5, 1975, Wyckoff.

Starkey, Herbert, Consultant, New Jersey State Department of Education; December 2, 1975, Trenton.

Steinfelt, Bernard, Deputy Assistant Commissioner for Administration and Finance, New Jersey State Department of Education; January 5, 1976, Trenton.

Swanson, Carl, Assistant Deputy Commissioner, New Jersey State Department of Education; December 4, 1975, Trenton.

Tantum, Anne, Division of Curriculum and Instruction, New Jersey State Department of Education; October 23, 1975, Trenton.

Tecker, Glenn, Director of Management Information, New Jersey School Boards Association; January 21, 1976, Trenton.

Tractenberg, Paul, Director, Education Law Center; March 18, 1976, Newark.

Ward, Robert, Office of the Deputy Commissioner, New Jersey State Department of Education; November 19, 1975, Trenton.

Weintraub, Joseph, Former Chief Justice, New Jersey Supreme Court; April 24, 1976, Orange.

Weiss, Stephen G., Office of the Attorney General, New Jersey; July 28, 1976, East Orange.

Wenzel, William, Deputy Assistant Commissioner for Vocational-Technical Education, New Jersey State Department of Education; December 16, 1975, Trenton.

Werenne, Lillian, President, New Jersey Personnel Guidance Association; March 16, 1976, Trenton.

White, John, New Jersey Legislative Services Agency; August 1, 1975, Trenton.

Wiley, Stephen B., New Jersey State Senator, Chairman, Senate Education Committee 1974–1976; August 22, 1975, Morristown.

Wilson, Sherwood, Director, Educational Improvement Centers, New Jersey State Department of Education; December 4, 1975, Trenton.

Woodford, Robert, Committee on Education, New Jersey Manufacturers Association; February 18, 1976, West Trenton.

APPENDIX B

Aggregate Inteviews: Public, Legislature, Department
of Education, and Interest Group

PUBLIC ATTITUDES

The discussion of public attitudes is based on studies done by the
New Jersey Poll, which is located at the Eagleton Institute of Politics, Rutgers University. The New Jersey Poll interviews by telephone approximately one thousand state residents, selected to reflect the county-by-county distribution of the state population, and
then randomly drawn within each county. All undated questions
reported below were asked during September 1975, but additional
questions, as indicated below, were posed to citizens in February and
April 1976.

New Jersey Supreme Court

*(1) Percentage of sample unable to respond to: "How would you rate the
job _____ is doing?"*

U.S. Congress	4%
U.S. Supreme Court	13%
N.J. Legislature	11%
N.J. Governor	5%
N.J. Supreme Court (September 1975)	27%
N.J. Supreme Court (April 1976)	15%

(2) *"How would you rate the job _____ is doing?"* (Scores are the mean of all scores assigned on a rating from one [lowest] to four [highest].)

| | Positive | | Negative | | |
	Excellent	Good	Only Fair	Poor	Score
U.S. Congress	1%	16%	54%	29%	1.88
U.S. Supreme Court	3	29	43	25	2.11
N.J. Legislature	2	21	53	25	2.00
N.J. Governor	1	21	42	35	1.88
N.J. Supreme Court:					
September 1975	4	37	47	12	2.33
April 1976	5	42	41	12	2.40

(3) *Relation of socio-ideological background to evaluation of New Jersey Supreme Court. Scores represent mean of all scores assigned to the court on a rating from one (lowest) to four (highest).*

Background	Score
Democrats	2.40
Republicans	2.35
Independents	2.28
Liberals	2.40
Conservatives	2.32
Age 18–29	2.29
30–49	2.35
59 or over	2.38
Income under $10,000	2.41
$10,000 to $15,000	2.30
Over $15,000	2.41
Less than high school education	2.27
High school graduates	2.37
College education	2.41

(4) *Rating of New Jersey Supreme Court compared to evaluation scores for other institutions, which range from one (lowest) to four (highest).*

Mean Score for Other Institutions

Rating of Court	New Jersey Governor	U.S. Supreme Court	New Jersey Legislature
Excellent	2.91	3.08	3.14
Good	2.67	2.73	2.73
Only fair	2.35	2.29	2.24
Poor	2.16	1.88	2.12

(5) *"Some people have recently argued that schools in poor and disadvantaged communities should be given more state aid than other schools. Others say that state aid should be distributed evenly among all school districts. Which side do you agree with?"*

More state aid for poor communities	27%
State aid should be distributed evenly	67
Don't know	6

(6) *"If the State Supreme Court decided that schools in poor and disadvantaged communities should receive additional state aid, would you approve or disapprove of the decision?"*

Approve	62%
Disapprove	32
Don't know	6

(7) *"If the New Jersey Supreme Court ruled that taxes in your community must be raised to provide more funds for schools in poor and disadvantaged communities, what do you think the local officials in your community should do—raise your local taxes, take no action, or oppose the Court efforts to raise local taxes?"*

Raise taxes	26%
Take no action	13
Oppose Court efforts	61

Attitudes Toward Education

(8) *"On the whole, how good a job do you think schools in the state are doing educating children?"*

Excellent	10%
Good	41
Only fair	33
Poor	16
Mean score (Four-point scale with four as excellent)	2.45

(9) *"Do you think public schools are teaching basic skills as well as they once did?"*

Yes	44%
No	56%

(10) *"If the state government spent more money for public schools, would that improve the quality of education in the state?"*

Agree	39%
Disagree	54
Don't know	6

Taxes and Fiscal Equity

(11) *"Which do you think is most important for state government to do—control spending and hold down taxes, provide programs and services to meet people's needs, or keep government honest and free from corruption?"*

Control spending	22%
Provide services	20
Keep government honest	53

(12) *"Would you be willing to pay more taxes if the additional money was to go toward paying for New Jersey's public schools, or are the schools getting enough money now?"*

Willing to pay	32%
Schools have enough	57
Depends/don't know	11

(13) *"Comparing New Jersey to other states in the nation, do you think New Jersey residents pay more, less, or about the same in overall state and local taxes?"*

More	52%
Less	14
About the same	26
Don't know/no opinion	8

(14) *"Compared to taxpayers in other states, do you think you are getting more for your money, less for your money, or about the same?"*

More	7%
Less	46
About the same	42
Don't know/no opinion	5

(15) *In February 1976, "Would you be in favor of an income tax which would raise enough money both to restore the budget cuts and to provide reductions in the local property tax?"*

Yes	62%
No	33
Don't know	5

(16) *"If the income tax–property tax reduction package passed by the Assembly [in March] 1976 were to become law, do you think property taxes in New Jersey would be reduced next year?"*

Yes	29%
No	56
Don't know	15

(17) *"If the tax package [passed by the Assembly in March 1976] became law, do you think the total taxes your family will pay next year would increase or decrease?"*

Increase	77%
Decrease	16
Don't know	7

Attitudes Toward *Robinson*

(18) *"How closely have you followed the Botter decision, that is, the State Supreme Court's* Robinson v. Cahill *school finance decision— very closely, somewhat closely, not very closely, or not at all?"*

	September 1975	April 1976
Very closely or somewhat closely	12%	22%
Not very closely	29	36
Not at all	55	41
Don't know	4	1

(19) *Relation of socio-ideological background to familiarity with* Robinson *decision.*

September 1975

	Characteristic	Somewhat or Very Closely	Not Very Closely	Not at All	Don't Know
Age	18–29	9%	20%	69%	2%
	30–49	13	35	49	3
	50 and over	12	29	53	6

	Characteristic	Somewhat or Very Closely	Not Very Closely	Not at All	Don't Know
Income	Under $10,000	14%	23%	57%	6%
	$10,000 to $20,000	10	34	53	3
	Over $20,000	17	29	53	1
Education	Less than high school education	10%	26%	58%	6%
	High school graduate/some college	8	32	57	3
	College graduate and over	28	25	45	2
Party	Democrat	11%	26%	58%	5%
	Republican	14	26	57	2
	Independent	14	32	53	2
					N=1003

April 1976

	Characteristic	Somewhat or Very Closely	Not Very Closely	Not at All	Don't Know
Age	18–29	24%	32%	44%	0%
	30–49	25	36	38	2
	50 and over	18	40	42	1
Income	Under $10,000	20%	37%	41%	2%
	$10,000 to $15,000	15	39	45	0
	Over $15,000	31	33	35	1
Education	Less than high school education	16%	42%	42%	1%
	High school graduate/some college	20	34	44	1
	College graduate and over	42	30	27	1
Party	Democrat	18%	42%	39%	1%
	Republican	21	35	41	3
	Independent	27	31	42	0
					N=1002

(20) "As you know, the Court ruled that New Jersey's present system for funding public schools is unconstitutional because its heavy reliance

on local property taxes does not guarantee students throughout the state a quality education. Do you approve or disapprove of this decision?"

	September 1975	February 1976	April 1976
Approve	43%	41%	41%
Disapprove	44	47	47
Don't know	13	12	12

(21) Relation of socio-ideological background to evaluation of Robinson *decision.*

	Characteristic	Approve	Disapprove	Don't Know
Income	Under $10,000	39%	46%	15%
	$10,000 to $20,000	46	48	6
	Over $20,000	53	43	4
Education	Less than high school education	34%	46%	20%
	High school graduate/some college	46	45	9
	College graduate and over	53	37	10
Municipal	City	27%	52%	22%
Environment	Older suburbs	39	49	12
	New suburbs	47	42	11
	Rural	46	40	14
Ideology	Liberal	57%	36%	7%
	Conservative	37	49	14

N=932

(22) Relation of evaluation of New Jersey Supreme Court and Public Schools to Robinson *decision, with four as excellent through one as poor.*

		Mean Court Rating Score	Mean School Performance Score
Evaluation	Approve	2.42	2.33
of Decision	Disapprove	2.33	2.46

(23) Relation of approval of Robinson *decision to agreement with statement: "The state has an obligation to spend more on public services*

for poor and disadvantaged people than it does on the average citizen."

Degree of Agreement

		Strongly or Mildly Agree	Strongly or Mildly Disagree	Don't Know
Evaluation	Approve	56%	36%	8%
of Decision	Disapprove	52	43	5
	Don't know	9	23	68
				N=745

(24) *Relation of approval of* Robinson *decision to willingness to pay additional taxes for New Jersey public schools.*

		Willing to Pay More	Schools Already Have Enough
Evaluation	Approve	36%	64%
of Decision	Disapprove	36	64
			N=735

(25) *Relation of approval of* Robinson *decision to willingness to pay additional taxes to help schools in poor and disadvantaged communities.*

		Willing to Pay More	Not Willing to Pay More
Evaluation	Approve	56%	44%
of Decision	Disapprove	45	55
			N=781

(26) *Relation of approval of* Robinson *decision to recognition of per pupil school district spending differences.*

		Spending Differs	Spending Pretty Much the Same
Evaluation	Approve	53%	43%
of Decision	Disapprove	47	57
			N=723

LEGISLATIVE ATTITUDES

The discussion of legislative attitudes in chapter three is based on interviews with 26 members of the New Jersey legislature, conducted between August and November 1975. The 14 assemblypersons and 12 senators were selected to be interviewed either because of their involvement in legislative debate triggered by *Robinson* or because they reflected the diversity of characteristics found within the legislature. The 26 interviewees comprised 22 percent of the legislature, 30 percent of the senate, and 18 percent of the assembly. In a session when the governor's income tax plan narrowly passed one house and was narrowly defeated in the other chamber, 13 of our 26 legislators supported the income tax program. Table A.1 compares the characteristics of the legislators interviewed with those of the entire legislative body. This comparison reflects the fact that the legislators interviewed here are generally more capable, more articulate, and more involved than the average legislator and more likely to represent well-to-do suburban areas.

Most interviews lasted between 1 and 1¼ hours. Some questions were closed-ended, with predetermined responses, and others were open-ended, with no specific alternative answers offered. Open-ended questions were coded independently by three interviewers, with minor disagreements being resolved through subsequent discussion. The specific questions and responses follow by topic.

TABLE A. 1

Comparison of Characteristics of Interviewed and All Legislators

Characteristic			All Legislators	Interviewed Legislators
Mean Age			47.0 years	46.2 years
Sex	Women		8%	8%
	Men		92	92
Race	Black		8	8
	White		92	92
Occupation	Lawyer		38	38
	Other		62	62
Party Affiliation	Democrat		80	77
	Republican		20	23
House	Senate		33	46
	Assembly		67	54
Mean Years of Service			4.7 years	5.6 years
District Per Capita Income, 1972			$4477	$4739
District Character	Urban		30%	19%
	Suburban		53	65
	Rural		18	15

New Jersey Supreme Court

(1) "How would you rate the job the New Jersey Supreme Court is doing?"

Excellent or good	17	(65%)
Only fair or poor	6	(23%)
No answer	3	(12%)

(2) "Among the people you talk to on a day-to-day basis, do you think that opinions about the New Jersey Supreme Court have changed in recent years? Why is that?" Responses to this question were coded as positive or negative for both a public and a personal or elite view of the Court.

	Public View	Personal or Elite View
Positive	2 (8%)	13 (50%)
Negative	18 (69%)	9 (35%)
No answer	6 (23%)	4 (15%)

(3) "The justices now serving on the New Jersey Supreme Court are at least as well qualified as justices in past decades."

Agree	17 (65%)
Disagree	1 (4%)
No answer	8 (31%)

(4) Relation of occupation and job rating of the New Jersey Supreme Court.

		Lawyers	Non-Lawyers
Court	High	7	10
Rating	Low	2	4

N=23

(5) "Although the Supreme Court should interpret the Constitution, in some of its recent decisions the Court has become too involved in political rather than legal questions."

Agree	11 (42%)
Disagree	8 (31%)
No answer	7 (27%)

(6) "If you told your constituents that the Court required you to vote for increased taxes, how do you think they would react? (Would the

Court's ruling be effective protection for voting for new taxes, an effective defense for constituency antagonism?)"

Coded as:

Yes, it would	3 (12%)
No, it would not	18 (69%)
No answer	5 (19%)

Public Schools

(7) "On the whole, how good a job do you think schools in the state are doing educating children?"

Excellent or good	10 (39%)
Only fair or poor	13 (50%)
No answer	3 (11%)

(8) "Public schools are not teaching basic skills as well as they once did."

Agree	20 (77%)
Disagree	2 (8%)
No answer	4 (15%)

(9) "How much room for improvement is there in the way school districts use their money?"

A great deal or some	19 (73%)
Little or not much	2 (8%)
No answer	5 (19%)

(10) "Do you think school teachers are treated better by government than most other groups in society, treated about the same, or treated worse?"

Treated better	17 (65%)
Treated same or worse	7 (27%)
No answer	2 (8%)

(11) "If the state government spent more money for public schools, would that improve the quality of education?"

Yes	1 (4%)
No	19 (73%)
Mixed	5 (19%)
No answer	1 (4%)

(12) *"Some people think that this controversy will simply increase the pay of teachers and expand the influence of the NJEA [New Jersey Education Association]. What do you think?"*

Coded as:

Agree	10 (38%)
Disagree	9 (35%)
No answer	7 (27%)

(13) *"If the state decided to move toward greater equality in per pupil expenditures throughout the state, are there any particularly difficult problems that might be encountered? What about local control of education?"*

Coded as:

Diluting local control a problem	5 (19%)
Diluting local control *not* a problem	16 (62%)
No answer	5 (19%)

(14) *"Local school boards should be permitted to establish school budgets without going directly to the voters for approval."*

Agree	9 (35%)
Disagree	14 (54%)
No answer	3 (11%)

(15) *"Would you say you devoted a great deal of time, a moderate amount of time, a little time, or no time to the problem of* school operations?*"*

Some or much	10 (38%)
Little or none	16 (62%)

(16) *"With all the other problems before the legislature, how much time would you say you have spent on the* school aid issue—*a great deal, a moderate amount, or none?"*

Some or much	19 (73%)
Little or none	7 (27%)

(17) *"Had you devoted much time to the questions of either state aid or school operations before this session of the legislatures?"*

Yes	11 (42%)
No	12 (46%)
No answer	3 (12%)

(18) *Relation of time devoted to school operations to evaluation of school performance.*

		Evaluation of School Performance	
		Good or Excellent	*Only Fair or Poor*
Time	Much or some	7	2
Devoted	Little or none	3	11

N=23

Taxes and Fiscal Equity

(19) *"Do you think that there is more public support for an income tax today than there was five years ago, or less support?"*

| More | 14 (54%) |
| Less or same | 12 (46%) |

(20) *"The state has a special obligation to spend more money on public services to help disadvantaged and poor people than it spends on services for the average citizen."*

Agree	18 (69%)
Disagree	2 (8%)
No answer	6 (23%)

(21) *"There should be some low-income housing in every community in the state regardless of the preferences of the local residents."*

Agree	9 (35%)
Disagree	12 (46%)
No answer	5 (19%)

(22) *"Are you in favor of ending minimum aid so that the funds can be used for equalization purposes?"*

Yes (opposes minimum aid)	11 (43%)
No (supports minimum aid)	9 (35%)
Mixed	3 (11%)
No answer	3 (11%)

(23) *"If the legislature does not act this fall, would you support the Court's ruling to redistribute minimum aid and save harmless aid?"*

Yes	12 (46%)
No	9 (35%)
No answer	5 (19%)

Robinson v. *Cahill*

(24) "Was the decision a good one for the Court to make? Is it a decision you approve of?"

Approve	16 (62%)
Disapprove	7 (27%)
No answer	3 (11%)

(25) "Different people view the Court's action in different ways. What major objectives do you think the Court was most concerned to accomplish with its decision?"

Coded as:

Fiscal objectives	10 (39%)
Educational objectives	3 (11%)
Both	9 (35%)
Other or no answer	4 (15%)

(26) "The whole school finance question should be settled by the Courts."

Agree	1 (4%)
Disagree	25 (96%)

(27) Relation of legislative approval of Robinson *to evaluation of school performance.*

Evaluation of Schools

	High	*Low*
Approve	6	8
Disapprove	3	4
		N=21

(28) Relation of approval of Robinson *to income tax support.*

	Support Tax	*Oppose Tax*
Approve	13	0
Disapprove	3	7
		N=23

(29) Relation of approval of Robinson *to general view of New Jersey Supreme Court.*

View of Court

	Positive	*Negative*
Approve	12	2
Disapprove	4	2
		N=20

(30) Relation of approval of Robinson *to attitudes toward increased teacher benefits.*

Impact on Benefits

	More	*Same*
Approve	2	9
Disapprove	6	0

N=17

(31) Relation of approval of Robinson *to belief that poor are treated worse by government.*

Attitude on Treatment of Poor People

	Treated Better	*Treated Same*	*Treated Worse*
Approve	2	4	10
Disapprove	3	2	1

N=22

Impact of Court Involvement on Legislative Attitudes

(32) "If the state government spent more money for public schools, would that make the school finance system fairer?"

More fair	12 (46%)
Not more fair	5 (19%)
It depends	9 (35%)

(33) "Were partisan considerations as important on the school controversy as they are on most other issues?"

As partisan	4 (15%)
Less partisan	15 (58%)
No answer	7 (27%)

(34) Relation of prior background in education issues to evaluation of schools.

Evaluation of School Performance

		Good or Excellent	*Only Fair to Poor*
Prior	Much or same	9	1
Background	Little or none	0	11

N=21

(35) Relation of support for minimum aid program to support of judicial decision to redistribute minimum aid.

		Attitude Toward Minimum Aid		
		Supports	*Opposes*	*Mixed*
Hypothetical	Supports	1	7	3
Court Ruling	Opposes	6	2	0
				N=19

DEPARTMENTAL AND INTEREST GROUP ATTITUDES

This section was compiled from interviews conducted between October 1975 and April 1976. These interviews gathered information about education politics in New Jersey and gauged reaction to the *Robinson* decision among two important communities: the New Jersey State Department of Education and various interest groups operating within the state.

The department interviews were conducted with about twenty people who are currently or were formerly associated with the department of education. Some individuals were selected to be interviewed because of their participation in events dealing with *Robinson,* while a few were chosen to represent organizational divisions within the department.

Representatives of 16 separate interest groups, representing both education and noneducation concerns, were interviewed. These groups included: the Advocate for Education, The League of Women Voters, the New Jersey Adult Education Association, the New Jersey Association of Elementary School Principals, the New Jersey Association of School Administrators, the New Jersey Association of Secondary School Principals, the New Jersey Congress of Parents and Teachers, the New Jersey Education Association, the New Jersey Federation of Teachers, the New Jersey Manufacturers Association, the New Jersey National Association for the Advancement of Colored People (NAACP), the New Jersey Personnel Guidance Association, the New Jersey School Boards Association, the New Jersey Taxpayers Association, and the Puerto Rican Congress.

One element of the interview was a written set of statements which requested an agree/disagree response. Not all department personnel or group representatives completed the questionnaire, and some groups may have been represented by more than one respondent.

The agree/disagree statements have been divided here into three basic sections: attitudes toward education, opinions about the New Jersey Supreme Court, and attitudes on other issues. The responses of the interest group representatives have been tabulated according to their status as either an education-oriented or non-education-oriented group.

Attitudes Toward Education

(1) "Public schools are not teaching basic skills as well as they once did."

| | | **Interest Groups** | | |
	Department of Education	Education Groups	Noneducation Groups	Total Groups
Agree	6 Respondents	0	5	5
Uncertain	1	1	2	3
Disagree	9	6	0	6

(2) "Teaching social values is an important purpose of the public schools."

| | | **Interest Groups** | | |
	Department of Education	Education Groups	Noneducation Groups	Total Groups
Agree	13 Respondents	7	5	12
Uncertain	2	0	1	1
Disagree	1	0	1	1

(3) "In general, the schools in the state are doing a good job educating children."

| | | **Interest Groups** | | |
	Department of Education	Education Groups	Noneducation Groups	Total Groups
Agree	14 Respondents	6	1	7
Uncertain	2	0	4	4
Disagree	0	0	2	2

Opinions About the New Jersey Supreme Court

(4) "The whole school finance question should be settled by the courts."

	Department of Education	Interest Groups Education Groups	Noneducation Groups	Total Groups
Agree	3 Respondents	0	2	2
Uncertain	1	0	0	0
Disagree	12	7	5	12

(5) "If the New Jersey Supreme Court ruled that teacher strikes violated the state's constitutional obligation to students, the state government should act promptly to prevent such strikes."

	Department of Education	Interest Groups Education Groups	Noneducation Groups	Total Groups
Agree	11 Respondents	3	6	9
Uncertain	3	1	0	1
Disagree	2	3	1	4

(6) "The justices now serving on the New Jersey Supreme Court are at least as well qualified as justices in past decades."

	Department of Education	Interest Groups Education Groups	Noneducation Groups	Total Groups
Agree	6 Respondents	5	4	9
Uncertain	9	2	3	5
Disagree	1	0	0	0

(7) "It is more important for the New Jersey Supreme Court to help the state address pressing public problems than to narrowly interpret the state constitution."

	Department of Education	Interest Groups Education Groups	Noneducation Groups	Total Groups
Agree	4 Respondents	3	1	4
Uncertain	4	3	2	5
Disagree	8	1	4	5

(8) "Although the Supreme Court should interpret the Constitution, in some of its recent decisions, the Court has become too involved in political rather than legal questions."

	Department of Education	Interest Groups Education Groups	Noneducation Groups	Total Groups
Agree	5 Respondents	1	2	3
Uncertain	3	1	2	3
Disagree	8	5	3	8

Attitudes on Other Issues

(9) "The state has a special obligation to spend more money on public services to help disadvantaged and poor people than it spends on services for the average citizen."

	Department of Education	Interest Groups Education Groups	Noneducation Groups	Total Groups
Agree	12 Respondents	5	3	8
Uncertain	2	1	3	4
Disagree	2	1	1	2

(10) "There should be some low-income housing in every community in the state, regardless of the preferences of the local residents."

	Department of Education	Interest Groups Education Groups	Noneducation Groups	Total Groups
Agree	10 Respondents	4	2	6
Uncertain	5	1	3	4
Disagree	1	2	2	4

(11) " New Jersey should adopt a personal income tax in the near future."

	Department of Education	Interest Groups Education Groups	Noneducation Groups	Total Groups
Agree	11 Respondents	4	6	10
Uncertain	4	1	1	2
Disagree	1	1	0	1

INDEX

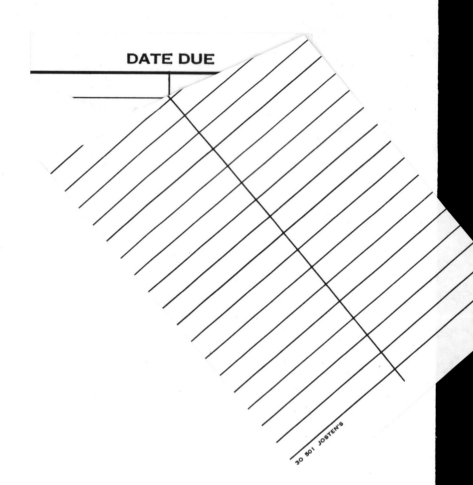

DATE DUE

30 501 JOSTEN'S